Labour Law and Sustainable Development

Studies in Employment and Social Policy

VOLUME 55

Editors

Professor Alan Neal (founding editor of the *International Journal of Labour Law and Industrial Relations*, and Convenor of the European Association of Labour Law Judges); Professor Manfred Weiss (past president of the International Industrial Relations Association); and Professor Birgitta Nyström (professor of private law at the Law Faculty, University of Lund, Sweden, and member of the European Committee of Social Rights).

Objective

Studies in Employment and Social Policy series seeks to provide a forum for highlighting international and comparative research on contemporary areas of significance for evaluation and regulation of the world of work.

Introduction

Launched in 1997, the Studies in Employment and Social Policy Series now boasts over fifty titles, addressing key policy and development issues in the fields of industrial relations, labour law, social security, and international labour regulation.

Content

With contributions from leading figures in the field, the series brings together key policymakers, academics, and regulators, providing a unique context in which to analyse and evaluate the rapid and dramatic work and social policy developments taking place around the globe.

The titles published in this series are listed at the end of this volume.

Labour Law and Sustainable Development

With Foreword by Tiziano Treu

Valentina Cagnin

Wolters Kluwer

Published by:
Kluwer Law International B.V.
PO Box 316
2400 AH Alphen aan den Rijn
The Netherlands
E-mail: international-sales@wolterskluwer.com
Website: lrus.wolterskluwer.com

Sold and distributed in North, Central and South America by:
Wolters Kluwer Legal & Regulatory U.S.
7201 McKinney Circle
Frederick, MD 21704
United States of America
Email: customer.service@wolterskluwer.com

Sold and distributed in all other countries by:
Air Business Subscriptions
Rockwood House
Haywards Heath
West Sussex
RH16 3DH
United Kingdom
Email: international-customerservice@wolterskluwer.com

ISBN 978-94-035-2074-2

e-Book: ISBN 978-94-035-2081-0
web-PDF: ISBN 978-94-035-2084-1

Original title: Diritto del Lavoro e Sviluppo Sostenibile" (Collana Universitá Ca' Foscari - Dipartimento di Economia - Collana del Centro Studi Giuridici), © Wolters Kluwer Italia, 2018

Table of Contents

Foreword			ix
Introduction			1
CHAPTER 1 The Crisis of Labour Law and the Research for a 'Sustainable Paradigm'			5
§1.01	The Crisis of Labour Law		5
	[A]	… and of the Labour Market	9
§1.02	Old and New Value Paradigms of Labour Law		11
§1.03	The Research for a New 'Sustainable' Paradigm		15
§1.04	The Concept of Sustainable Development: A Controversial Notion		19
	[A]	The 'Founding' Pillars	22
	[B]	From 'Very Weak' to 'Very Strong Sustainability'	25
§1.05	Value Profiles		26
§1.06	Jurisprudential Remarks		30
CHAPTER 2 Labour Law and Multi-level Sustainability in the International, European and Compared Institutional Fields			43
§2.01	Sustainable Development in the Institutional Context		43
§2.02	The International Context		44
	[A]	The ILO and the Social Dimension of Sustainable Development	44
	[B]	United Nations: Global Compact, Millennium Development Goals and Agenda 2030	48
	[C]	The OECD and the Guidelines for Multinationals	51
	[D]	WTO and Sustainable Development	52
§2.03	The European Context		54
	[A]	The Regulatory Framework	54
	[B]	The Special Incentive Scheme for Sustainable Development and Good Governance (GSP +)	58

[C] The Horizontal Social Clause (Article 9 TFEU) and Evaluations on Sustainability of European Policies 60
[D] The Promotion of CSR 62
§2.04 An Overlook at National Experiences 66
[A] The Election of Sustainable Development to a Constitutional Principle 66
[B] Italy and Sustainable Development Goals: Delays and Progress 70

CHAPTER 3
Labour Law and Sustainable Development: Value Analogies and Application Profiles in the National Context 77
§3.01 Value and Methodological Analogies Between the Objects of Investigation 77
§3.02 Generational Solidarity in the Labour Market and in the Enterprise 77
[A] Solidarity Tools for Generational Turnover 78
§3.03 Equality of Possibilities: The Theory of Capabilities Applied to Labour Law 84
[A] 'Smart Work': A 'Double Win' for the Reconciliation of Work-Life Balance and the Increase in Productivity 86
[B] The Enhancement of Individual Autonomy and the Problem of the Type 90
[C] Sustainable Development as a Source of Legitimacy of the Capability Approach in Subordination 94
§3.04 The Balance Between Different Axiological Perspectives 99
[A] The Dismissal in the 'Flexicurity': An Idea of Sustainable Development 99
§3.05 Mutually Reinforcing Axiological Profiles in Labour Law 106

CHAPTER 4
Sustainable Development: A New Paradigm for Labour Law 109
§4.01 Spaces of Sustainability 109
[A] The Insiders Versus Outsiders Conflict 110
[B] The 'Unsustainability' of the Current Pension System 114
[C] Gender Inequality and Gender Pay Gap 118
§4.02 Labour Law: A Sustainability Law 120

Annexes 127

ANNEX 1 The Most Significant Evolutionary Stages of Sustainable Development 129

ANNEX 2 The Ten Principles of the UN Global Compact 133

ANNEX 3 The UN Millennium Development Goals (MDGs) 135

ANNEX 4 The UN Sustainable Development Goals (SDGs) 137

ANNEX 5 Goal n. 8 of the UN Sustainable Development Goals 'Promote Lasting, Inclusive and Sustainable Economic Growth, Full and Productive Employment and Decent Work for All': Targets, Indicators and Progress in 2019 139

ANNEX 6 The European Pillar of Social Rights in 20 Principles 143

Bibliography 151

Foreword

This book deals with two fundamental matters that go beyond the Italian debate: the issue of the crisis of labour law and that of new possible perspectives of development inspired by the Sustainability paradigm. The ambitious objective of the book is to compare theoretical hypotheses, normative tendencies and practices present in the International and Italian scenario in order to verify if Sustainable Development could be relevant as a guiding criterion for the future labour law, that is 'to be useful in order to guide the exit from the crisis and, at the same time, to define the founding values of a new sustainable labour law' (p. 4).

The author is aware of the complexity of the issues involved and deals with them with great care, almost cautiously, avoiding emphatic proclamations and easy generalizations, both of which are not infrequent in dealing with these issues. Rather than definitive solutions, arguments are explained with the aim of providing the reader with a reasoning basis to verify whether the proposed indications are convincing and practicable. The presentation and discussion of the plurality of national and international texts and sources give many useful hints even to expert readers.

These sources provide a well-prepared analytical basis of different materials covering many fields, which have grown out of proportion in recent years and which show rich cultural and also regulatory content. These are essential cognitive elements in order to knowingly deal with these issues, which are scarcely acquired in our debate, even though they are often presupposed by those who intervene in the matter.

The second chapter of the essay well emphasizes how in recent years, concerning Sustainable Development and its different economic and social implications, we have seen the dawning, at the various supranational levels, of a network of principles, agreements, practices and even (soft, or scarcely binding) norms that represent a major institutional innovation in the world scenario.

The international indications have not only been a stimulus to theoretical reflection, but they have activated a series of interactions between different legal, national and supranational systems with implications that are not yet all perceived. They have nourished intertwined forms of dialogue between different public and private actors of the various systems able to give life to forms of horizontal harmonization between the principles and practices of these systems: a tendency to isomorphism sometimes under trace but no less significant.

An area where this tendency is evident, as I have also been able to investigate personally, is constituted by the social clauses of international trade treaties, whose contents and procedures have manifested significant convergences precisely because of the intertwining and mutual influence of principles and practices coming from this network of different supranational sources. It is the influence of this network that guarantees the acquisition, until recently taken for granted, of the need to consider the various dimensions of sustainability together, not only the original environmental but also the economic and social dimensions.

The heuristic and political importance of this integrated vision is convincingly illustrated by the author with precise references to its (first) implications. It is for this reason as well that the concept of Sustainability has taken on multiple (and in some cases indeterminate) meanings, presenting itself, following some definitions reported in the text that seem to me significant, as an umbrella principle or as a matrix of useful principles to constitute a window through which labour law looks with a new orientation at the future of its subject matter. The book analyses two possible implications, strategic and methodological, that the application of the principle of sustainability can assume both for the interpretation and for the (possible) evolution of labour law.

Under the first profile, the text discusses the assonance among the values of labour law (in particular, solidarity and equality of opportunity) and Sustainable Development. In interpreting and revising its values, our subject matter has always had to reconcile different interests, the needs of economy and enterprises with those of protection and dignity of work. It has done so with different orientations and outcomes according to the various economic and political contexts, often pressed by contingencies induced by these contexts.

The horizon of Sustainability induces to widen the scopes and terms of the reconciliation of interests, recalling the need not only to emphasize the qualitative aspects of development and work, but to always consider a medium-long-term perspective, to take into account the multiplicity of the stakeholders interested in economic, social and environmental issues and, in particular, to practice an approach that achieves intergenerational equity. Adopting this last approach is a real strategic leap for both legislators and social actors, including labour Unions, whose solidarity, even when taking into account general interests, has focused on the destinies of present generations, sometimes to the detriment of future ones (and sometimes even of young people).

According to the author, Sustainable Development reinforces the capabilities approach and together with this, it would contribute to a more dynamic and sustainable labour law. Our subject matter has tasks that go beyond the traditional ones, not only that of protecting weak part of the employment contract but also that of social protection: to contribute to the sustainability of development in its social, economic and environmental multiple dimensions, and also to promote the capabilities of workers.

Here we can find controversial issues, raised in fact by the theory of capabilities, which deal with the crisis of subordination and with the possibility of enhancing individual autonomy in the current world of (subordinate but independent) labour. The recent legislation on smart work, dealt with extensively by the author, can foster a better combination, a true virtuous circle, among personal needs to reconcile one's own hours, flexible organization of companies and reduction of external and internal costs to companies. However, at the same time, the law unprecedentedly recognizes a major role to individual contract in the regulation of very delicate aspects of the employment relationship, and this is a critical aspect even for workers in the new economy.

The question that cannot be avoided is how to strengthen the capacity of such workers to make the management of this new form of work sustainable, with what new individual rights and what collective support. Furthermore, the theses on capabilities have been criticized for underestimating the importance of collective action for the regulation of labour relations and for the exercise of individual autonomy.

Certainly, the perspectives of trade union relations need to be reconsidered no less than those of the individual labour law because they are challenged by the same structural factors that are at the basis of the crisis of our subject matter and that directly invest in the possibilities and the very meaning of the collective action. But this reconsideration must be conducted with the same convictions needed to ponder on the new job forms and their possible rules.

I think that the principle of Sustainability can also be useful here because the ambitious goals of reorienting development in all its dimensions can hardly be pursued without the participation, in new ways to be identified, of workers as individuals and their organizations.

The second implication of the sustainability approach - the methodological one - is no less rich than the first implication- the strategic one - for labour law. This approach emphasizes in new ways the value of interdependence, between disciplinary profiles and between different decision-making levels, necessary to grasp the evolution and the sense of development. As far as I concerned, it is useful to identify the orientations of our subject matter that are necessary to make it capable of interpreting new realities and responding to the different needs of workers and companies.

Interdependence is one of the fundamental characteristics of modernity, and it is also present in different dimensions, according to social-economic choices, by geopolitical areas and by time sequences. This is why the analytical and proactive approach to Sustainable Development must be 'matrix-oriented'. Thus it can help labour law go out of the traditional boundaries within which it has developed, the world of subordinate work and, if you will, the working class, on which it has concentrated its choices and the related mediations of interests.

This area has historically promoted not only the cause of work but also the well-being of most populations (however, only in advanced countries). But it has become increasingly inadequate, on the one hand, with the diversification of social groups and individual fortunes and, on the other hand, with the involvement of entire populations that have been so far excluded in the world scene. All this requires that our subject matter, as well as its protagonists, broaden their horizon on the different fields indicated by the multiple dimensions of sustainability.

Facing these new areas of action may involve difficult political and even juridical choices, such as those between the needs of growth and of environmental protection that have often been excluded and that are at the origin of persistent conflicts. On another front, the unprecedented implications of markets and global politics must be addressed by the national actors in relation to each other and by the fragile supranational institutions if both want to contribute to the directions of development where the latter are now decisively determined.

Finally, the prolongation of life and the diversity of its cycles widen and complicate the contents of solidarity between generations, and this also requires new social and economic policies to make these relations sustainable and to avoid the fracturing of the generational pact that has held together modern societies so far.

In the third and fourth chapters of the book, the author presents the implications of the Sustainability approach for some critical areas of our labour law. The enhancement of individual autonomy has already been mentioned above; the pension system is analysed in the book by noting the criticalities that make it unsustainable and by pointing to the urgency of interventions to promote intergenerational solidarity.

The flexicurity policies are analysed underlining how the European design of the latter is in line with the idea of Sustainability because it reinterprets the balance between the need for flexibility and security in the current context of mobile and transitional markets, even if the implementation practices, especially in the Italian case, have been unbalanced.

Gender and wages inequalities constitute a profound contradiction with respect to equality of opportunity, which is one of the founding principles of Sustainability. The contrast of these inequalities also requires a broadening of the horizons of labour law and its actors, so that they can be mobilized, with the necessary alliances, to make it a central objective of development policies.

The research conducted in the book allows the author to legitimately ask the question of whether labour law can be a Sustainability law. The question is founded, the answer is uncertain. But that is enough in order to continue investigation like this that can offer promising ideas, as the author also believes, both for the reconsideration of many parts of the current normative texts and for proposing new solutions.

The current context of our country does not offer easy elements to support these perspectives. However, many of the founding principles of Sustainable Development are already present and active in the institutional fabric and in international sources. They help in guiding the steps towards the construction of a more modern and supranational law that may be useful to sustainability; and from the fragile indications of international actors, there may be stimulus to reinforce the attempts made in some countries to undertake a path towards Sustainable Development.

Tiziano Treu

Introduction

It is a generally shared opinion, even though not universally accepted, that the global crisis of the past decade has, on the one hand, highlighted the social unsustainability of ultra-liberal economic theories,[1] which, along with the drastic reduction of the constraints deriving from labour law legislation, represent the precondition of economic and social development, consistent with the imperatives of globalization; on the other hand, it has highlighted the criticalities of the traditional labour law system, in many ways incapable of adapting its cognitive and normative structures to an economic, social and cultural context in profound transformation.[2]

If it is true that labour law has never been characterized by a linear and uninterrupted development, since the setbacks and crises are part of its constitutive status, as is - after all - appropriate to a discipline so deeply intertwined with the economic structure and conditioned by the political-social context in which we from time to time operate,[3] the current crisis of the discipline shows a profound destabilization of the matter, so much so that it can be described in terms of genetic mutation,[4] or of change of scientific paradigm.[5]

The traditional protective legislation of labour law has indeed been *under fire*[6] for a long time: a fire fuelled by the continuous criticism of excessive rigidity of the subject centred on the protection of the weak part of the employment contract, with the consequent negative effects in terms of production and employment. As a matter of

1. R. B. Reich, *Supercapitalismo: come cambia l'economia mondiale e i rischi per la democrazia*, Fazi, Roma, 2008; P. Krugman, *Il ritorno dell'economia della depressione e la crisi del 2008*, Garzanti, Milano, 2009.
2. R. Del Punta, *Epistemologia breve del diritto del lavoro*, in L. Nogler, L. Corazza (a cura di), *Risistemare il diritto del lavoro. Liber amicorum Marcello Pedrazzoli*, Franco Angeli, Milano, 2012, p. 330.
3. D. Gottardi, F. Guarriello (a cura di), *Massimo Roccella, Manuale di diritto del Lavoro, Mercato del lavoro e rapporti di lavoro*, Giappichelli, Torino, 6a edizione, 2015.
4. V. Speziale, *La mutazione genetica del diritto del* lavoro, in *Dir. lav. mer.*, 2016, 2.
5. A. Perulli, *Il contratto a tutele crescenti e la Naspi: un mutamento di 'paradigma' per il diritto del Lavoro?*, in A. Perulli, L. Fiorillo (a cura di), *Contratto a tutele crescenti e Naspi, Decreti legislativi 4 marzo 2015, n. 22 e n. 23*, Giappichelli, Torino, 2015.
6. A. Goldin, *Some Defining Components of a Labour Law Influx*, Pompeu Fabra University, Barcelona, 2013.

fact, on the basis of neoliberal logics, this alleged rigidity is considered as an obstacle to development, innovation, productivity and attractiveness of foreign investments, as well as being responsible for the current problems in the labour market, both in terms of unemployment, and of strong and increasingly growing dualisms and segmentations.

It is because of the prevalence of the standard economic logic and of the continuous pushes to a greater flexibility (in entry, functional and out of the employment relationship) that we are facing the very well-known phenomena of deregulation of the matter that have affected many European labour law systems.[7] Such paths of deregulation (or re-regulation) have led, reform after reform, to a progressive devastation of the founding pillars and to a real regulatory crisis of the subject matter.[8] A crisis that can be understood as the final outcome of the continuous and tiring process of adapting the discipline to a social and economic context that is very different from that in which the subject was conceived and has gradually developed, so much so as to question the same paradigm and the same values on which labour law has been founded so far. Therefore, labour law is now wondering more than ever about its future and its disciplinary matrix,[9] as well as about the need, accelerated by the economic crisis that is still in many ways ongoing,[10] for a new paradigm of reference.

The overcoming of these profound critical issues that affect labour law and its very epistemological essence cannot in fact set aside the adoption of new criteria and

7. T. Papadopoulos, A. Roumpakis, *The Meta-regulation of European Industrial Relations: Power Shifts, Institutional Dynamics and the Emergence of Regulatory Competition*, in *International Labour Review*, 2013, vol. 152, p. 256; A. Lyon-Caen, T. Sachs, *La legge sulla «sécurisation de l'emploi»: DNA di una riforma*, in *Lav. dir.*, 2013, p. 435; A. Lyon-Caen, T. Sachs, *L'ADN d'une réforme*, in *Revue de droit du travail*, 2013, p. 162; E. Peskine, *Les accords de maintien dans l'emploi. Ruptures et continuités*, in *Revue de droit du travail*, 2013, p. 168; F. Ferrando García, *El reforzamiento del poder de direccion tras la reforma laboral de 2012*, in *Revista de Derecho Social*, 2013, vol. 61, p. 71; A. M. Romero Burillo, *La regulación de la movilidad geográfica tras las reformas laborales 2010-2012*, in *Revista de Derecho Social*, 2013, vol. 64, p. 43; M. Rodríguez-Piñero, F. Bravo Ferrer, F. Valdés Dal-Ré, M. E. Casas Baamonde, *La huida del derecho del trabajo hacia el 'emprendimiento', las reformas de la Reforma Laboral de 2012 y otras reformas: la L 11/2013 y el RDL 11/2013*, in *Relaciones Laborales*, 2013, n. 10, p. 1; J. M. Morales Ortega, *Movilidad geográfica y modificaciones sustanciales tras la reforma de 2012: ¿una mal entendida flexiseguridad?*, in *Temas Laborales*, 2013, vol. 119, p. 55; A. Baylos Grau, *La desconstitucionalización del trabajo en la reforma laboral del 2012*, in *Revista de Derecho Social*, 2013, vol. 61, p. 27; M. T. Diaz Aznarte, *Crisi economica e riforma del diritto del lavoro in Spagna. Le ricette neoliberali producono occupazione?*, in *Riv. giur. lav.*, 2015, 4, p. 893.
8. Therefore, we shifted from talking about labour law of the crisis (or labour law of emergency) of the last two decades of the twentieth century, to talking about the crisis of labour law. Cfr. R. De Luca Tamajo, L. Ventura (a cura di), *Il diritto del lavoro nell'emergenza*, 1979, Jovene, Napoli; G. Giugni, *Prospettive del diritto del lavoro per gli anni '80*, in AA.VV., *Atti del VII Congresso nazionale di diritto del lavoro – AIDLASS, svoltosi a Bari nelle giornate del 23-25 aprile 1982*, Giuffrè, Milano, 1983.
9. A. Perulli, *L'idea di diritto del lavoro, oggi*, in A. Perulli (a cura di), *L'idea di diritto del lavoro, oggi. In ricordo di Giorgio Ghezzi*, Cedam, Padova, 2016, p. XLI.
10. G. Davidov, *The Reports of My Death Are Greatly Exaggerated: 'Employee' as a Viable (Though Over-Used) Legal Concept*, in G. Davidov, B. Langille (eds), *Boundaries and Frontiers of Labour Law: Goals and Means in the Regulation of Work*, Hart Publishing, Oxford, 2006; K. V. W. Stone, *The Decline of the Standard Contract of Employment in the United States: A Socio-Regulatory Perspective*, in K. V. W. Stone, H. Arthurs (eds), *Rethinking Workplace Regulation: Beyond the Standard Contract of Employment*, Russell Sage Foundation, New York, 2013, pp. 58-78.

new conceptual categories on which to reconstruct the legitimizing foundation of the matter. Starting from this reference context, the idea that I intend to develop here consists in proposing Sustainable Development as a new orientation paradigm for labour law.

If the most commonly proposed definition of the term is given by the Brundtland Report according to which Sustainable Development 'satisfies the needs of the present without compromising the ability of future generations to satisfy their own',[11] it immediately appears as evident that this is a concept all the way other than monolithic. It takes the form of an essentially controversial[12] and fluid notion, that is to say a meaning that may differently manifest itself in relation to the specific field of reference. It is a sort of 'motherhood and apple-pie concept', that is, something known by everyone, but of which everyone offers a different version.[13]

Mentioning Sustainable Development in the present era therefore means confronting a multifaceted and ambivalent concept; it means investigating its several forms in areas ranging from environmental protection to the economy, from architecture to natural sciences, from philosophy to medicine, to social sciences. The interdisciplinary and the indeterminate nature of the concept of Sustainable Development, while on the one hand give the concept an unprecedented propulsive force – legitimizing its application in the most varied and even juridical fields – on the other hand, represent at the same time a source of criticality of the model, which can appear as an elusive concept and lacking in concrete contents and, therefore, in potential applications that can be usefully investigated.

For this reason, in order to grasp its characteristic traits, its different delineations (or pillars) and its normative validity, we should reconstruct a definitive framework of Sustainable Development, both retracing the original debate on the subject and retracing its original jurisprudential physiognomy. If at first (indicatively up to the first half of the 1990s), Sustainable Development applied to juridical matters was mostly confined to environmental protection issues, in the last few years the concept has experienced a wider and more correct connotation, delineated in a triple environmental, economic and social dimension, thus assuming a certain value both in terms of constitutional principle and as a global *policy* tool.

Its entry into the legislative and institutional frameworks at European level, as well as at international and comparative level, justifies its application also in the field of labour law, which, as we shall see, can aspire to become part of the Sustainable Development model with its natural vocation to reconcile conflicting logics and rationalities. Starting from a preliminary reflection on the possible axiological commonalities that can be found between labour law and Sustainable Development, the

11. Brundtland Report, *Our Common Future*, elaborated by the 1983 UN World Commission on environment and development, hosted by Gro Harlem Brundtland, Norwegian Prime Minister, from whom it got its name.
12. There are endless disputes on the meaning and the degree by which we can obtain all the things that are indicated by the concept. Cfr. J. R. Ehrenfeld, *Sustainability Needs to Be Attained, Not Managed*, in *Sustainability: Science, Practice & Policy*, 2008, vol. 4, p. 1.
13. K. Pittel, *Sustainability and Endogenous Growth, New Horizons in Environmental Economics*, Edward Elgar, Cheltenham UK, 2002.

thesis that lies ahead is to enhance the spaces acquired by Sustainability *in* labour law and *for* labour law, not only in a historical key but also in perspective, pondering about the applicative potential of the principle of Sustainable Development to the subject matter.

The aim of this work is therefore to provide the reader with a reasoning basis to assess whether the choice to elect Sustainable Development as a new paradigm of reference for labour law is feasible, and if in particular, this choice can be useful in order to guide the exit from the crisis and, at the same time, to define the founding values of a new 'sustainable' labour law.

CHAPTER 1

The Crisis of Labour Law and the Research for a 'Sustainable Paradigm'

§1.01 THE CRISIS OF LABOUR LAW

The transformations that have in the past years affected economy, society, science and technology have given the jurists of the third millennium a world that is profoundly different from the one in which the fundamental categories of labour law have been created and defined (as closely related to that particular economy and society): transformations which, in an accelerated *continuum* of causes and effects and for reasons that have nothing to do with the law, are putting to test the foundations and the structure of the juridical (paradigm of the) labour law system.[1]

The inability of labour law to adapt its cognitive and evaluative structures, in a word, its rationality, to a profoundly transformed[2] economic, social and cultural context has determined a convulsive mutation[3] of the subject matter, that is, a genetic mutation that has altered its 'DNA', transforming it into something else.[4]

A mutation that began at the end of the twentieth century,[5] often described and resulting in terms of the now self-evident 'labour law crisis', precisely in order to

1. D. GAROFALO, *Lavoro, impresa e trasformazioni organizzative, Relazione alle giornate di studio Aidlass 2017, Frammentazione organizzativa e lavoro: rapporti individuali e collettivi*, Cassino, 18-19 Maggio 2017, p. 96.
2. A. PERULLI, *Efficient breach, valori del mercato e tutela della stabilità. Il controllo del giudice sui licenziamenti economici in Italia, Francia e Spagna*, in *Riv. giur. lav.*, 2012, 1, p. 561.
3. L. CORAZZA, R. ROMEI, *Il puzzle delle trasformazioni*, in L. CORAZZA, R. ROMEI (a cura di), *Diritto del lavoro in trasformazione*, il Mulino, Bologna, 2014, p. 14.
4. V. SPEZIALE, *La mutazione genetica del diritto del lavoro*, in M. P. IADICICCO, V. NUZZO (a cura di), *Le riforme del diritto del lavoro. Politiche e tecniche normative*, Editoriale Scientifica, Napoli, 2016.
5. Crisis and ending of labour law were concepts debated already since the 1980s. G. LYON-CAEN, *La crise du droit du travail*, in F. GAMILLSCHEG et al. (eds), *In Memoriam Sir Otto Kahn Freund*, Munich, C.H. Beck'sche Verlagsbuchhandlung, 1980, pp. 517-524; G. LYON-CAEN, *Le droit du travail: une tecnique reversible*, Dalloz, Paris, 1995; U. ROMAGNOLI, *Un diritto da ripensare*, in *Lav. dir.*, 1995, p. 467; B. HEPPLE, *The Future of Labour Law*, in *Comparative Labor Law & Policy*

effectively indicate the profound destabilization suffered by the subject matter in the postmodern era in the face of the new context, so different from the late Fordist era or from that of the Italian Workers' Statute of the 1970s.[6]

Such crisis has been described by the doctrine with a wide range of adjectives and delineations. The keywords are crisis of impotence, of legitimacy, as well as of an existential, empirical, normative, conceptual or spiritual crisis.[7] It seems that labour law has lost its soul,[8] or at least that the continuous external solicitations have overturned it: its traditional privatistic, microeconomic and conflictual features, centred on the protection of the worker implicated in the relationship through mandatory rules set by the law or collective autonomy, in its turn guaranteed or supported by the law itself, now coexist with different public, macroeconomic and participatory characteristics, attentive to the interrelations between the discipline of work on the one hand, and the functioning of the company and of the whole economic system on the other, in the awareness that this functioning affects the very possibility of actually meeting the workers' needs.[9]

In a context of great changes, mainly due to the economic and financial crisis and to the progressive globalization of the markets, the capacity of labour law to act as a seismograph of trends, that is to say as a branch of the law being more sensitive to social and institutional[10] transformations, has risked compromising its foundations: the continuous search for adaptation to the new context, so very different from that of the period of its formation, has entailed, through countless reforms, an irreversible

---

Journal, 1996, vol. 17, p. 626; S. Simitis, *Il diritto del lavoro ha ancora un futuro?*, in *Giorn. dir. lav. rel. ind.*, 1997, 4, p. 609; A. Jeammaud, *Il diritto del lavoro alla prova del cambiamento*, in *Lav. dir.*, 1997, 3, p. 339; L. Mariucci, *Il diritto del lavoro della seconda Repubblica*, in *Lav. dir.*, 1997, 2, p. 163; J. Rifkin, *La fine del lavoro, Il declino della forza lavoro globale e l'avvento dell'era post-mercato*, Mondadori, Milano, 2014; P. Lokiec, *Il faut sauver le droit du travail*, Odile Jacob, Paris, 2015.

6. S. Deakin, F. Wilkinson, *Il diritto del Lavoro e la teoria economica. Una rivisitazione*, in *Giorn. dir. lav. rel. ind.*, 1999, 84, 4, p. 588; R. Del Punta, *L'economia e le ragioni del diritto del Lavoro*, in *Dir. lav. rel. ind.*, 2001, 1, p. 3; M. Rodriguez-Piñero, B. Ferrer, *La grave crisi del diritto del lavoro*, in *Lav. dir.*, 2012, 1, pp. 3-18. Sulla dottrina internazionale: B. Langille, *Labour Law's Back Pages*, in G. Davidov, B. Langille (eds), *Boundaries and Frontiers of Labour Law*, Hart Publishing, Oxford, 2006; G. Davidov, B. Langille, *Introduction: Goals and Means in the Regulation of Work*, *ibid.*; K. V. W Stone, *Rethinking Labour Law: Employment Protection*, *ibid.*; A. Hyde, *What Is Labour Law?*, *ibid.*; K. V. W. Stone, H. Arthurs, *The Transformation of Employment Regimes: A Worldwide Challenge*, in K. V. W. Stone, H. Arthurs (eds), *Rethinking Workplace Regulation*, Russell Sage Foundation, New York, 2013.
7. M. D'Antona, *Diritto del lavoro di fine secolo, una crisi d'identità?*, in *Riv. giur. lav. prev. soc.*, 1998, 1, p. 312; H. Arthurs, *Labour Law After Labour*, in G. Davidov, B. Langille (eds), *The Idea of Labour Law*, Oxford University Press, Oxford, 2011; B. Langille, *Labour Law's Theory of Justice*, *ibid.*, p. 101; B. Caruso, *Nuove traiettorie del diritto del lavoro nella crisi europea. Il caso italiano*, in *WP C.S.D.L.E. 'Massimo D'Antona'.INT – 111/2014*, p. 1; L. Zoppoli, *Il diritto del Lavoro dalle ideologie alla numerologia? L'insostenibile pesantezza delle politiche, del diritto e dei tecnici del diritto*, in M. Brollo, M. Marazza (a cura di), *Quad. arg. dir. lav.*, 2015, 13, p. 137.
8. L. Mariucci, *Il diritto del lavoro della seconda Repubblica*, in *Lav. dir.*, 1997, 2, p. 168.
9. A. Vallebona, *Istituzioni di diritto del lavoro, Il diritto sindacale*, Ottava edizione, Cedam, Padova, 2012, p. 53.
10. L. Mariucci, *Il diritto del lavoro della seconda Repubblica*, in *Lav. dir.*, 1997, 2, p. 168.

disintegration of the regulatory pillars of the subject matter.[11] We are dealing with a slow but inexorable process, characterized by measures of deregulation, that is to say by a progressive reduction of the traditional mandatory protective legislation of labour law, carried out under the continuous pressure of labour flexibility in response to criticism of excessive rigidity of the matter, considered as an obstacle to development and innovation.[12]

A flexibility that was achieved in Italy, as well as in most developed economies, both in hiring (through the multiplication of flexible contract typologies such as fixed-term contracts, temporary work, contract work, intermittent work, subordinate work, voucher work), both in dismissals (refer to the reduction of the reinstatement discipline of dismissals with a view to the progressive monetization of protection) and in the context of the relationship itself (refer, for example, to the power granted to proximity bargaining[13] or to the recent modifications of *jus variandi*, provided for in 2103 c.c.[14]).

---

11. Massimo D'Antona individuates four pillars of labour law: the State-nation, the big factory, the full employment, and the general representation through Unions. Cfr. M. D'Antona, *Diritto del lavoro di fine secolo, una crisi d'identità?*, in *Riv. giur. lav. prev. soc.*, 1998, 1, pp. 312-319.
12. C. Zoli, *Le recenti riforme del diritto del lavoro tra continuità e discontinuità*, in L. Mariucci (a cura di), *Dopo la flessibilità, cosa? Le nuove politiche del lavoro*, il Mulino, Bologna, 2006, pp. 395-408.
13. The reference here is to Art. 8, Law 148/2011, pursuant to which, as is known, the corporate or territorial collective agreements stipulated by the comparatively more representative trade unions on the national or territorial level or by their company union representatives, on condition of being signed on the basis of a majority criterion, can apply to all interested workers' specific agreements aimed at greater employment, at the quality of employment contracts, at the adoption of forms of labour participation, at the emergence of irregular work, at increases in competitiveness and of wages, at the management of company and employment crises, at investments and at the start-up of new activities, also in dispensation of the provisions of the law and collective agreement. On this point G. Santoro Passarelli, *Accordo interconfederale 28 giugno 2011 e art. 8 d. l. 138/2011 conv. con modif. l. 148/2011*, in *Arg. dir. lav.*, 2011; S. Centofanti, *L'articolo 8 d. l. n. 138/2011 conv. in l. n. 148/2011: una norma lesiva dei principi del diritto del lavoro*, in *Lav. giur.*, 2011, 11; C. Zoli, *Contrattazione in deroga*, in F. Carinci (a cura di), *Da Pomigliano a Mirafiori: la cronaca si fa storia*, Milano, Ipsoa, 2011, pp. 41-56; R. Pessi, *Indisponibilità del tipo e disponibilità regolativa dell'autonomia collettiva. Sull'art. 8 della manovra bis*, in *Riv. it. dir. lav.*, 2011, 1; A. Perulli, V. Speziale, *L'articolo 8 della legge 14 settembre 2011, n. 148 e la 'rivoluzione di Agosto' del Diritto del lavoro*, in *WP C.S.D.L.E. 'Massimo D'Antona'.IT – 132/2011*; G. Ferraro, *Il contratto collettivo oggi dopo l'art. 8 del decreto n. 138/2011*, in *WP C.S.D.L.E. 'Massimo D'Antona'.IT – 129/2011*; R. De Luca Tamajo, *Prime valutazioni e questioni di legittimità costituzionale dell'art. 8 l. n. 148 del 2011*, in *Arg. dir. lav.*, 2012, 1, p. 19; U. Carabelli, *I profili di incostituzionalità dell'art. 8 con riferimento all'efficacia erga omnes dei contratti collettivi da esso previsti*, in *Riv. giur. lav.*, 2012, pp. 539 ss; A. Lassandari, *Dopo l'accordo del 28 giugno 2011 (e l'art. 8 della l. n. 148): incertezze, contraddizioni, fragilità*, in *Lav. dir.*, 2012, 1, pp. 55-80; M. Barbieri, *Il rapporto tra l'art. 8 e l'accordo interconfederale del 28 giugno 2011*, in *Riv. giur. lav*, 2012, 3; C. Zoli, *Dall'accordo interconfederale 28 giugno 2011 all'art. 8 del d. l. n. 138/2011*, in F. Carinci (a cura di), *Contrattazione in deroga*, Ipsoa, Milano, 2012, pp. 137-154; A. Garilli, *L'art. 8 l. n. 148 del 2011 nel sistema delle relazioni sindacali*, in *Arg. dir. lav.*, 2012, 1; A. Perulli, *La contrattazione collettiva 'di prossimità': teoria, comparazione e prassi*, in *Riv. it. dir. lav.*, 2013, 4; P. Lambertucci, *La contrattazione collettiva di prossimità e gli assetti contrattuali del Testo unico del 2014: modelli di relazioni industriali a confronto*, in *Dir. mer. lav.*, 2014, 1-2.
14. On the topic: M. Brollo, *La disciplina delle mansioni dopo il Jobs Act*, in *Arg. dir. lav.*, 2015, 6, pp. 1156-1185; A. Perulli, L. Fiorillo (a cura di), *Tipologie contrattuali e disciplina delle mansioni: Decreto legislativo 15 giugno 2015, n. 81*, Giappichelli, Torino, 2016; C. Zoli, *La*

The modalities in which labour law has tried to respond to the needs of flexibility, productivity, and cost-effectiveness manifested by the business world, have in fact overshadowed the need for protection of the worker, as a weak contractual party. The economic objectives have in fact become the characteristic of legislative actions: refer, for example, to the rewriting of the discipline regarding dismissals, which, in relation to its greater or lesser degree of reduction of the entrepreneurial power to interrupt the contract, is analysed in relation to its ability or not to affect employment levels. Or to the spread of flexible contractual types, evaluated in consideration of its ability to fluidify the market (guaranteeing a more dynamic turnover between entries and exits) and to better meet the organizational needs of the companies. Or, again, to the more or less accentuated flexibility of working time, which is also functional to the level of productivity of the company, with needs that are clearly predominant on the protection of the safety and life of the worker.[15]

Such pushes to deregulation and flexibility have also been accelerated by globalization, which in addition to entailing unprecedented competition between the various national labour law systems has proven to be able to erode their capacity and effectiveness by decreeing a loss of sovereignty, not only on a theoretical juridical level but also above all on the level of political decisions.[16] The fundamental characteristics of labour law have undergone a complex phase of *denationalization*, since they no longer identified with the nation-state (as a political actor, as a normative power, as a national community).[17] Further, we are facing the multiplication of regulatory levels, given that the internal regulations are confronted with the international standards of the International Labour Organization (ILO) and those of the European Union (EU):[18] the latter, as a matter of fact, are ever less conditioning the labour law sector in view

---

disciplina delle mansioni, in A. Perulli, L. Fiorillo (a cura di), *ibid.*, ivi; G. Zilio Grandi, E. Gramano (a cura di), *La disciplina delle mansioni prima e dopo il Jobs Act. Quadro legale e profili problematici*, Giuffrè, Milano, 2016; G. Vidiri, *La disciplina delle mansioni nel jobs act: una (altra) riforma mal riuscita*, in *Arg. dir. lav.*, 2016, 3, p. 465; M. Brollo, *La mobilità professionale dei lavoratori dopo il Jobs Act: spunti dal caso Fiat/FCA*, in *Riv. it. dir. lav.*, 2016, pp. 306-323; G. Vidiri, *La disciplina delle mansioni nel jobs act: una (altra) riforma mal riuscita*, in *Arg. dir. lav.*, 2016, 3, p. 465; P. Lambertucci, *I poteri del datore di lavoro nello Statuto dei lavoratori dopo l'attuazione del c.d. jobs act del 2015: primi spunti di riflessione*, in *Arg. dir. lav.*, 2016, 3, p. 514.

15. V. Speziale, *La trasformazione del diritto del lavoro*, in *Lav. dir.*, 2016, 4, pp. 719-720.
16. S. Scarponi (a cura di), *Globalizzazione e diritto del lavoro: il ruolo degli ordinamenti sovranazionali*, Giuffrè, Milano, 2001; F. Guarriello, S. Leonardi (a cura di), *Globalizzazione e relazioni industriali*, Ediesse, Roma, 2003; M. Napoli, *Globalizzazione e rapporti di lavoro*, Vita e Pensiero, Milano, 2006; S. Cassese, *Il diritto globale*, Einaudi, Torino, 2009; P. Lambertucci, *Globalizzazione e diritto del lavoro: brevi spunti di riflessione*, in *Dir. merc. lav.*, 2010, 1; A. Perulli, *Globalizzazione e Dumping sociale, quali rimedi?*, in *Lav. dir.*, 2011, 1; M. R. Ferrarese, *Diritto sconfinato: Inventiva giuridica e spazi nel mondo globale*, Laterza, Roma, 2015.
17. M. D'Antona, *Diritto del lavoro di fine secolo, una crisi d'identità?*, in *Riv. giur. lav. prev. soc.*, 1998, 1, p. 319.
18. On this point, it is sufficient to recall that the Community normative production, with a view to harmonizing the discipline of the labour market and labour relations within the individual Member States of the EU, has significantly affected the evolution of internal legislation of our country, in the field of collective dismissals, outsourcing, part-time and fixed-term work, working hours, workers' rights to information and protection against discrimination. On the topic, E. Ales, *Diritti sociali e discrezionalità del legislatore nell'ordinamento multilivello: una prospettazione giuslavoristica*, in *Giorn. dir. lav. rel. ind.*, 147, 2015, 3.

of a legislative harmonization among the twenty-eight Member Countries but are, on the contrary, characterized by a mercantile logic that ended up contributing to the crisis of the European social model in the face of an unprecedented expression of economic freedoms.[19]

Finally, a further shock to the foundations of labour law was given by the advent of the fourth industrial revolution: the impressive and unstoppable technological evolution allowed an epoch change in the productive and organizational methods of work, transforming the concepts of work, of worker and of workplace themselves, thus questioning the terms in which the basic concepts of the subject had been defined (among which, first of all, the dichotomy autonomy-subordination in the processes of qualification of the contractual relationship).[20]

In a short time, therefore, labour law was affected by a series of phenomena that undermined its foundations and, consequently, its ability to effectively regulate labour relations and the labour market.

[A] ... and of the Labour Market

The labour law crisis clearly manifests itself in the current labour market situation, characterized by a growing dualism between those who benefit from protection and those who are deprived of it, by a structural malfunction, unemployment and gender gap, both in Italy and at international level.[21]

Let us take as a reference, for example, the employment rate, given that full employment is the fundamental indicator of the labour market efficiency.

If, for the first time after a decade, in 2017, there was a decrease in the unemployment rate in Italy towards pre-crisis levels, as well as a tendency to reduce the employment gender gap, the current figures of the market are still alarming: the

19. The reference is to the sentences of the European Court of Justice of Laval Quartet: case C-438/05 of 11 December 2007 (*Viking*); case C-341/05 of 18 December 2007 (*Laval*); case C-346/06 of 19 June 2008 (*Rüffert*); case C-319/06 of 19 June 2008 (*Commission v. Luxembourg*). On the topic, M. Freedland, J. Prassl (eds), *Viking, Laval and Beyond*, Hart Publishing, Oxford and Portland, Oregon, 2014.
20. The historical dichotomy of subordinate work versus independent work, with a respective annexation or tout court exclusion from the area of labour law protection, no longer results as adequate to represent the concrete phenomenology of labour relations in the new productive scenario, since the technological progress, the gig economy and the platform work have overturned the concept of work and of worker. These developments make the prescient analyses of Massimo D'Antona more and more present. He pointed out that 'If labour law has so far identified itself with the typical figure of the subordinate worker ... now that total identification with the typical social figure wanes, and labour law seems to go back the way that goes from "work" (typical subordinate) to "jobs" (subordinate or independent), which means to go back to dealing with the whole range of contracts through which, in the multiple forms allowed by a productive organization that today is much less rigid than the past, it is possible to realize the integration of the mainly personal work in the economic activity of others.' Cfr. M. D'Antona, *Diritto del lavoro di fine secolo, una crisi d'identità?*, in *Riv. giur. lav. prev. soc.*, 1998, 1, p. 322.
21. With reference to global data, more that 201 million workers in the world are currently unemployed, with an increase of 3.4 million compared to 2016. Global unemployment is 5.8% and such percentage is not going to decrease in the short term. Cfr. International Labour Organization, *World Employment and Social Outlook 2017: Sustainable Enterprises and Jobs: Formal Enterprises and Decent Work*, International Labour Office, Geneva, 2017.

general unemployment rate (35.1%), youth unemployment (32.7%) and NEET[22] **(24.3%**[23]**), as well as the gender gap in employment rates (18.4%)** result as significantly far from the European average (27.1%, 17.3%, 14.2% and 10.4% respectively[24]), moreover, an average that is far from optimal levels.[25]

If there is no doubt that the economic crisis has contributed heavily to worsen the situation, it is equally true that national labour regulation systems have proved inefficient, by contributing to exacerbating the phenomenon of unemployment; in fact, 'where labour markets are governed by more efficient rules, less dramatic employment effects of the crisis have been reported'.[26]

To the current inefficiency of the labour market, we may add the possible repercussions of the fourth industrial revolution on employment levels: the technological innovation and the automation of production processes could lead to mass technological unemployment, to the obsolescence of professionalism and skills, as well as to the deterioration of the already high misalignment between demand and supply of labour.

However, concerning the impact of artificial technology and intelligence on the professions of the next decade, the experts are divided, estimating either a loss of millions of jobs, or a high risk of replacing the workforce, or an increasing automation that creates and at the same time destroys jobs.[27]

If, as history teaches, the evolution of technology can create jobs, we should not expect any long-term mass unemployment. Industry 4.0 can, however, present a dual

22. NEETs are young people between 15 and 29 years of age who are *not engaged in Education, Employment or Training*, that is to say excluded from the training and work circuit. Despite the fact that this is a much higher average than Germany (8.8%), France (14.4%) and the United Kingdom (12.3%), the ISTAT survey shows that only one NEET out of four is inactive, unavailable or interested in work, since 43.4% of NEETs are looking for employment and 32.6% are part of the potential labour force. Therefore most of NEETs, contrary to popular opinion, are characterized by a growing interest in the labour market. To deepen the topic, M. S. Agnoli (curated by), *Generazioni sospese. Percorsi di ricerca sui giovani Neet*, Franco Angeli, Milano, 2014; A. Rosina, *NEET. Giovani che non studiano e non lavorano*, Vita e Pensiero, Milano, 2015.
23. The European data does not deny the statistical results of the ISTAT: considering the different age group between 15 and 24, the percentage of NEETs in Italy is 19.9%, against an average in the continent of 11.5%. *Source*: European Commission, Annual Survey on Employment and on Social Developments in Europe (ESDE), July 2017.
24. 2017 ISTAT Report: Labour Market: The Slow Upswing and the Disparity in Social Groups.
25. On the topic, M. Brollo, M. Marazza (curated by), *Diritto del lavoro e mercato. L'impatto delle riforme del lavoro nell'analisi giuridica dei dati sull'occupazione*, Cedam, Padova, 2015.
26. B. Caruso, *Nuove traiettorie del diritto del lavoro nella crisi europea. Il caso italiano*, in *WP C.S.D.L.E. 'Massimo D'Antona'.INT – 111/2014*, p. 23.
27. For example, the World Economic Forum estimates a loss of five million jobs from 2016 to 2020. According to the latest McKinsey research, only 5% of jobs will disappear completely, while 49% of jobs currently performed by individuals will be automated and the technology will create 2.6 jobs for each one that destroys them. Frey and Osborne, on the other hand, predicted in 2015 that technological development would put to high risk of substitution: 47% of the US workforce within a decade. Cfr. J. Rifkin, *The End of Work: The Decline of the Global Labor Force and the Dawn of the Post-market Era*, Putnam Publishing Group, New York, 1995; C. B. Frey, M. A. Osborne, *The Future of Employment: How Susceptible Are Jobs to Computerization?*, in *Oxford Martin School Working Paper*, Oxford, 17 September 2013; World Economic Forum, *'Future Jobs' Report*, 2016; McKinsey Global Institute, *A Future That Works: Automation, Employment, and Productivity*, January 2017.

risk: (i) wage competition among the same workers from all over the world, who, thanks to the new technologies and the work performed on demand on the platform, find themselves able to compete in a new global labour market, without borders;[28] (ii) an imbalance in the job offer towards high-level professional figures and a parallel exclusion from the labour market of the currently least-qualified figures.

§1.02 OLD AND NEW VALUE PARADIGMS OF LABOUR LAW

The crisis of the labour law discipline has not only affected the labour market but, as anticipated, also the scientific reflection on labour law and on the founding paradigms of the matter, as if the emersion of a new axiological system had corrupted its original purity.[29]

Leaving aside a historical digression on the evolution of labour law in Italy in the past fifty years, for the purposes of this reflection, it is sufficient to recall that the labour law system has made a persistent effort to approach new contextual criticalities over the years, questioning many consolidated structures of the subject, by virtue of the strong sensitivity of the discipline to the economic and social context. Moreover, it is known that labour law is naturally permeable to the demands that come from the social-economic context of reference, undertaking a continuous work of redefining its postulates, so as to be able to contribute to the governance of the changes that occur.[30]

Its postulates have in fact been redefined several times, abandoning some regulatory techniques that have characterized labour law in the twentieth century, in order to internalize other values commonly considered as more suitable for the regulation of the new contextual phenomena: the centrality of the company as an

28. About the effects of *gig economy* and of the fourth industrial revolution on labour law, please refer to: P. Tullini, *Digitalizzazione dell'economia e frammentazione dell'occupazione. Il lavoro instabile discontinuo informale: tendenze in atto*, in *Riv. giur. lav.*, 2016, 4; P. Tullini (a cura di), *Web e lavoro: Profili evolutivi e di tutela*, Giappichelli, Torino, 2017; A. Perulli, *Lavoro e tecnica ai tempi di Uber*, in *Riv. giur. lav.*, 2017, 1, pp. 195-218; P. Loi, *Un'introduzione al tema del lavoro nella gig economy*, in *Riv. giur. lav.*, 2017, 2, p. 23; A. Salento, *Industria 4.0 ed economia delle piattaforme: spazi di azione e spazi di decisione*, *Riv. giur. lav.*, 2017, 2, ivi, p. 29; A. Lassandari, *Problemi di rappresentanza e tutela collettiva dei lavoratori che utilizzano le tecnologie digitali*, in *Riv. giur. lav.*, 2017, 2, ivi, p. 59; R. Voza, *Il lavoro reso mediante piattaforme digitali tra qualificazione e regolazione*, in *Riv. giur. lav.*, 2017, 2, ivi, p. 71; T. Treu, *Rimedi, tutele e fattispecie: riflessioni a partire dai lavori della Gig economy*, in *Lav. dir.*, 2017, 3-4, pp. 367-406; M. Lai, *Evoluzione tecnologica e tutela del lavoro: a proposito di smart working e di crowd working*, in *Dir. rel. ind.*, 2017, 4, p. 985; G. Santoro Passarelli, *Lavoro etero-organizzato, coordinato, agile e telelavoro: un puzzle non facile da comporre nell'impresa in via di trasformazione*, in *Dir. rel. ind.*, 2017, 3, p. 771; F. Seghezzi, *La nuova grande trasformazione. Lavoro e persona nella quarta rivoluzione industriale*, Adapt University Press, Modena, 2017; M. Tiraboschi, *Il lavoro agile tra legge e contrattazione collettiva: la tortuosa via italiana verso la modernizzazione del diritto del lavoro*, in *Dir. rel. ind.*, 2017, 4, p. 921; V. Cagnin, *Gig-economy ed il problema qualificatorio dei gig-workers; uno sguardo oltreconfine*, in A. Perulli (a cura di), *Lavoro Autonomo ed Economia delle Piattaforme*, Cedam, Padova, 2018.

29. L. Corazza, R. Romei, *Il puzzle delle trasformazioni*, in L. Corazza, R. Romei (a cura di), *Diritto del lavoro in trasformazione*, il Mulino, Bologna, 2014, p. 10.

30. L. Fiorillo, *Il lavoro agile: continua il processo di ridefinizione del Diritto del lavoro*, in L. Fiorillo, A. Perulli (a cura di), *Il jobs act del lavoro autonomo e del lavoro agile*, Giappichelli, Torino, 2018, p. 165.

economic and social actor, labour flexibility, regulatory differentiation inspired by non-homogenizing logics and the reconsideration of the Welfare State. However, the emersion of this new path of labour law does not correspond to formalizing either the end of labour or the end of labour law, therefore the crucial issue is to wonder whether, and to what extent, these changes are modifying the labour law paradigm.[31]

Thus, if the entire evolutionary process of labour law in the second half of the past century is based on the protection of the subordinate worker, understood as a weak contracting party of the labour relation, it is precisely the paradigm (or value) of subordination that is now in crisis. The very notion of subordination, pursuant to Article 2094 of the Civil Code,[32] results as incapable of giving an account of the growing multiformity of real relationships, given the blurring of the dualistic vision between subordination and autonomy, by virtue of the constant expansion of the grey area to the detriment of the prevalence of the classic social type of subordinate worker.[33]

The symbol of this incapacity is both the emersion, even in the normative fabric, of the notion of 'organized' work, which can be traced back to the sphere of labour law

31. G. Cazzetta, *Giuslavorisi e costruzione della memoria nell'Italia repubblicana*, in G. Cazzetta, G. G. Balandi (a cura di), *Diritti e lavoro nell'Italia repubblicana: materiali dall'incontro di studio, Ferrara, 24 ottobre 2008*, Giuffrè, Milano, 2009, p. 13.
32. Pursuant to Art. 2094 of the Italian Civil Code, the employee is 'a person who commits, in return for a remuneration, to cooperating in the undertaking ... in service and under the direction of the employer'.
33. On the topic of subordination and autonomy, P. Ichino, *Subordinazione e autonomia nel diritto del lavoro*, Giuffrè, Milano, 1989; M. Pedrazzoli (curated by), *Lavoro subordinato e dintorni. Comparazioni e prospettive*, il Mulino, Bologna, 1989; L. Gaeta, *In tema di frammentazione della subordinazione: a proposito di un paio di sfasature e di un viaggio nel passato*, in M. D'Antona (curated by), *Politiche di flessibilità e mutamenti di diritto del lavoro: Italia e Spagna*, Editoriale Scientifica, Napoli, 1990, pp. 119-132; L. Menghini, *Autonomia e subordinazione: sollecitazioni dottrinali e risposte della giurisprudenza*, in *Riv. giur. lav.*, 1991, 42, p. 208; A. Perulli, *Il diritto del lavoro tra crisi della subordinazione e rinascita del lavoro autonomo*, in *Lav. dir.*, 1997, pp. 173 ss; R. De Luca Tamajo, R. Flammia, M. Persiani, *La crisi della nozione di subordinazione e della sua idoneità selettiva dei trattamenti garantistici. Prime proposte per un nuovo approccio sistematico in una prospettiva di valorizzazione di un tertium genius: il lavoro coordinato*, in AA.VV., *Subordinazione e autonomia: vecchi e nuovi modelli*, UTET, Torino, 1998; M. Dell'Olio, *La subordinazione nell'esperienza italiana*, in *Arg. dir. lav.*, 1998, p. 697; G. Ferraro, *Dal lavoro subordinato al lavoro autonomo*, in *Giorn. dir. lav. rel. ind.*, 1998, p. 429; F. Lunardon, *L'evoluzione del concetto di subordinazione nell'elaborazione dottrinale*, in *Quad. dir. lav. rel. ind.*, 1998, 26; L. Gaeta, *Contro l'unificazione tra lavoro autonomo e subordinato*, in F. Amato (curated by), *I 'destini' del lavoro. Autonomia e subordinazione nella società post-fordista*, Franco Angeli, Milano, 1998, pp. 123-127; A. Supiot, *Au-delà de l'emploi*, Flammarion, Paris, 1999; A. Supiot, *Lavoro subordinato e lavoro autonomo*, in *Dir. rel. ind.* 2000, pp. 217 ss; P. Davies, *Lavoro subordinato e lavoro autonomo*, in *Dir. rel. ind.*, 2000, pp. 207 ss; M. Pedrazzoli, *La parabola della subordinazione: dal contratto allo status. Riflessioni su Barassi e il suo dopo*, in *Arg. dir. lav.*, 2002, p. 263; A. Perulli, *Lavoro autonomo e dipendenza economica, oggi*, in *Riv. giur. lav.*, 2003, 1, pp. 221-270; M. Persiani, *Individuazione delle nuove tipologie tra subordinazione e autonomia*, in *Arg. dir. lav.*, 2005, 1; E. Ghera, *Subordinazione, statuto protettivo e qualificazione del rapporto di lavoro*, in *Giorn. dir. lav. rel. ind.*, 2006, 1, pp. 1-37; E. Ghera, *Il nuovo diritto del lavoro. Subordinazione e lavoro flessibile*, Giappichelli, Torino, 2006; A. Perulli, *Lavori atipici e parasubordinazione tra diritto europeo e situazione italiana*, in *Riv. giur. lav.*, 2006, 4; M. T. Carinci, *Il dialogo fra Pino Santoro Passarelli e la dottrina. Dalla parasubordinazione al lavoro economicamente dipendente: la rivincita di un'idea*, in *Arg. dir. lav.*, 2007, 4-5, pp. 906-927; M. Roccella, *Lavoro subordinato e lavoro autonomo, oggi*, in *WP C.S.D.L.E. 'Massimo D'Antona'.IT – 65/2008*; P. Tosi, *Autonomia, subordinazione e coordinazione*, in *Labor*, 2017, 2, p. 245.

protections (Article 2, paragraph 1, D. lgs. 81/2015) and the resurgence of the forms of para-subordinate work and independent collaborations, which, despite the abrogation of project work (Article 52), have been confirmed by the Jobs Act[34] as evidence of the complex and non-linear situation of the labour market also in the area of independent work.

The traditional labour law narrative was then based on the absolutization of the value of the stability of the full-time and open-ended employment relationship, as a unique form of attraction of the protections and as identification of the right to work (Article 4 of the Constitution) with stable subordinate work.[35] If, at least on paper, the full-time and open-ended contract is still understood as the common form of employment contract,[36] over the years the forms and the use of flexible or atypical work have increased, making the 'standard' employment contract much less 'typical'.

Over the years, we have faced a deterioration in the principle of inderogability[37] (and consequently, the principle for the *favour* of the weak contractor) that had always been considered not a mere technique but the super-principle of labour law,[38] since in such principle lies nothing less than the foundation of all labour law systems, which have always been recognized in the disparity of power between the parties of the employment contract.[39]

---

34. The Jobs Act is the labour reform introduced by the Renzi government which aims to bring about important changes with respect to contractual forms, social safety nets, the reconciliation of working times and private life.
    Delegated Law 183/2014 is the law that identifies the points of the Jobs Act and delegates the government to issue the individual decrees implementing the labour reform.
35. B. Caruso, *Nuove traiettorie del diritto del lavoro nella crisi europea. Il caso italiano*, in *WP C.S.D.L.E. 'Massimo D'Antona'.INT – 111/2014*, p. 19.
36. Article 1, para. 7, letter b), 10 December 2007/n. 183. The same formula is contained in the Preamble of the Directive 1999/70/EC of the Council of 28 June 1999, relating to the framework agreements CES, UNICE and CEEP on fixed-term work 8, p. 6: 'considering that permanent employment contracts represent the common form of labour relations and contribute to the quality of life of the workers concerned and to improve their performance'.
37. The inderogability of the norm, the proof of the historical difference between labour and common laws, has since always constituted an axiological peculiarity of the subject matter. On inderogability, A. Ichino, *A chi serve il diritto del lavoro, Riflessioni interdisciplinari sulla funzione economica e la giustificazione costituzionale dell'inderogabilità delle norme giuslavoristiche*, in *Riv. it. dir. lav.*, 1994; P. Tullini, *Indisponibilità dei diritti dei lavoratori: dalla tecnica al principio e ritorno*, in *Giorn. dir. lav. rel. ind.*, 2008; C. Cester, *La norma inderogabile: fondamento e problema del diritto del lavoro*, in *Giorn. dir. lav. rel. ind.*, 2008, pp. 341 ss; G. Fontana, *Dall'inderogabilità alla ragionevolezza*, Giappichelli, Torino, 2010; A. Zoppoli, *Il declino dell'inderogabilità?*, in *Dir. lav. merc.*, 2013, pp. 53 ss; R. De Luca Tamajo, *Il problema dell'inderogabilità delle regole a tutela del lavoro: passato e presente*, in *Giorn. dir. lav. rel. ind.*, 2013, 4, pp. 715 ss; G. Santoro Passarelli, *Autonomia privata individuale e collettiva e norma inderogabile*, in *Riv. it. dir. lav.*, 2015, 1, pp. 61 ss.
38. R. De Luca Tamajo, *La norma inderogabile nel diritto del lavoro*, Jovene, Napoli, 1976; M. Novella, *L'inderogabilità nel diritto del lavoro. Norme imperative e autonomia individuale*, Giuffrè, Milano, 2009.
39. B. Langille, *Labour Law's Theory of Justice*, G. Davidov, B. Langille (eds), *The Idea of Labour Law*, Oxford University Press, Oxford, 2011, p. 104.

One of the most evident changes to the traditional labour law[40] system can also be found in the progressive reduction of the judicial role,[41] especially in the area of control of entrepreneurial prerogatives:[42] the exclusion of the necessary linkage of temporary contracts to a causal, the continuous changes in terms of *jus variandi* and of power to control of the employer, as well as the more recent limitation of the judge's discretionality in the choice of the sanctionatory remedies applicable in the case of illegitimate dismissal, in order to render the 'separation' costs more contained and foreseeable for the employer, has entailed a process of judicial disintermediation,[43] that is, a devaluation of the fundamental role of mediation carried out by the jurisprudence.

Finally, the discipline seems to have lost the strong values of *universality* and *solidarity* that have characterized the labour law model in the Fordist era: refer, in this regard, to the current fragmentation of collective bargaining under the progressive decentralization of the contractual system and to the ever-widening spaces of derogability of the national collective bargaining regulations on the part of the company contract, a process culminating in the adoption of a norm (Article 8 of Law No. 143/2011) which even enables proximity bargaining to derogate *in pejus* from the same law regulation and from the parallel tendency to re-evaluate the individual autonomy with the inevitable consequences in terms of weakening of the solidarity among workers belonging to the same sector, or even to the same company.

Thus, beside the old and solid values of the labour law discipline of the twentieth century, such as *subordination, irrevocability, stability, rigid judicial control, national trade union bargaining, universality* and *solidarity*, in the course of time, along the process of transformation (still in progress) of the subject, new values of reference for

40. A. Lo Faro, *Compatibilità economiche, diritti del lavoro e istanze di tutela dei diritti fondamentali. Qualche spunto di riflessione dal caso italiano*, in *Giorn. dir. lav. rel. ind*, 2014, 2, p. 297.
41. On this point, an illustrative reference is Art. 30 of the so-called collegato-Lavoro, approved with law n. 183 of 4 November 2010, which establishes that, with reference to the regulations that contain general clauses, including the rules on the establishment of an employment relationship, the exercise of the employer's powers, the transfer of the company and withdrawal, the judicial control of the deeds of exercising the employer's powers is limited exclusively, in accordance with the general principles of the order, to the ascertainment of the assumption of legitimacy and cannot be extended to the merit on the technical, organizational and productive assessments that are the responsibility of the employer or the client. For the doctrine on the subject, refer to the writings of: A. Vallebona, *Il Collegato Lavoro: un bilancio tecnico*, in *Mass. giur. lav.*, 2010, p. 900; M. Tiraboschi, *Clausole generali, onere della prova, ruolo del giudice*, in G. Proia, M. Tiraboschi (a cura di), *La riforma dei rapporti e delle controversie del lavoro*, Giuffrè, Milano, 2011, p. 31; O. Mazzotta, *La giustizia del lavoro nella visione del 'collegato': la disciplina dei licenziamenti*, in M. Cinelli, G. Ferraro (a cura di), *Il contenzioso del lavoro nella Legge 4 novembre 2010, n. 183 (Collegato Lavoro)*, Giappichelli, Torino, 2011, XXVII; G. Ferraro, *Il controllo giudiziale sui poteri imprenditoriali, ibid.*, 2011, 5 ss; L. Nogler, *Opinioni sul Collegato Lavoro*, in *Giorn. dir. lav. rel. ind.*, 2011, p. 124; M. T. Carinci, *Clausole generali, certificazione e limiti al sindacato del giudice. A proposito dell'art. 30, l. n. 183 del 2010*, in O. Mazzotta (a cura di), *Il diritto del lavoro dopo il 'collegato' (Legge 4 novembre 2010, n. 183)*, in *Quaderni di Questione Lavoro*, 2011, 1, p. 15.
42. A. Perulli, *Il controllo giudiziale dei poteri dell'imprenditore tra evoluzione legislativa e diritto vivente*, in *Riv. it. dir. lav.*, 2015, 1, pp. 83-126.
43. B. Caruso, *La rappresentanza delle organizzazioni di interessi tra disintermediazione e re-intermediazione*, in *WP C.S.D.L.E. 'Massimo D'Antona'.IT – 326/2017*, pp. 6-7.

labour law have been created: *competitiveness*, *efficiency*, *flexibility*, *simplicity*, *certainty* (inflected within an individual dimension of protection of the employer's interests in the predetermination of costs and the marginalization of reintegration[44]), *individualization* and *competition*. These are new values of labour law, which have become part of the fabric of the discipline under the relentless pressure of a series of regulatory interventions aimed at adapting the subject matter to the changing context of the new millennium, and they must be carefully examined to reflect on the guidelines and on the new keys to reading the change in progress, that is to understand the new and problematic scientific paradigm of labour law that allows the subject matter to elaborate its 'point of view' on the reality and to solve on this basis the cognitive and pragmatic problems it faces.[45]

§1.03 THE RESEARCH FOR A NEW 'SUSTAINABLE' PARADIGM

In light of the scenario mentioned above, the need for a cognitive refounding of the subject[46] is evident, which entails a verification of the 'functioning' of labour law in the light of the precepts of economic efficiency.[47]

But in this verification of economic compatibility, the new paradigm of labour law cannot completely lose its original axiological status. In short, what emerges is a work of reaffirmation of the constitutive characteristics of the subject matter, in order to reaffirm the epistemological autonomy of this branch of law and at the same time to 'prevent economic rationality from being the only parameter of evaluation of the effects of the juridical norms and the basis of the proposals of reforms of the juridical system'.[48] Moreover, conscious of being, as Gérard Lyon-Caen said, *a droit de perpétuel compromis*, labour law does not ask, nor has it ever asked, to become other-than-itself. It longs for conservative restorations. It asks for improved maintenance. In short, it only asks for what it needs from time to time to avoid being caught in the orbit of the market economy, without thereby wanting or being able to get out of it completely.[49]

Such an operation of conservative re-modulation of the labour law presupposes, however, having in mind a reference model, a society utopia, a vision,[50] or a new

44. A. Olivieri, *Le tutele dei lavoratori dal rapporto al mercato del lavoro: alla postmodernità giuridica verso la modernità economica?*, Giappichelli, Torino, 2017, p. XIX.
45. P. Costa, *Cittadinanza sociale e diritto del lavoro nell'Italia repubblicana*, in G. Cazzetta, G. G. Balandi (a cura di), *Diritti e lavoro nell'Italia repubblicana: materiali dall'incontro di studio, Ferrara, 24 ottobre 2008*, Giuffrè, Milano, 2009, p. 24.
46. R. Del Punta, *Epistemologia breve del diritto del lavoro*, in *Lav. dir.*, 2013, 1, pp. 37 ss.
47. R. Del Punta, *L'economia e le ragioni del diritto del lavoro*, in *Giorn. dir. lav. rel. ind.*, 2001, 1, p. 9.
48. V. Speziale, *La mutazione genetica del diritto del lavoro*, in M. P. Iadicicco, V. Nuzzo (a cura di), *Le riforme del diritto del lavoro. Politiche e tecniche normative*, Editoriale Scientifica, Napoli, 2016.
49. U. Romagnoli, *Giuristi del lavoro. Percorsi italiani di politica del diritto*, Donzelli editore, Roma, 2009, p. 192.
50. D. Garofalo, *Lavoro, Impresa e trasformazioni organizzative, Relazione alle Giornate di Studio AIDLASS 2017, Frammentazione organizzativa e lavoro: rapporti individuali e collettivi*, Cassino, 18-19 Maggio 2017.

guiding paradigm that replaces the previous active paradigms, applied and undermined by contemporary labour law.[51]

Recalling the definition elaborated by Thomas Kuhn, a paradigm is a set of statements capable of defining the 'theoretical field' (the object and method) of a discipline and as such implicitly or explicitly shared by the enthusiasts of that specialistic knowledge. The paradigm is the window through which the discipline looks at the world, a sort of interface between the 'inside' and the 'outside', among the cognitive strategies of a specialized knowledge and the magmatic intertwining of social interaction.[52]

Starting from the assumption that the labour law paradigm of the twentieth century is now inadequate and insufficient to address the complexity of the problems posed by globalization, technological transformation and business[53] organization, it is necessary to identify this new window from which labour law can look at the world.

And the opportunity to identify and adopt a new paradigm for the labour law discipline, which contains 'the indelible traces of the changing compromise resulting from the encounter and the clash with the knowledge and powers concerned by the same complex of knowledge',[54] can be offered precisely from the crisis, as its Chinese ideogram suggests, composed of two different characters, the first indicating the 'danger' and the second 'the opportunity'. The crisis could therefore represent not only a threat to labour law discipline in the sense of a progressive dismantling, but, at the same time, the opportunity to adopt a new regulatory paradigm and to invert, or better to correct, the route so far followed characterized by a downward trend in reformism.[55]

As a matter of fact, even if in the Italian language the term 'crisis' has an essentially negative[56] connotation, by recalling the etymology of the term deriving from the Greek *krisis* (that is to say the verb *krino*, which means 'to separate, to sort out and decide'[57]), it is possible to grasp a positive sense. The crisis can be interpreted differently in a perspective of 'separation' and at the same time of 'passage' towards a

51. Labour law science tends to make its own history, since it is aware of the intrinsically historical character of the paradigms it is constructing, applying and putting into question. Cfr. P. Costa, *Cittadinanza sociale e diritto del lavoro nell'Italia repubblicana*, in G. Cazzetta, G. G. Balandi (a cura di), *Diritti e lavoro nell'Italia repubblicana: materiali dall'incontro di studio, Ferrara, 24 ottobre 2008*, Giuffrè, Milano, 2009, p. 24.
52. T. S. Kuhn, *La tensione essenziale: cambiamenti e continuità nella scienza*, Torino, Einaudi, 1985; T. S. Kuhn, *La struttura delle rivoluzioni scientifiche*, Torino, Einaudi, 1995.
53. B. Caruso, *Nuove traiettorie del diritto del lavoro nella crisi europea. Il caso italiano*, in B. Caruso, G. Fontana (a cura di), *Lavoro e diritti sociali nella crisi europea. Un confronto fra costituzionalisti e giuslavoristi*, il Mulino, Bologna, 2015.
54. A. Somma, *Dal lavoratore al consumatore. Cittadinanza e paradigma giuslavoristico nell'economia sociale di mercato*, in G. Cazzetta, G. G. Balandi (a cura di), *Diritti e lavoro nell'Italia repubblicana: materiali dall'incontro di studio, Ferrara, 24 ottobre 2008*, Giuffrè, Milano, 2009, p. 132.
55. V. Cagnin, *Crisi e diritto del lavoro: la via della sostenibilità*, in *IANUS*, 2012, 7.
56. The crisis can be defined as 'the deterioration of an objective condition with consequent social-political instability and decadence of civil institutions' (Corriere della Sera Dictionary) or again, a 'transitory state of particular difficulty or disturbance, in the life of a man or a company '(*Garzanti* dictionary).
57. The crisis therefore evokes, in a neutral sense, the transition between two phases and/or moments, so much so that it can also be described as 'the decisive turn that a business undertakes', or again, as a 'remarkable and sudden change'.

new state, or as a necessary moment of reflection, of evaluation in the sense of a change for an improvement and/or for a rebirth: 'Therefore, we have a dimension of separateness and therefore of the overcoming of one system towards another, within the crisis, but also a dimension of the decision on 'what to do' in facing the crisis.'[58]

In this sense, we could also refer to the concept of 'creative destruction' that could lead the current de-construction of labour law (triggered by the economic and global crisis) to its subsequent reconstruction and rebirth.[59]

A paradigm shift could therefore prove to be the fundamental step of the postmodern era to adapt the labour law discipline to the new social-economic context and to recover its lost legitimacy.

The idea is to accept the challenge of change for labour law, but without the discipline abdicating from itself.[60] According to some authors it is simply a matter of facing the problem of developing new techniques (means) to apply the old values (goals) to the new empirical[61] realities, without any need for a paradigm shift.[62]

Others, however, suffering from what has been (good-naturedly) defined as 'the paradigm shift syndrome[63]', strongly hope for it.

The doctrinal solutions are based on radically different approaches,[64] for example: (i) the adoption of a discursive paradigm, which compares labour law with other social sciences, in an open and transparent communication process,[65] as well as different alternatives on the epistemological and paradigmatic future of the discipline: constitutional and statutory traditionalism; (ii) strongly self-controlled change, marked by the preservation of the twentieth-century noble tradition; (iii) or again, a paradigm

58. A. Perulli, *La crisi come categoria del discorso e le aporie della nuova disciplina sui licenziamenti economici*, in *Il diritto del lavoro al tempo della crisi, Atti AIDLASS del XVII Congresso Nazionale di Diritto del Lavoro, Pisa, 7-9 giugno 2012*, Giuffrè, Milano, 2013, p. 273.
59. J. A. Schumpeter, *Teoria dello sviluppo economico*, ETAS, Milano, 2002. Translation of the sixth German edition (1964), also in the wake of the 1934 English edition of the *Theorie der wirtschaftlichen Entwicklung*, 1911, with Introduction of P. Sylos Labini.
60. L. Fiorillo, *Il lavoro agile: continua il processo di ridefinizione del Diritto del lavoro*, in L. Fiorillo, A. Perulli (a cura di), *Il jobs act del lavoro autonomo e del lavoro agile*, Giappichelli, Torino, 2018, p. 175.
61. B. Langille, *Labour Law's Theory of Justice*, in G. Davidov, B. Langille (eds), *The Idea of Labour Law*, Oxford University Press, Oxford, 2011, p. 101.
62. Manfred Weiss claims that a paradigm shift is not necessary for labour law: 'Labour law does not need to be reinvented; there is no need for a new paradigm. Labour law still has its unique function in the context of employment in its broadest sense ... However, there is an urgent need for adaptation to new circumstances'. Cfr. M. Weiss, *Re-inventing Labour Law?*, in G. Davidov, B. Langille (eds), *The Idea of Labour Law*, Oxford University Press, Oxford, 2011, p. 56.
63. L. Zoppoli, *Le fonti (dopo il jobs act): autonomia ed eteronomia a confronto*, in O. Mazzotta (a cura di), *Lavoro ed esigenze dell'impresa fra diritto sostanziale e processo dopo il Jobs Act*, Giappichelli, Torino, 2017, p. 14.
64. V. Speziale, *La mutazione genetica del diritto del lavoro*, in M. P. Iadicicco, V. Nuzzo (a cura di), *Le riforme del diritto del lavoro. Politiche e tecniche normative*, Editoriale Scientifica, Napoli, 2016. Also Franco Carinci claims that the expression 'change of paradigm' has by now become up-to-date, as an expression of a synthetic evaluation on the reform carried out by the Jobs Act. Cfr. F. Carinci, *Licenziamento e tutele differenziate*, in O. Mazzotta (a cura di), *Lavoro ed esigenze dell'impresa fra diritto sostanziale e processo dopo il Jobs Act*, Giappichelli, Torino, 2017, p. 119.
65. R. Del Punta, *Epistemologia breve del diritto del lavoro*, in *Lav. dir.*, 2013, 1, pp. 37 ss.

of law and economics tempered by flexicurity; (iv) or rather a controlled modernization, 'in the sense of innovation that is rooted in tradition not denying it, but changing it, even radically, in the realized alchemy'.[66] Another hypothesis was a change in the 'fundamental paradigm' of the subject, replacing the property rule with the liability rule with respect to the workplace, so that the reintegration gives way to a predetermined compensation indemnity, losing the nature of main protection of the worker in favour of the protection in the labour market.[67]

Other positions in the doctrine see in the Jobs Act a change of paradigm long studied and announced in the context of an overall and profound redistribution of social and economic power for the benefit of the company and the market.[68] The real challenge of the present would be to bring out the positive virtualities of the old paradigm in the new and reconstruct a course of social legitimacy of labour law norms based not only on a procedural reason but also based on a substantial axiological core: this means, at the very least, reintroducing anthropology into politics and, with it, regaining that profound sense of the mediation of interests and their right balance.[69]

An assumption, that of mediation and adaptation of interests, which responds to the need for compatibility (and not strict submission) with the values expressed by the economy, the market and the company that is at the basis of Sustainable Development.

From this point of view, it is precisely Sustainable Development that could be taken as a new paradigm for the subject matter: after all, without a reference framework based on the results for development, social and labour standards tend to be considered as 'subsidiary' social goods that promote and support economic growth or other humanitarian objectives. Consequently, they can be immediately sacrificed when they hinder the achievement of such objectives because they are purely instrumental.[70]

Sustainable Development could therefore constitute the new framework of value reference for the discipline, or the orientation compass, the new polar star to use as a guide when selecting new values and new techniques that are the foundation of the discipline of the second millennium.

However, a reflection on the appropriateness of electing Sustainable Development as a reference value paradigm for the new labour law requires a preliminary

66. B. Caruso, *Impresa, lavoro, diritto nella stagione del Jobs Act*, in *Giorn. dir. lav. rel. ind.*, 2016, pp. 255-289 and in A. Perulli (a cura di), *L'idea di diritto del lavoro, oggi. In ricordo di Giorgio Ghezzi*, Cedam, Padova, 2016, p. 255.
67. Such is the opinion of Ichino according to Franco Carinci on the matter of paradigm change, in F. Carinci, *Licenziamento e tutele differenziate*, in O. Mazzotta (a cura di), *Lavoro ed esigenze dell'impresa fra diritto sostanziale e processo dopo il Jobs Act*, Giappichelli, Torino, 2017, p. 119.
68. A. Perulli, *Il contratto a tutele crescenti e la Naspi: un mutamento di 'paradigma' per il diritto del Lavoro?*, in A. Perulli, L. Fiorillo (a cura di), *Contratto a tutele crescenti e Naspi, Decreti legislativi 4 marzo 2015, n. 22 e n. 23*, Giappichelli, Torino, 2015, p. 5.
69. A. Perulli, *L'idea del diritto del lavoro, oggi*, p. LIX, citando G. Ghezzi, *Presentazione*, in E. Gragnoli, A. Perulli (a cura di), *La riforma del mercato del lavoro e i nuovi modelli contrattuali. Commentario al decreto legislativo 10 settembre 2003, n. 276*, Cedam, Padova, 2004.
70. *See*, in this sense, T. Novitz, *Core Labour Standards Conditionalities: A Means by Which to Achieve Sustainable Development?*, in J. Fandez, C. Tan (eds), *International Economic Law, Globalization and Developing Countries*, Edward Elgar, Cheltenham, 2010, pp. 234-251.

investigation on the meaning of the term itself, by definition controversial, polyhedral and multidisciplinary: a sort of 'motherhood and apple-pie concept', something known to everyone, but of which everyone offers a different recipe.[71]

To this end, in the next paragraphs, the doctrinal debate on the meaning and value of Sustainable Development will be reconstructed, and then the most significant referrals in court will be analysed.

§1.04 THE CONCEPT OF SUSTAINABLE DEVELOPMENT: A CONTROVERSIAL NOTION

In an attempt to reconstruct a precise defining framework of Sustainable Development, the doctrine immediately faces the difficulty of tracing a single and shared notion.

The indeterminateness of the application boundaries of the term and its unquestionable interdisciplinarity,[72] if on the one hand constitute an element of strength of the concept, on the other hand are a source of criticism and, even, of scepticism: 'sustainability is an empty concept, lacking from substance and containing embedded ideological positions that are, under the best interpretation, condescending and paternalistic'.[73] At first glance, one could then have the impression of confronting an 'empty' concept, devoid of any juridical-applicative content.

However, a more in-depth analysis allows us to reach different conclusions, highlighting the value of the Sustainable Development paradigm and the potential applications in the field of labour law.

The term 'Sustainable Development' goes back to the Brundtland Report, elaborated by the World Commission on the Environment and Development of the United Nations (UN), where it is defined as 'the development that meets the needs of the present without compromising the ability of future generations to satisfy their own'.[74]

Specifically, this is a new concept of 'development', understood as an objective not only for developing countries but also, and above all, for those already developed, since Sustainable Development 'requires the satisfaction of basic needs of all and to extend to everyone the possibility of implementing their aspirations for a better life'.[75]

Such definition therefore implies a need for reconciliation between present and future needs that is expressed in the concept of social equity between each generation[76]

71. K. Pittel, *Sustainability and Endogenous Growth, New Horizons in Environmental Economics,* Edward Elgar, Cheltenham UK, 2002.
72. Sustainable Development is the subject of research in matters of ecology, e-economy, environmental policies, medicine, architecture and many other disciplines, without any risk of undue appropriation of the term.
73. J. Fortune, J. Hughes, *Modern Academic Myths,* in F. A. Stowell, R. L. Ison, R. Armson, J. Holloway, S. Jackson, S. McRobb (eds), *System for Sustainability: People, Organizations and Environments,* Plenum Press, New York and London, 1997, pp. 125-130.
74. Brundtland Report, *Our Common Future,* elaborated by the 1983 World Commission on the Environment and Development of the United Nations, chaired by Madame Gro Harlem Brundtland, Norwegian Prime Minister, from whom the Report was named.
75. *Ibid.,* p. 43.
76. *'Even the narrow notion of physical sustainability implies a concern for social equity between generations, a concern that must logically be extended to equity within each generation'.* Cfr.

and in the adoption of a long-term approach in the management of economic, social and environmental resources in the present.[77] This presupposes a strong solidaristic connotation among generations, both at an intra-generational level – that is to say among the same living but geographically distant generations – and at intergenerational level – that is to say among successive generations – so that the satisfaction of the current human needs does not lead to an irreversible destruction of natural resources and to the jeopardization of the biosphere's balance, but that allows future generations to have a natural heritage (and if possible, of quality) and to choose the way to satisfy their own needs, being aware that 'the availability of each generation is influenced by the consumption of previous generations'.[78]

Starting from the Brundtland Report, the doctrine, in the most diverse fields of discipline, has over the years offered different definitions of the term, in an attempt to concretize, limit and further specify the concept.

According to one of the most respected doctrinal interpretations, the term would indicate 'an improvement in the quality of life, without exceeding the capacity of the underlying ecosystems',[79] or 'the potential of an ecosystem to subsist over time, without any change',[80] or' the precondition for ensuring lasting development over long periods of time'.[81] Furthermore, Sustainable Development is defined as 'the development that offers basic environmental, social and economic services to all members of a community, without threatening the operability of the natural, urban or social systems from which the supply of such services depends'.[82] In this sense, the concept implies the ability of a development process to sustain over time the reproduction of the world capital composed of economic capital (that is 'built' by individuals), human/social capital (that is the individuals of a society) and natural capital (that is the natural environment and natural resources of society).[83] This concept is also defined as a path of economic and social transformation, whose primary objective is the achievement of an equally distributed economic well-being, which may be perpetually

Brundtland Report, *Our Common Future*, elaborated by the 1983 World Commission on the Environment and Development of the United Nations, chaired by Madame Gro Harlem Brundtland, Norwegian Prime Minister, p. 43.

77. *Ibid.*, pp. 4, 43–44.
78. N. Georgescu-Roegen, *Energia e miti economici*, Torino, Boringhieri, 1982.
79. Cfr. Caring for the Earth: *A Strategy for Sustainable Living*, World Conservation Union (IUCN), United Nations Environment Programme (UNEP) and World Wide Fund for Nature (WWF), 1991; R. Repetto, *The Global Possible-Resources, Development and the New Century*, Yale University Press, New Haven, 1985, p. 10.
80. Y. Jabareen, *A New Conceptual Framework for Sustainable Development*, in *Environment, Development and Sustainability*, 2008, vol. 10, p. 181.
81. L. Davico, *Lo Sviluppo Sostenibile. Le dimensioni sociali*, Carocci, Roma, 2004, 18.
82. ICLEI, *International Council for Local Environmental Initiatives*, https://iclei.org/.
83. Repetto describes it perfectly in terms of '*a development strategy that manages all assets, natural resources, and human resources, as well as financial and physical assets, for increasing long-term health and well-being. Sustainable development, as a goal rejects policies and practices that support current living standards by depleting the productive base, including natural resources, and that leaves future generations with poorer prospects and greater risks than our own*'. Cfr. R. Repetto, *World Enough and Time*, Yale University Press, New Haven, 1986, p. 15.

repeated for many generations,[84] having to leave to future generations a similar patrimony of resources, or better than what was inherited.[85] Hence, the common expression 'not cheating on your kids', taken as a slogan in Anglo-Saxon countries to immediately explain the concept of 'justice extended to the future',[86] which is inflected in terms of responsibility and solidarity among the different generations, in the awareness that the availability of each generation is influenced by the consumption of the previous generations.[87]

Sustainable Development could otherwise be defined in terms of application of the principle of responsibility promoted by Hans Jonas, considered the precursor of development understood in terms of sustainability. Jonas promotes a concept of ethical normative oriented to the future, suggesting to act 'in such a way that the effects of one's action are compatible with the continuation of an authentically human life', considering the future consequences of any choice or act, no longer responding to one's own deeds *ex post*, but *ex ante*, showing that these actions will not cause potential damage because 'attention must be placed on the risks that anyone provokes to others and to the community'.[88]

In this perspective, the solution will only emerge when humans, faced with the extreme situation that technical-scientific development has led to, will succeed in becoming aware of the irreversible transformations induced by the technique on natural processes and of the long- and super long-term effects that put into question the very existence of future generations. This sense of danger and threat will lead man to a new ethical commitment of responsibility, and therefore humans will feel responsible towards nature and for this reason towards themselves and their existence. Only at this point will Prometheism (or the principle of hope) be replaced by a new global ethic, based essentially on the heuristic of fear, that is, the idea that, by valuing the long-term negative effects of certain choices, humans might take ethical decisions, avoiding choices that lead to catastrophe.[89]

Moreover, in broader terms, Sustainable Development is defined in terms of 'a renewed vision of the world, rather than a notion: it is a plural, multiple, complex thought, that in the contamination between knowledge and different languages ... moves towards a re-conception of the ways of acting of our civilization, on the social, economic and juridical level'.[90]

---

84. R. Goodland, G. Ledec, *Neoclassical Economics and Principles of Sustainable Development*, in *Ecological Modelling*, 1987, vol. 38, nos 1-2, pp. 19-46.
85. *'Sustainable development is about being fair to the future. It is about living the next generation a similar, or better, resource endowment than that which inherited.'* Cfr. D. Pearce, *Sustainable Development: An Economic Perspective*, in *Gatekeeper Series*, n. 89-01, London Environmental Economic Centre, 1989.
86. H. E. Daly, J. B. Cobb, *For the Common Good*, Beacon Press, Boston, 1989.
87. N. Georgescu-Roegen, *Energia e miti economici*, Torino, Boringhieri, 1982.
88. E. Levinas, *Autrement qu'ètre ou au- delà de l'essence*, 1974, trad. it. di S. Petrosino, M. T. Aiello, *Altrimenti che essere o al di là dell'essenza* (introd. di S. Petrosino), Jaca Book, Milano, 1983.
89. H. Jonas, *Il Principio di Responsabilità*, Einaudi, Torino, 2014.
90. R. Bifulco, A. D'Aloia, *Le generazioni future come nuovo paradigma del diritto costituzionale*, in R. Bifulco, A. D'Aloia (a cura di), *Un diritto per il futuro. Teorie e modelli della responsabilità intergenerazionale*, Jovene, Napoli, 2008, p. 10.

As can be seen from the proposed definitional framework, the doctrine has not (yet) reached a universal definition of Sustainable Development and the debate on this point is still very intense, so much so that the same literature considers such definitions as for the most part abstract, vague,[91] lacking in operativeness,[92] often confused or even contradictory.[93]

Probably, adopting a single definition of the term within such a complex concept would mean limiting its meaning and its application: 'there is not, and should not be, any single definition of sustainability that is more logical and more productive than other definitions',[94] For this reason, in defining the concept of Sustainable Development it is more appropriate to resort to its triple delineation (economic, social and environmental) or to the different degrees of sustainability.

[A] The 'Founding' Pillars

Another approach, proposed both in doctrinal and institutional terms, defines Sustainable Development by inflecting it on a plurality of dimensions: social, environmental, economic and institutional.

Environmental sustainability means the ability to maintain the quality and reproducibility of natural resources over time, to preserve biological diversity and to guarantee the integrity of ecosystems. In this sense the concept of sustainability hopes for a development that preserves the natural resources essential to human life (water, air, soil and species diversity) and that pushes to protect non-renewable resources in a constant attempt to reduce energy consumption, pollutants and emissions of greenhouse gases. Environmental sustainability may therefore result as the ability to preserve over time the three functions of the environment: the function of resource supplier, the function of receiving waste and the function of direct source of utility. As regards the entrepreneurial activity, for example, the adoption of a logic of ecologically sustainable development cannot be separated from an analysis both of the compatibility between business activity and the maintenance of ecosystems, and the impact of activity and products in terms of resource consumption, waste production and polluting emissions. Finally, within a territorial system, environmental sustainability means the ability to enhance the value of environment as a 'distinctive element' of the territory, while guaranteeing the protection and renewal of natural resources and patrimony.

Economic sustainability concerns the ability of a system to generate lasting growth of economic indicators, through the creation of income and work for the sustenance of populations, achieving eco-efficiency intended as the rational use of

91. D. Gow, *Poverty and Natural Resources: Principles for Environmental Management and Sustainable Development*, in *Environmental Impact Assessment Review*, 1992, pp. 49-65.
92. C. Villanueva, *Community Development and the Futures of Sustainable Communities in the Philippines*, in Y. Kaoru (ed.), *Sustainable Global Community in the Information Age: Vision from Future Studies*, Praeger Studies on the 21st Century, Praeger, Santa Barbara, 1997.
93. M. R. Redclift, *Sustainable Development: Exploring the Contradictions*, Methuen, London, 1987.
94. C. V. Kidd, *The Evolution of Sustainability*, in *Journal of Agricultural and Environmental Ethics*, 1992, vol. 5, n. 1, pp. 1-26.

available resources and as a reduction in the exploitation of non-renewable resources. In an entrepreneurial logic, for example, Sustainable Development should imply the development of the company's operating area, as well as its stakeholders, the respect for the principles of good competition, the absence of corruption or abuse of dominant position.[95]

Social sustainability concerns the ability to guarantee access to goods considered as fundamental (work, safety, health, education) and conditions of well-being (enjoyment, serenity, sociability) in an equitable manner within today's and future communities. Declined on this specific dimension, sustainability, or durability[96] implies the transmission to future generations of resources, possibilities and rights – specifically social ones – that will allow them access to well-being to the extent that it is conceived nowadays, in terms of social cohesion, equity and lifestyle. In this sense, we may also talk about the distribution of equity, or intra-generational and intergenerational equity, emphasizing the need of present and future generations to share the capacity for well-being.[97] Social sustainability can therefore be defined as the ability to guarantee conditions of human well-being (work, safety, health, education) equally distributed by classes and gender.

Recently, a fourth dimension (or pillar) has also been identified: the institutional dimension, or the capacity to ensure conditions of stability, democracy, participation, information, training and justice, which has the objective of developing forms of inter-institutional coordination and cooperation that are able to build shared programmes, binding commitments and certain implementation times, in compliance with the principle of subsidiarity.[98] It is precisely this dimension that justifies, legitimizes and encourages the adoption of actions, policies and guidelines by institutions at national, European and international level, which promote the dissemination and the concrete application of Sustainable Development among States, legislators, businesses, citizens and consumers.

In the various forms, the common aspect between the pillars of Sustainable Development is the transmission of a patrimony to future generations: the transmission from one generation to another of natural resources essential to human life (water, air, the soil and the diversity of natural and vegetal species (*environmental sustainability*),

---

95. E. Reynaud (a cura di), *Le développement durable au cœur de l'entreprise*, Dunod, Paris, 2006.
96. The term 'durability' derives from the French translation of Sustainable Development in *développement durable*, where the idea of the adjective 'sustainable' is exactly well rendered in terms of durability over time.
97. J. K. Boyce, A. R. Klemer, P. H. Templet, C. E. Willis, *Power Distribution, the Environment, and Public Health: A State-Level Analysis*, in *Ecological Economics*, 1999, vol. 1, n. 29, pp. 127-140; R. M. Solow, *Sustainability: An Economist's Perspective*, in R. Dorfman, N. Dorfman (eds), *Economics of the Environment*, 3rd edition, W. W. Norton, New York, 1991; S. Stymne, T. Jackson, *Intra-generational Equity and Sustainable Welfare: A Time Series Analysis for the UK and Sweden*, in *Ecological Economics*, 2000, vol. 2, n. 33, pp. 219-236.
98. The institutional dimension is extrapolated starting from Chapter 8 of UN Agenda 21, dedicated to the topic of *Integrating Environment and Development in Decision-Making*, whereby the following goals for States are found: (a) *integrating environment and development at the policy, planning and management levels*; (b) *providing an effective legal and regulatory framework;* (c) *making effective use of economic instruments and market and other incentives;* (d) *establishing systems for integrated environmental and economic accounting*.

of productive capacity (intended as human, industrial and natural capital) (*economic sustainability*), and of the same opportunities guaranteed today for the community (noting, in this case, both traditional social themes such as work, education, equity, employment, human rights, social justice and other themes, of a more advanced matrix, such as identity, culture, health and safety, well-being, the quality of life of a subject, social cohesion and social inclusion) (*social sustainability*).[99]

The different dimensions of Sustainable Development can be defined as 'inter-dependent and mutually reinforcing',[100] since they are strongly correlated and equally pondered over in the definition of the concept in question. To be precise, they are defined as 'pillars' because the loss of one of them would undermine the very meaning of Sustainable Development, which is based on the balance between these three dimensions and their hoped convergence over time.

Promoting sustainable development therefore means looking for the balance among these three different components. In particular, we are dealing with a dynamic equilibrium, since it is continually called into question by the pressures due to change that various subjects (public, social, private) promote, and which continually calls into question the priorities among the three fundamental objectives. The attainment and above all the maintenance over time of the balance involved is not immediate: the triple delineation of sustainability has a concrete difficulty, given by the tension and the permanent confrontation, which sometimes results in a conflict among the three dimensions. The task of institutions and economic operators is to resolve the dilemmas existing among the three profiles, negotiating compromises among the different stakeholders that underlie each dimension. In this way, each dimension could be evaluated from time to time as an objective, a means, a condition, or, as a constraint, depending on the position assumed, or, depending on the pillar on which the focus is.[101]

Sustainable Development therefore implies an equal focus on economic, social and environmental needs, entering into a process of civilization that moves from requests of conciliation of economic effectiveness to social equity and environmental protection, in the direction of '*un monde vivable, sur une planète viable, avec une société equitable*'.[102] The promotion of environmental protection and economic and social development, which must be carried out locally, nationally and globally,[103] is in fact essential for '*the recherche d'une preservation social et environnementale dans un contexte de développement économique*'.[104]

In conclusion, we are dealing with a development that promotes social and environmental values beside economic values, in a logic of reciprocal reconciliation

99. A. Colantonio, *Social Sustainability: Linking Research to Policy and Practice*, Oxford Brookes University, Oxford, 2009.
100. See United Nations, *World Summit on Sustainable Development*, 4 September 2002.
101. E. Reynaud (a cura di), *Le développement durable au cœur de l'entreprise*, Dunod, Paris, 2006.
102. M. Capron, *Evaluer les stratégies de développement durable des entreprises: l'utopie mobilisatrice de la performance globale (en collaboration avec Françoise Quairel)*, in *La Revue de l'Organisation Responsable*, 2006, 1.
103. *See* the 1992 Johannesburg Declaration on Sustainable Development.
104. A. Hugon, *Les mutations du droit de l'entreprise et l'objectif de développement durable*, Université de Limoges, 10 novembre 2010.

among them, without privileging one typology or the other, in order not to undermine the environmental and social grounds on which the same capacity for development is based.[105]

[B] From 'Very Weak' to 'Very Strong Sustainability'

As described in the preceding paragraphs, Sustainable Development is often defined in terms of the transmission of 'capital' which guarantees future generations the possibility of satisfying their needs, given by the aggregation of an *economic* capital, that is the generic productive capacity of an economy, which consists of physical capital, intangible assets and natural resources, exploited or developed for the use in economic transformation processes; an *ecological* capital, that is the total stock of renewable resources (both used and non-used within the production process), semi-natural and natural land, ecological factors such as the nutrient cycle and climatic conditions, which represent the part of natural capital that determines the general quality of the ecosystem; a *natural* capital, or the basic natural resource of a geographical area, which is made up of ecological capital and stocks of non-renewable resources.

On the basis of the importance attributed to the preservation of capital and to the trust (or mistrust) about its reproducibility, which may allow to maintain the total capital (given by the sum of the economic, ecological and natural ones) constant in time, four different levels of sustainability can be defined:

(i) a *very weak sustainability*, which implies a perfect substitutability among the different forms of capital: it can be considered as the most risky, and the most trusting in the capacity of future generations (difficult to imagine in actuality) to successfully deal with the environmental consequences of our actions;[106]
(ii) a *weak sustainability*, which requires a policy of protection and safeguarding of the natural capital at risk, since not entirely replaceable, even if there is confidence in a certain reproducibility of natural resources through human activity and technological development;[107]
(iii) a *strong sustainability*, defined with respect to ecological capital, which requires compliance with certain constraints regarding the ecosystem's ability to perform basic environmental functions.[108] More generally, in this level of sustainability, it is believed that natural capital should be safeguarded through measures aimed at protecting non-renewable resources and

105. G. Bologna, *Manuale della sostenibilità*, Edizioni Ambiente, Milano, 2008, p. 283.
106. M. Common, C. Perrings, *Towards an Ecological Economics of Sustainability*, in *Ecological Economics*, 1992, vol. 6, n. 1, pp. 7-34.
107. D. Pearce, A. Markandya, E. Barbier, *Blueprint for a Green Economy*, Earthscan, London, 1989; G. A. J. Klassen, J. B. Opschoor, *Economics of Sustainability or the Sustainability of Economics: Different Paradigms*, in *Ecological Economics*, 1991, vol. 4, n. 2, pp. 93-115.
108. R. Costanza (ed.), *Ecological Economics: The Science and Management of Sustainability*, Columbia University Press, New York, 1991.

ensuring the reproducibility of renewable ones, since this degree of sustainability implies that natural resources cannot be replaced with man-made resources;

(iv) a *very strong sustainability*, which instead represents the most restrictive version of sustainability, with a series of stationary constraints that must be imposed in terms of guaranteeing some environmental functions, since this theory rejects any degree of substitutability among natural resources and other resources. In general, within this level of sustainability, the conservation of natural capital is considered as necessary on the basis of an ideal of justice because any form of activity implies the dispersion of energy and some form of destruction and pollution.

Therefore, according to the proposed classification, the degree of substitutability of resources is inversely proportional to the degree of sustainability of development, that is to say that sustainability decreases with increasing substitutability.

For the purposes of this research, it is important to highlight how the above-mentioned conceptual definition, although it represents one of the defining methods most widely used in doctrine especially in the international context, does not consider the social dimension of Sustainable Development. To this end, if sustainability were to be described in terms of the substitutability of the social capital, that is the patrimony of social rights possessed by the citizens in a certain period, it would be appropriate to speak of a very strong sustainabilty since these rights are replaceable neither with natural nor with economic, let alone with ecological, capital.

§1.05 VALUE PROFILES

The doctrine also adjudicated on the so-called value of Sustainable Development, investigating its prescriptive valence and potential significance, in order to legitimize its use and diffusion, as well as the related application profiles.

For example, the concept is described as 'the value of values'; that is, in a hypothetical hierarchy, as 'the super-ordered value precisely because of its general value as it marks not only the degree of civil life but the right of those who will come after us, or future generations',[109] or again, as an ideal or, better, 'a broad, vague, indefinite and general idea of perfection we should aim at'.[110]

In the legal-philosophical thought of Luigi Mengoni, the 'values' have a foundation of rationality, considered as objective idealities that can be traced back to the cognitive process (as ideas of 'value') and considered as positive, juridical concepts capable to direct the search for law and to control the results.[111] In this sense,

109. V. PEPE, *Riforma dell'art. 41 della Costituzione per uno Sviluppo Sostenibile: la sostenibilità come etica pubblica*, in *L'Italia Forestale e Montana / Italian Journal of Forest and Mountain Environments*, 2012, vol. 67, p. 54.

110. J. VERSCHUUREN, *Sustainable Development and the Nature of Environmental Legal Principles*, in *Potchefstroom Electronic Law Journal*, 2006, vol. 9, n. 1, p. 219.

111. L. MENGONI, *Diritto e valori*, il Mulino, Bologna, 1985; M. GRANDI, *Lavoro e valori: note sulla prospettiva assiologica di Luigi Mengoni*, in *Arg. dir. lav.*, 2006.

Sustainable Development could be both an orientation value in the process of changing labour law and a reference point to *ex post* verify (and hopefully *ex ante*, too) the sustainability of political and legislative choices in matter.

There are also significant divergences in the doctrinal opinions on the possible classification of Sustainable Development as a 'juridical',[112] or rather 'meta-juridical'[113] principle, having been elevated for many countries even on a constitutional basis (see below). Moreover, some define it as an umbrella principle *'bringing together various legal norms as well as policy elements'*,[114] which opens in case of need and withdraws when not required due to the presence of other rules or interpretative principles.

Despite the fact that Sustainable Development has been repeatedly highlighted as a decision-making criterion within matters that are mostly related to environmental protection both by the International Court of Justice and by the European Court of Justice,[115] the doctrine continues to question whether Sustainable Development may be considered as a legal principle of international environmental[116] law to be applied to any environmental matter due to the peculiarity or speciality of the subject, or if, in broader terms, it could rather be considered as a full principle of contemporary international law concerning any sector, according to the logic of environment-development integration. In this sense, Sustainable Development could be understood as a transversal and universal principle of contemporary law, which tends to unify, standardize and harmonize the whole juridical system and consequently to influence, among others, the labour law field.

Moreover, some people, considering it as a set of principles, think it more appropriate to define it in terms of 'conceptual matrix',[117] that is a joint realization of a series of principles, such as the precautionary principle, the *polleur-payeur* principle and the principle of intergenerational responsibility.[118]

---

112. Cfr. P. Sands, *International Law in the Field of Sustainable Development*, in *British Yearbook of International Law*, 1994, pp. 303 ss.
113. C. Curti Gialdino, *L'Unione Europea ed il Principio dello Sviluppo Sostenibile*, Lecture presented at the 2nd level Seminar organized by the Public Education Ministry and by the Veneto Region, on the subject of 'Italian Constitution, European integration and Sustainable Development', Venice, San Servolo Island, 22-24 October 2007.
114. I. Kaya, *Implications of the Danube River Dispute on International Environmental Law*, in *Review of International Law & Politics*, 2008, vol. 4, n. 16, pp. 97-117.
115. At international level, as we will see in detail in §1.06, we see interesting references to Sustainable Development in the sentence of 25 September 1997 of the International Court of Justice, in the *Shrimp* case of 20 September 1999 of the WTO, in the sentence of the Permanent Court of Arbitration of 24 May 2005 of the *Iron Rhine* case, and in that of the International Court of Justice of 20 April 2010, the *Pulp Mills* case. At European level, reference is made to judgments C-91/05 of 20 May 2008, C-43/10 of 11 September 2012, C-195/12 of 26 September 2013, C-201/15 of 21 December 2016 (on the subject of collective dismissal) and the conclusions of the Advocates General Léger of 7 March 2000 (C-371/98), Jacobs of 26 October 2000 (C-379/98) and Bot of 8 May 2013 (C-204/12 and C-208/12).
116. By principle we mean the rules of conduct aimed at guiding and standardizing the behaviour of States, without binding effect.
117. Cfr. P. M. Dupuy, *Ou en est le droit international de l'environnement à la fin du siècle?*, in *Rev. Gén. Droit Int. Pub.*, 1997, p. 886.
118. Article 174 of the ECT (Art. 191 TFEU), which indicates the objective of environmental sustainability as instrumental to the protection of health, then sets out a series of very

A further interesting interpretation in the doctrinal field is that proposed by Lowe, who defined Sustainable Development in terms of *interstitial norm*, that is 'a concept that serves to concile the development of environmental, social and economic norms within international law, in the interest of present and future generations'.[119] The *interstitial norms* are also defined as 'a growing body of law that can be characterized as the implicit rules operating in and around explicit regulatory frameworks',[120] that is to say, a body of rules in course of definition, characterized by implicit rules operating inside and outside of explicit regulatory frameworks. These norms emerge within the international regulatory system and do not derive from the *opinion juris* or State practice, that is from the traditional mechanisms for the creation of international norms, but reflect 'the spirit of the time', as if 'a wide range of social concepts and pressures came to configure these *interstitial norms*, as in the case of international law'.[121]

In this sense, Sustainable Development could therefore act as a *gap* that fills or modifies the primary norms,[122] or as a balancing instrument in the event of conflict between two primary legal norms:[123] the function of *interstitial norms* is precisely that of 'directing the way conflicting and competing rules with their own normativity should interact in practice'.[124]

Other interpretations of the above-mentioned principle (even though they are less shared in the doctrinal field) consider, on the contrary, Sustainable Development as an 'independent legal cause of action',[125] recognizing also to the individual the opportunity to act before a tribunal or a court against a violation of Sustainable Development by a State or a market player, or rather as a customary norm of international law, therefore provided with a legally binding value. The term *customary norms*[126] is in fact used to identify 'international customs which are juridically

important principles: from the high level of protection to the prevention and correction of damage to the source, to the precautionary principle, to the polluter pays principle, which can easily be traced back to the conceptual matrix of Sustainable Development.

119. M. C. C. Segger, *Sustainable Development Law: Principles, Practices, and Prospects*, Oxford University Press, Oxford, 2004, p. 464.

120. M. Finnemore, J. S. Toope, *Alternatives to 'Legalization': Richer Views of Law and Politics*, in A. Beth, S. Steinberg, S. Richard (eds), *International Law and International Relations*, Cambridge University Press, Cambridge, 2007, p. 187.

121. V. Lowe, *The Politics of Law Making: Are the Method and Character of Norm Creation Changing?*, in M. Byers (ed.), *The Role of Law in International Politics: Essays in International Relations and International Law*, Oxford University Press, Oxford, 2001, p. 220.

122. V. Lowe, *Sustainable Development and Unsustainable Arguments*, in A. Boyle, D. Freestone (eds), *International Law and Sustainable Development: Past Achievements and Future Challenges*, Oxford University Press, Oxford, 1999, pp. 19 ss.

123. *Ibid.*, p. 34.

124. V. Lowe, *The Politics of Law Making: Are the Method and Character of Norm Creation Changing?*, in M. Byers (ed.), *The Role of Law in International Politics: Essays in International Relations and International Law*, Oxford University Press, Oxford, 2001, p. 216.

125. K. W. Junker, *The Progression of the Sustainability Concept in Environmental Law*, in *Umwelt und Gesundheit Online*, 2012, 5, pp. 13 ss.

126. The *customary norms* of international law were formed in international practice, gradually, as a rule. Historically, a customary norm of international law appears as the result of repeated actions by States. The element of repetition is the starting point of its formation. In most cases it is precisely the repetition of certain actions in similar situations that leads to such practices

binding',[127] in the awareness of the increasing importance of the customary norm and of the principles, considered to all extents as sources of international law.[128]

In addition, interesting is, although not so widespread in the doctrinal sphere, the definition of Sustainable Development in terms of the obligation of means,[129] that is the obligation to provide the necessary means to achieve it. On the contrary, more extreme are the visions of those who define Sustainable Development as 'a new independent branch of international law',[130] or those who modestly interpret it as 'an important philosophical or political but not normative objective'.[131]

Finally, rich in ideas is the opinion of Bosselmann, who suggests electing Sustainable Development as a norm or universal principle: '*sustainability emerges as an overarching norm or principle that calls for development based on ecological sustainability in order to meet the needs of people living today and in the future. Understood in this way, the concept provides content and direction. It can be used in society and enforced through law.*'[132] In this way, the concept assumes a defined content and a precise direction because it could be used in society and reinforced, subsequently, by law. More specifically, Sustainable Development should be assumed as a Grundnorm, that is, as a 'fundamental, general and presupposed' rule, within both the juridical and moral order, representing the common source, or 'unity in plurality of all the norms that form an order'.[133] Therefore, Sustainable Development would get to the point of being defined in terms of supreme 'presupposed' norm, since - as it happens with the Kelsenian Grundnorm - 'it cannot be set by an authority, whose competence should lie on an even higher standard. Its validity can no longer be deduced from a superior norm, the foundation of its validity can no longer be discussed'.[134] In other words, if it were set (by an authority), it would not be supreme, that is, fundamental. It would therefore not be a matter of producing a *Grundnorm* of

becoming a rule of conduct; in any case it is possible that the element of repetition is missing and that the rule of conduct results from a single precedent, even if these situations are rare.

127. G. I. Tunkin, *Remarks on the Juridical Nature of Customary Norms of International Law*, in *California Law Review*, 1961, vol. 49, n. 3, p. 419.
128. Article 38.1 of the Statute of the International Court of Justice states: 'The Court, whose function is to decide on the basis of international law the controversies submitted, applies: a) both general and particular international conventions, which establish rules expressly recognized by the disputing states; b) international custom, as proof of a general practice accepted as a right; c) the general principles of law recognized by civilized nations; d) subject to the provisions of article 59, the judicial decisions and the doctrine of the most qualified authors of the various nations as subsidiary means for determining the juridical norms'.
129. V. Barral, *Sustainable Development in International Law: Nature and Operation of an Evolutive Legal Norm*, in *European Journal of International Law*, 2012, p. 385.
130. N. Schrijver, *The Evolution of Sustainable Development in International Law, Recueil des Cours*, 2007, p. 217; N. Schrijver, *The Evolution of Sustainable Development in International Law: Inception, Meaning and Status*, Brill Nijoff, Leiden, 2008.
131. G. Fievet, *Réflexions sur le concept de développement durable: prétentions économiques, principes stratégiques et protection des droits fondamentaux*, in *Rev. Belge Droit Int.*, 2001, p. 143.
132. K. Bosselmann, *The Principle of Sustainability: Transforming Law and Governance*, Ashgate, London, 2008, pp. 81 ss.
133. *Ibid.*, p. 83.
134. H. Kelsen, *ReineRechtslehre*, Wien, 1960; trad. it. T. Treves (a cura di), *La dottrina pura del diritto*, Einaudi, Torino, 1966, p. 218.

sustainability, but judges should limit themselves only to 'ascertaining that this norm … is presupposed as a fundamental rule in attributing a foundation to the objective validity of juridical norms and in interpreting a coercive order, effective in its broad outlines, as a system of objectively valid legal norms'.[135] In this perspective, therefore, sustainability can be interpreted as an ideal of civilization, both nationally and internationally,[136] which is the starting point both for the production of law and for the interpretation of norms, acting as a beacon for jurisprudence in decisions concerning a balance among conflicting interests.

§1.06 JURISPRUDENTIAL REMARKS

Beyond the different doctrinal classification, the debate reported so far highlights how the concept of Sustainable Development has gained over the years a growing attention, so much so that it has been promoted in various fields and has become a jurisprudential principle aimed at guiding the judicial decisions at international and European level.

The first significant reference to Sustainable Development in the judicial field can be found in the famous sentence of 25 September 1997 of the International Court of Justice, in the context of the dispute between Hungary and Slovakia concerning the case *Gabcìkovo-Nagymaros* (case at the head on the topic of Sustainable Development) relative to the Danube dam building project. On that occasion, the Court left the parties the task of finding a shared solution,[137] recalling that 'the need to reconcile economic development with environmental protection is rightly expressed by the concept of Sustainable Development'. The above-mentioned case turns out to be particularly significant both because the above citation marked the entry of Sustainable Development into the international jurisprudence as a legitimate objective to condition the interpretation and application of international norms[138] and because on that occasion, the then vice president of the Court, Christopher Gregory Weeramantry, in his dissenting opinion, declared that the principle of Sustainable Development '*is a recognized principle of contemporary international law*',[139] necessary to reconcile the

---

135. *Ibid.*, p. 229.
136. K. Bosselmann, *The Principle of Sustainability: Transforming Law and Governance*, Ashgate, London, 2008, p. 4.
137. *Gabcìkovo-Nagymaros Project (Hungary/Slovakia), Judgment*, I.C.J. Reports, 1997, p. 78, paras 140-141.
138. The citation reported is recalled later by the judgment of the Permanent Court of Arbitration of 24 May 2005, relating to the case of the *Iron Rhine Railway*, where it is reiterated that the duty to prevent or at least mitigate the environmental damage caused by development has now become 'a general principle of international law' (p. 59). The *Iron Rhine* case saw Belgium and the Netherlands contrasting: while the latter had created nature reserves along the route of the historic 'Iron Rhine' line, trying to prevent it from being reactivated, Belgium aimed at strengthening the line, arguing that this project had helped to reduce road transport, contributing to the reduction of greenhouse gases and (to promote) Sustainable Development. (*Permanent Court of Arbitration in the Arbitration Regarding the Iron Rhine Railway, between the Kingdom of Belgium and the Kingdom of the Netherlands* (24 May 2005) at 59, 114, Award of the Arbitral Tribunal.)
139. Original version: '*His opinion states that both the right to development and the right to environmental protection are principles currently forming part of the corpus of international*

right to development and the right to environmental protection, both being part of the corpus of international law. On that occasion, the importance of the principle was emphasized above all for future disputes on environmental matters,[140] since sustainability is an '*integral part of the modern international law*',[141] precisely because of its '*broad and general acceptance by the global community*' and its nature of '*customary law*'.[142]

Another famous example of international law where Sustainable Development is assumed as a decision-making beacon – in this case by the judicial organs of the World Trade Organization (WTO) – is the *Shrimp* case, in terms of syndication on the legitimacy of the ban on importing shrimps placed by the United States for the protection of sea turtles.[143] Although the above-mentioned prohibition clearly constituted a deviation from the objectives of the General Agreement on Tariffs and Trade (GATT), that is to say a discrimination between shrimp-exporting countries,[144] it was considered as legitimate because it was justified by the protection of inderogable global interests and values, first and foremost that of Sustainable Development.

law. They could operate in collision with each other unless there was a principle of international law which indicated how they should be reconciled. That principle is the principle of sustainable development which, according to this opinion, is more than a mere concept, but is itself a recognized principle of contemporary international law', in *Summaries of Judgments, Advisory Opinions and Orders of the International Court of Justice.*

140. Cfr. Separated opinion of Vice-President Christopher Gregory Weeramantry, p. 85: '*Since sustainable development is a principle fundamental to the determination of the competing considerations in this case, and since, although it has attracted attention only recently in the literature of international law, it is likely to play a major role in determining important environmental disputes of the future, it calls for consideration in some detail. Moreover, this is the first occasion on which it has received attention in the jurisprudence of this Court.*'
141. Cfr. Separated opinion of Vice-President Christopher Gregory Weeramantry, p. 86: '*The principle is the principle of sustainable development and, in my view, it is an integral part of modern international law.*'
142. Cfr. Separated opinion of Vice-President Christopher Gregory Weeramantry, p. 104: '*Happily for international law, there are plentiful indications, as recited earlier in this opinion, of that degree of general recognition among States of a certain practice as obl igatory to give the principle of sustainable development the nature of customary law.*'
143. United States – Import Prohibition of Certain Shrimp and Shrimp Products (20 September 1999), WTO. Doc. WT/DS58/AB/R (Appellate Body Report). Per approfondimenti vedi A. Bonfanti, *Imprese multinazionali, diritti umani e ambiente. Profili di diritto internazionale pubblico e privato*, Giuffrè, Milano, 2012, pp. 133 ss.
144. Going into the details of the case involved, the Appellate Body of the WTO considered that the measures imposed by the United States (US) to react to the use of shrimp fishing techniques that caused the death of sea turtles, which is especially in danger of extinction and protected by American legislation, on which the restrictions on imports disputed by India, Malaysia, Pakistan and Thailand were based, were not justifiable pursuant to Art. XX g) of the GATT 1994, as imposed by the US without having first experienced a serious attempt to reach an agreed solution with the counterparts. The contents of the Art. XX del GATT, Art. XX, General Exceptions: '*Subject to the requirement that such measures are not applied in a manner which would constitute a means of arbitrary or unjustifiable discrimination between countries where the same conditions prevail, or a disguised restriction on international trade, nothing in this Agreement shall be construed to prevent the adoption or enforcement by any contracting party of measures: ... g) relating to the conservation of exhaustible natural resources if such measures are made effective in conjunction with restrictions on domestic production or consumption;* (...)'.

Recalling the importance and legitimacy of environmental protection as an objective of international and national policies,[145] the WTO appeal body reached this decision by recalling the Preamble of the WTO agreement,[146] which states that '*while allowing for the optimal use of the world's resources in accordance with the objective of sustainable development, seeking both to protect and preserve the environment and to enhance the means for doing so in a manner consistent with their respective needs and concerns at different levels of economic development*'.[147] in this way the appeal body decided how the optimal use of natural resources should be carried out '*in accordance with the objective of Sustainable Development*'.[148]

The first significant reference to the principle of Sustainable Development in Europe is found instead in the conclusions of Advocate General Philippe Léger regarding the case C-371/98.[149] The prejudicial matter, posed by the United Kingdom division of the European Court of Justice, concerned the interpretation of Directive 92/43/EEC, concerning the conservation of natural and semi-natural habitats and of the wild flora and fauna of Member States, through, among other instruments, the designation of special areas of conservation. In particular, the High Court asked the European Court to specify the scope of the Member States' powers in the designation of such special areas of conservation and, more precisely, to declare whether, in order to compile the list of sites that could be chosen as sites of Community importance, a Member State had the obligation or only the faculty to take into account the needs, in

145. *See* point 129 of 12 October 2008 WTO report (WT/DS58/AB/R), United States – Import prohibition of certain shrimp and shrimp products, Report of the Appellate Body: '*While Article XX was not modified in the Uruguay Round, the preamble attached to the WTO Agreement shows that the signatories to that Agreement were, in 1994, fully aware of the importance and legitimacy of environmental protection as a goal of national and international policy. The preamble of the WTO Agreement – which informs not only the GATT 1994, but also the other covered agreements – explicitly acknowledges the objective of sustainable development*'.
146. *See* §2.02[D] WTO and Sustainable Development.
147. *See* p. 152 of WTO report (WT/DS58/AB/R): '*At the end of the Uruguay Round, negotiators fashioned an appropriate preamble for the new WTO Agreement, which strengthened the multilateral trading system by establishing an international organization, inter alia, to facilitate the implementation, administration and operation, and to further the objectives, of that Agreement and the other agreements resulting from that Round. In recognition of the importance of continuity with the previous GATT system, negotiators used the preamble of the GATT 1947 as the template for the preamble of the new WTO Agreement. Those negotiators evidently believed, however, that the objective of "full use of the resources of the world" set forth in the preamble of the GATT 1947 was no longer appropriate to the world trading system of the 1990's. As a result, they decided to qualify the original objectives of the GATT 1947 with the following words: ... while allowing for the optimal use of the world's resources in accordance with the objective of sustainable development, seeking both to protect and preserve the environment and to enhance the means for doing so in a manner consistent with their respective needs and concerns at different levels of economic development, ...*'
148. *See* p. 153 of the WTO sentence: '*We note once more that this language demonstrates a recognition by WTO negotiators that optimal use of the world's resources should be made in accordance with the objective of sustainable development. As this preambular language reflects the intentions of negotiators of the WTO Agreement, we believe it must add colour, texture and shading to our interpretation of the agreements annexed to the WTO Agreement, in this case, the GATT 1994. We have already observed that Article XX(g) of the GATT 1994 is appropriately read with the perspective embodied in the above preamble.*'
149. Conclusions of the Advocate General Philippe Léger, presented on 7 March 2000, case C-371/98, *First Corporate Shipping*, sentence of 7 November 2000 (Racc. pp. I-9235, I-9237).

particular the economic ones, enshrined in Article 2.3 of the Directive involved. The Advocate General, presenting the normative context, considered that the purpose of the Directive concerning *habitats*, that is to favour the maintenance of biodiversity, while taking into account the economic, social, cultural and regional needs contributed to '*the general objective of lasting development* ...',[150] and explained how the concept of lasting (or sustainable) development '*does not mean that the interests of the environment must necessarily and systematically prevail over the interests supported by other policies pursued by the Community in accordance with art. 3 of the EC Treaty (now, after amendment, Article 3 EC). On the contrary, it highlights the necessary balance among different interests, sometimes contradictory, but that should be conciliated*'.[151] Moreover, recalling the definition of Sustainable Development contained in the Brundtland Report, the Advocate General specified the need emphasized therein 'not to contrast development and environment, but on the contrary to make them evolve in a coordinated way'.[152] Besides, significant is the connection of the principle involved to the principle of integration contained in its conclusions: '*in order to conciliate these different interests in the prospect of "lasting development", the Treaty on European Union has introduced the principle of "integration" which requires the Community legislator to comply with the requirements of environmental protection in the definition and implementation of other policies and actions carried out. The integration of the environmental dimension therefore constitutes the foundation of the durable development strategy simultaneously sanctioned by the Treaty on European Union and by the fifth program «environment», entitled "Towards a durable development". The fifth program expressly states that the success of this process presupposes that the five chosen sectors of the economy – industry, energy, transport, agriculture and tourism – fully contribute to it. It is therefore hoped to limit the trends and practices that are harmful to these sectors*'.[153] In the light of these considerations, the Advocate General established that the activity of designating the Special Areas of Conservation should consist, without prejudice to the respect of the objective of 'durable development' and the principle of 'integration', in assessing the interests at stake, in verifying whether the maintenance of human activities in the area involved was compatible or not with the aim of conservation, that is, restoration of natural habitats as well as of wild fauna and flora.[154]

The Conclusions of the Advocate General Jacobs of 26 October 2000, in the context of the C-379/98 proceeding, concerning the free circulation of goods, are equally decisive for the process of affirmation of Sustainable Development in court. In that occasion, the Advocate recalled the '*deep concern for environment*', demonstrated by the changes to the Treaties adopted in Amsterdam, highlighting the importance of Article 6, according to which '*the requirements connected with the protection of the*

150. *Ibid.*, p. 53.
151. *Ibid.*, p. 54.
152. *Ibid.*, p. 56.
153. *Ibid.*, p. 57.
154. *Ibid.*, p. 58.

environment must be integrated into the definition and implementation of the Community policies and actions pursuant to Article 3', including therefore the internal market, and then, he added: *'in particular in the perspective to promote Sustainable Development'*.[155]

The Advocate General identified in Sustainable Development a real obligation to be respected, declaring that *'as shown by its formulation, the art. 6 is not of a merely programmatic nature; it imposes juridical obligations'*. The Advocate General then concluded by highlighting the obligation of *'taking into particular consideration environmental concerns in the interpretation of the Treaty provisions on the free circulation of goods. Furthermore, damage to the environment, even when they do not constitute an immediate threat – as is often the case – for the health and life of men, animals and plants protected by art. 36 of the Treaty, can represent a more serious threat, even if in the longer term, for the ecosystem as a whole. In such circumstances it would be difficult to justify the fact of reserving to the environment a lower degree of protection than that reserved to the interests recognized in the Treaties on trade concluded many decades ago and recalled in the text of the art. 36 of the EC Treaty, unchanged since its adoption in 1957'*.[156] Therefore, on this occasion, the Advocate General chose Sustainable Development as an interpretative criterion of the Treaty on the free movement of goods, marking an important step in the process of affirming the principle in the jurisprudential field, proposing a necessary balance between economic and environmental interests.

In 2008, after a decade of the introduction of the principle of Sustainable Development in International Courts, we have the first reference to Sustainable Development in the sentences of the European Court of Justice:[157] the occasion was that of a proceeding on request on the part of the Commission of the European Communities: (i) to cancel Council Decision 2004/833/CFSP, implementing joint action 2002/589/CFSP, in view of an EU contribution to ECOWAS[158] in the framework of the moratorium on small calibre weapons; (ii) to declare inapplicable, as illegitimate, the joint action of the Council 12 July 2002, 2002/589/CFSP, on the EU's contribution to the fight against the destabilizing accumulation and spread of portable and light weapons. According to the Commission, the joint action involved should not have been adopted because the project should not have been financed by a Council policy, but by the 9th European Development Fund under the Cotonou Agreement concluded between the EU and the states of Africa, the Caribbean and the Pacific – in order to promote and accelerate the economic, cultural and social development of the latter, thus contributing to peace and security and promoting a stable and democratic political context.[159] The Council therefore usurped with its decision an exclusive

155. Conclusions of Advocate General Jacbos of 26 October 2000, in the field of the proceeding *Preussen Elektra AG v. Schhleswag AG*, Case C-379/98, p. 230.
156. *Ibid.*, p. 232.
157. European Court of Justice, C-91/05, *Commission of European Communities v. European Union Council*, 20 May 2008.
158. Economic Community of Western Africa States.
159. Indeed, this partnership aims to reduce and eliminate poverty, in line with the objectives of sustainable development and the gradual integration of these into the world economy. The

competence of the Community, recognized by Article 47 Treaty of the European Union (TEU). In judging on the limitation of the respective sectors of the Community policy on cooperation to development and of the Common Foreign and Security Policy (CFSP), the judges emphasized that there could not be '*Sustainable Development and the elimination of poverty without peace and without security and that the pursuit of the objectives of the new Community development policy necessarily goes through the promotion of democracy and respect for human rights.*'[160] Furthermore, the Court recalled Articles 177–181 TEU, concerning cooperation with developing countries, which 'aim not only at the sustainable economic and social development of these Countries, at their harmonious and progressive integration into the world economy and the fight against poverty, but also to the development and consolidation of democracy and the rule of law, as well as the respect of human rights and fundamental freedoms, while observing the commitments made within the United Nations and other international organizations'.[161] In addition, evaluating the purpose of the contested decision, the judge stated that '*the excessive and uncontrolled accumulation and spread of small arms and light weapons not only threatens peace and security, but also reduces the prospects for Sustainable Development, particularly in West Africa*'.[162] Despite the decision of the Council impugned by the Commission aimed at preventing further accumulation of small arms and light weapons in West Africa by strengthening the capacity of a group of developing African countries to fight against a phenomenon that constitutes '*an obstacle to their Sustainable Development*',[163] the judges ordered the annulment of the action of the Council considering that the latter, by adopting the 2004/833 decision, had violated Article 47 TEU because it was a matter of exclusive competence of the Community (that is the subject of policy community of cooperation to development).[164] In such a circumstance, Sustainable Development was not evoked to achieve a balance among conflicting interests, but it turned out to be, more properly, a main criterion for evaluating the division of competences in Europe, recognizing a full internalization of the principle under investigation in the Community context.

A concrete reference to Sustainable Development can also be found in the sentence of 20 April 2010 of the International Court of Justice (*Pulp Mills* case), concerning the balance between the interest in economic development (of Uruguay) and that of environmental protection (of Argentina), in the field of the plans to build a paper mill along the Uruguay river. On that occasion, the judges recalled the concept of Sustainable Development '*which takes into consideration the need to safeguard the continuity in the conservation of the river environment and the right of economic*

agreement involved explicitly mentions among the activities to support the fight against the accumulation of small arms and light weapons and excludes the financing by the CFSP of actions already contemplated in the agreement.

160. Case C-91/05, p. 66 and the reference to p. 57 of Case C-403/05.
161. Case C-91/05, p. 65.
162. *Ibid.*, p. 93.
163. *Ibid.*, p. 98.
164. The judge came to a decision contrary to the Conclusions of the Advocate General Paolo Mengozzi, presented on 19 September 2007, who suggested rejecting the Commission's appeal.

development of the States adjacent to the river',[165] and the need '*to conciliate the interests of neighbouring states, in a trans-boundary context, and in particular in the use of shared natural resources, but also the need to balance the use of water and the protection of the river, in accordance with the objective of Sustainable Development*',[166] and eventually decided not to obstruct the construction of the paper mill, as it was not of environmental damage.

The decision is particularly exemplary as it enhances the triple essence of Sustainable Development, that is the same value of its components: Sustainable Development must not in fact be evoked for the exclusive purpose of environmental protection, but to induce an assessment of balance of interests and of opposite axiological values. In this case the interest in economic development, having no particular repercussions in environmental or social terms, has been protected precisely by virtue of Sustainable Development.[167]

With the sentence of the European Court of Justice of 11 September 2012,[168] the interpretation of Directive 92/43 on the conservation of natural and semi-natural habitats of wild flora and fauna, in light of the objective of *Sustainable Development*,[169] allows to justify the authorization for the transformation of a natural river ecosystem into an anthropized river and lake ecosystem.[170]

On that occasion, the judges considered that the directive involved, having the purpose '*to promote the maintenance of biodiversity, while taking into account economic, social, cultural and regional needs*', contributed '*to the general objective of a Sustainable Development*':[171] in the wake of this 'Article 6, paragraph 4, first paragraph, of Directive 92/43 ...'[172] must be interpreted. Consequently, the Court clarified that Directive 92/43 – and in particular Article 6, paragraph 4, first paragraph, of the

165. *See* para. 80, *Pulp Mills on the River Uruguay (Argentina v. Uruguay)*, Provisional Measures, Order of 13 July 2006, I.C.J. Reports 2006.
166. *See* para. 177, *Pulp Mills on the River Uruguay (Argentina v. Uruguay)*, Provisional Measures, Order of 13 July 2006, I.C.J. Reports 2006: '*it is the view of the Court that its formulation reflects not only the need to reconcile the varied interests of riparian States in a trans-boundary context and in particular in the use of a shared natural resource, but also the need to strike a balance between the use of the waters and the protection of the river consistent with the objective of sustainable development.*'
167. In compliance with the above-mentioned Conclusions of Advocate General Philippe Léger, presented on 7 March 2000, case C-371/98, p. 54.
168. The sentence C-43/10 concerns a matter proposed in the context of various appeals for annulment proposed by the prefectural administration of a province of Greece (Aitoloakarnania) and by other bodies and associations against certain Greek Ministers, concerning acts related to the plans of partial deviation of the upper course of the waters of the Acheloo river (western Greece) towards the Peneus river, in Thessaly. Specifically, the sentence focuses on the interpretation of three different directives: Directive 2000/60/EC of 23 October 2000, which establishes a framework for Community action in the field of water, Directive 2001/42/EC of 27 June 2001, concerning the assessment of the effects of certain plans and programmes on the environment and Council Directive 92/43/EEC of 21 May 1992 on the conservation of natural and semi-natural habitats and wild flora and fauna.
169. Article 6 TFCE: 'The needs connected with the protection of the environment must be integrated into the definition and implementation of the community policies and actions pursuant to Article 3, in particular with a view to promoting Sustainable Development.'
170. Case C-43/10, p. 134.
171. *Ibid.*, p. 137.
172. *Ibid.*, p. 138.

same Directive – '*interpreted in the light of the objective of Sustainable Development, it authorizes, ... the transformation of a natural fluvial ecosystem in an anthropized fluvial and lake ecosystem, provided that the conditions set out in the cited provision of this Directive are met*'.[173] The reference on this occasion to Sustainable Development is decisive because it marks an important step in the affirmation of Sustainable Development as an interpretative criterion of European Directives and was adopted, for the first time, by European judges as a criterion of choice and guide in the resolution of a dispute, interpreting a directive, that is a primary source of European law, '*in light of the objective of Sustainable Development*', enhancing the necessary balance among the needs of economic development and those of environmental protection.

The following year, in September 2013,[174] the European Court of Justice was consulted in the context of the dispute that opposed the *Industrie du Bois de Vielsalm&Cie SA* to the Walloon Region concerning the latter's refusal to grant the benefit of a reinforced support regime in the field of biomass cogeneration because its cogeneration plant used only wood or wood waste and not other types of waste.[175] The request for preliminary ruling submitted by the Constitutional Court of Belgium concerned in fact the interpretation of Article 7 of Directive 2004/8/EC of the European Parliament and of the Council, dated 11 February 2004, on the promotion of cogeneration, based on a useful heat demand in the internal energy market, in order to understand whether the unequal treatment implemented by the Belgian Government between biomass cogeneration plants that exploit wood or wood waste and those that exploit all other types of waste is legitimate or not. The Luxembourg judges, in response, acknowledged a discretionary power to Member States in deciding to treat different biomass categories differently, leaving them free to provide for a reinforced support measure such as the one in the main proceeding.[176] Beyond the specific conclusions elaborated by the Court, what we want to highlight here is the reference made by the judges to Sustainable Development, recalling that: '*The promotion of renewable energy sources is a high priority objective at the Union level, and is justified taking into account, in particular, the fact that the exploitation of these energy sources contributes to the protection of the environment and to Sustainable Development and that it can in addition to contributing to the security and diversification of energy supplies and enabling the objectives of the Kyoto protocol to be achieved more quickly.*'[177] In this sense, Sustainable Development is therefore used as a justification for the achievement of a further objective of the Union, the promotion of renewable energy sources.

173. *Ibid.*
174. Sentence of the Court (Fourth Section), C-195/12, *Industrie du bois de Vielsalm & Cie (IBV) SA v. Région wallonne* del 26 settembre 2013.
175. Transmissible title granted to green electricity producers pursuant to Art. 38, para. 3 of the 2001 regional law, intended to support the development of production facilities through the obligations imposed on suppliers and network operators of green electricity.
176. Case C-195/12, p. 81.
177. *Ibid.*, p. 56.

With the most recent AGET Iraklis sentence of 21 December 2016,[178] Sustainability fully enters into a labour law dispute.[179]

The case involved concerned a dispute arising from the Greek Ministry of Labour's decision to not authorize a collective dismissal proposed by a company controlled by the French multinational Lafarge (precisely the AGET Iraklis) due to the lack of a plan in order to move the workers involved in the other plants of the group. The company, in opposition to the ministerial act, had filed an appeal before the Council of State, stating that the Greek law on dismissals was detrimental to the freedom to conduct business in providing (in the absence of a Union agreement) the possibility of veto for the Prefect or the Minister on the basis of assessments carried out '*regarding the conditions of the labour market, the situation of the company and the interest of the national economy*'.

The preliminary matters were therefore related to doubts as to the conformity of the Greek legislation (l. N. 1387/1983) with the Directive 98/59/CE[180] concerning collective redundancies, as well as Articles 49 and 63 Treaty on the Functioning of the European Union (TFEU), concerning respectively the freedom of establishment and the free movement of capital.

Although, as we shall see, the Luxembourg Court considered this appeal as founded, thus assuming an economic position, the sentence involved undoubtedly deserves to be valued: on the one hand, because the balance achieved between economic freedom and social rights is much more sensitive to the fact that collective dismissals concern not only the interests of companies but also those of workers, and, not least, of society in the broad sense;[181] on the other, because for the first time in European judicial history the judges invoke the principle of Sustainable Development to judge the legitimacy of a legislation on dismissals: the balance in this case does not in fact concern economic freedom and environmental protection, as it happens more often, but the economic freedom and the interest in social protection and high level of employment, primary objectives of the EU, as well as, precisely, of Sustainable Development.

The judges began by recalling how '*the Union not only establishes an internal market, but works for Europe's Sustainable Development, which is based in particular*

178. Sentence CGE /Great Section) of 21 December 2016, C-201/15.
179. For the doctrine, N. Countouris, A. Koukiadaki, *The Glass Half Full: Collective Redundancies, Public Interest, and the (Unfulfilled) Potential of Europe's 'Highly Competitive Social Market Economy'*, in *Giorn. dir. lav. rel. ind.*, 2017, 153, 1; G. Orlandini, *Libertà di stabilimento versus diritto al lavoro: ancora un bilanciamento 'sbilanciato' tra libertà economiche e diritti dei lavoratori*, in *Giorn. dir. lav. rel. ind.*, 2017, 153, 1; A. Olivieri, *Le tutele dei lavoratori dal rapporto al mercato del lavoro: Dalla postmodernità giuridica verso la modernità economica?*, Giappichelli, Torino, 2017, p. 138; D. Garofalo, *Lavoro, impresa e trasformazioni organizzative, Relazione alle giornate di studio Aidlass 2017, Frammentazione organizzativa e lavoro: rapporti individuali e collettivi*, Cassino, 18-19 Maggio 2017, p. 66; A. Allamprese, G. Orlandini, *Licenziamenti e regole di mercato. Il caso greco davanti alla Corte di Giustizia (prime note sulla sentenza AGET Iraklis)*, Roma, 31 gennaio 2017.
180. Directive that abrogates Directive 75/129/EEC.
181. N. Countouris, A. Koukiadaki, *The Glass Half Full: Collective Redundancies, Public Interest, and the (Unfulfilled) Potential of Europe's 'Highly Competitive Social Market Economy'*, in *Giorn. dir. lav. rel. ind.*, 2017, 153, 1, p. 198.

on a highly competitive social market economy, which aims at full employment and to social progress, and it promotes, in particular, social protection'.[182] Given the Union's not only economic but also social purpose, '*the rights deriving from the provisions of the Treaty relating to the free circulation of goods, people, services and capital must be balanced with the objectives pursued by social policy, including ... the promotion of employment, the improvement of living and working conditions - allowing their equalization in the progress - adequate social protection, social dialogue, the development of human resources aimed at enabling a high and lasting employment level and the fight against exclusion*'.[183]

In the same perspective, the Luxembourg Court recalls that, pursuant to Article 147 TFEU, both that '*the Union contributes to a high level of employment by promoting cooperation between Member States*' and that '*in defining and implementing the policies and activities of the Union, the objective of high employment level is taken into account*', expressly mentioning, moreover, the Horizontal Social Clause contained in Article 9 TFEU, pursuant to which '*in defining and implementing its policies and actions, the Union shall in particular take into account the needs connected with the promotion of a high level of employment and the guarantee of adequate social protection*'.[184]

The strong importance given to the social dimension of the EU is also reaffirmed by recalling a previous sentence (*Viking*[185]), which, despite the imbalance achieved on that occasion in terms of economic freedoms and social rights, clarified '*that, pursuant to art. 3, n. 1, lett. c) and j), EC, the Community action involves not only an internal market characterized by the elimination, among Member States, of obstacles to the free movement of goods, people, services and capital*' but also '*a policy in the social sector*'. Article 2 EC indeed affirms that the Community has the task, in particular, of promoting 'a *harmonious, balanced and sustainable development of economic activities' and 'a high level of employment and social protection*'.[186]

The Court, on the basis of these statements, despite considering that Article 49 TFEU must be interpreted in the sense that it hinders the Greek national legislation, declares that Directive 98/59/EC does not, *in principle*, preclude the legislation involved.[187] However, in the context of such a national regulation, aimed at a conciliation and a fair balance between the protection of workers and employment on the one hand, and the freedom of establishment and freedom of enterprise on the other, the juridical criteria that the competent authority must apply in order to oppose a collective dismissal plan (that is to say, the *evaluations made regarding the conditions of the labour market, the situation of the company and the interest of national economy*), cannot, in particular, be formulated in a generic and imprecise manner, so

182. C-201/15, p. 76.
183. *Ibid.*, p. 77.
184. *Ibid.*, p. 78.
185. C-438/05.
186. The Court recalls the points 78-79 of the 11 December 2007 sentence, International Workers' Federation and Finnish Seamen's Union, C-438/05.
187. C-201/15, p. 34.

that the Court is concerned with returning to the judge the task of verifying that the legislation, 'in the light of the three evaluation criteria to which such legislation refers to and the concrete application that the aforementioned public authority[188] gives', does not deprive the provisions of the Directive '*of their useful effect*'.[189]

This is for the purpose of enhancing the need for certainty of companies and the proper functioning of the market.

Although this decision has been defined by authoritative doctrine as 'another step forward in the process of erosion of what remains of the European social model',[190] it nevertheless must be emphasized how the judgment of the Court of Justice seems to take, albeit timidly, distances from its excesses of the past,[191] placing itself in profound contrast with the opinion of Advocate General Wahl. The incipit of his Conclusions ('*The European Union is based on a free market economy, which implies that companies must be free to manage their business in the way they consider as advantageous*'[192]) made his declaration already predictable in judging the Greek rules opposite to Directive 98/59/EC, to Article 49 TFEU, and to Article 16 of the Charter of Fundamental Rights of the EU (on business freedom) by virtue of the possibility of proceeding with a prior examination of dismissals.

Although in this latest work of balancing social rights and economic freedoms, the latter still prevailed, the ruling in question seems to open up positive perspectives for Sustainable Development also in the judicial sphere since the Court, unlike the Advocate General, on the basis of the emphasis given to the social dimension of the EU and the objective of Sustainable Development, does not *tout court* exclude the limitation of collective dismissals[193] but insists on the generality and imprecision of criteria to be assessed for the dismissals' legitimacy.

188. *Ibid.*, p. 44.
189. Such a reference to the principle of useful effect could even change the rationale of the directive, whose function would not only be the 'social' one of protecting workers through the involvement of their union representatives in the processes of transformation of the productive organization but also the 'economic' one, to guarantee the employer the freedom to proceed with dismissals, once the Union confrontation is over. Cfr. G. Orlandini, *Libertà di stabilimento versus diritto al lavoro: ancora un bilanciamento 'sbilanciato' tra libertà economiche e diritti dei lavoratori*, in *Giorn. dir. lav. rel. ind.*, 2017, 153, 1, p. 207.
190. Cfr. G. Orlandini, *Libertà di stabilimento versus diritto al lavoro: ancora un bilanciamento 'sbilanciato' tra libertà economiche e diritti dei lavoratori*, in *Giorn. dir. lav. rel. ind.*, 2017, 153, 1, p. 217.
191. N. Countouris, A. Koukiadaki, *The Glass Half Full: Collective Redundancies, Public Interest, and the (Unfulfilled) Potential of Europe's 'Highly Competitive Social Market Economy'*, in *Giorn. dir. lav. rel. ind.*, 2017, 153, 1, p. 201. Il riferimento è ai casi C-438/05 *Viking*, C-341/05 *Laval*, C-426/11 *AlemoHerron*.
192. Conclusions of Advocate General Nils Wahl, presented on 9 June 2016, C-201/15, p. 1.
193. C-201/15, p. 83: 'In light of these different aspects, it must first be noted that the mere fact that a Member State provides, in its national legislation, that collective redundancy plans must, before any implementation, be notified to a national authority, which has powers of control that gives itself, under certain circumstances, the power to oppose such a plan for reasons relating to the protection of workers and employment, cannot be considered as contrary to the freedom of establishment guaranteed by the Article 49 TFEU nor to the freedom to conduct business enshrined in Article 16 of the Charter.'

Undoubtedly, the measure of this success will depend on the intervention of the referring Court and on the subsequent measures by the Greek authorities regarding collective redundancies, but the AGET *Iraklis* sentence can, in any case, be considered the milestone of reference in the social delineation of Sustainable Development in judicial sphere, in the field of labour law.

CHAPTER 2

Labour Law and Multi-level Sustainability in the International, European and Compared Institutional Fields

§2.01 SUSTAINABLE DEVELOPMENT IN THE INSTITUTIONAL CONTEXT

In the past few years, the concept of Sustainable Development has always been more frequently evoked in multiple normative documents of different nature (Constitutions, Treaties, Conventions, Declarations, commercial agreements, etc.), in which it is identified either as a value, as an objective, or as a regulatory paradigm of reference for legislators and economic actors, in particular for multinational companies.

If at the beginning - approximately until the first half of the 1990s - the concept of Sustainable Development was used almost exclusively in the context of legislative initiatives aimed at protecting the environment, restrictively interpreted as an environmental pillar,[1] over time we had several concrete examples of a more properly social and economic delineation of the concept, in line with a more conscious acceptance of the triple dimension of Sustainable Development. This happened both in the jurisprudential and in the institutional context: both at international level (the reference is

1. We invite you to refer to the most significant doctrine on the debate on Sustainability, strictly associated to the conservation of environmental quality: I. MOFFATT, *The Evolution of Sustainable Development Concept: A Perspective from Australia*, in *Australian Geographical Studies*, 1992, vol. 30, pp. 27-42; R. E. MUNN, *Towards Sustainable Development*, in *Atmospheric Environment*, 1992, vol. 26, n. 15, pp. 2715-2731; J. T. HEINEN, *Emerging, Diverging and Converging Paradigms on Sustainable Development*, in *International Journal of Sustainable Development and World Ecology*, 1994, vol. 1, pp. 22-23; C. MITCHAM, *The Concept of Sustainable Development: Its Origins and Ambivalence*, in *Technology in Society*, 1995, vol. 17, n. 3, pp. 311-326; D. A. MCENTIRE, *The History, Meaning and Policy Recommendations of Sustainable Development: A Review Essay*, 2005, vol. 4, n. 2, pp. 106-118; J. A. DU PISANI, *Sustainable Development – Historical Roots of the Concept*, in *Environmental Sciences*, 2006, vol. 3, n. 2, pp. 83-96.

mainly to the WTO, UN, ILO and OECD documents), as well as at European level (TFEU, Treaty of Lisbon, Charter of Nice, etc.) and at national level (several national legal systems such as France, Switzerland and Portugal have modified their Constitutions to promote it as a constitutional principle).

The framework proposed below demonstrates how Sustainable Development has become part of both the so-called *hard* and *soft* sources, reflecting the necessary complementarity in regulating the phenomena of the modern era,[2] with an extremely peculiar path. On the one hand, in fact, the concept of Sustainable Development was initially relegated to the issues of environmental[3] protection and, subsequently, it was delineated in the broader economic, institutional and social version; on the other hand, this principle spread at an international level and only at a later time (and rather slowly), it was accepted and recognized also at a macro-regional level (with reference to Europe) and even later, at a national level.

The original investigation carried out in this chapter is therefore preliminary to a subsequent reasoning on the applicability of Sustainable Development to national labour law, given that, as we shall see, the concept has been able to find concrete spaces in the institutional, international and European scenario, so much so that it can be reflected in terms of a true regulatory paradigm.

§2.02 THE INTERNATIONAL CONTEXT

[A] The ILO and the Social Dimension of Sustainable Development

The ILO, a crucial regulatory reference point for the respect of the dignity of the worker,[4] has always played a key role in the process of affirmation and diffusion of the concept of Sustainable development.

Already in 1977 the ILO underlined the importance of development as being connected to social objectives in the Tripartite Declaration on the principles concerning multinational companies and politics,[5] in which for the first time, multinationals were invited to '*take full account of the objectives of general policy that the countries where they operate have set*', given that '*their activities should be harmonized with the priorities of development and with the social structures and objectives of the Country in which they operate*', being able to '*contribute to the promotion of economic and social well-being, to the improvement of living standards and the satisfaction of basic needs, to*

2. For an interesting approach to the issue, with reference to labour law, *see* B. Langille, *Hard Law Makes Bad Cases: The International Labour Organization (Nervously) Confronts New Governance Institutions*, in *International Journal of Comparative Labour Law and Industrial Relations*, 2016, vol. 32, pp. 407-423.
3. *See* Annex 1: The Most Significant Evolutionary Stages of Sustainable Development.
4. G. Donata, F. Guarriello (a cura di), *Massimo Roccella. Manuale di diritto del lavoro*, Sesta edizione, Giappichelli, Torino, 2015, p. 21.
5. The Tripartite Declaration of the ILO on the principles concerning multinational companies and social policies dates back to 1997 and was revised in 2000, in 2006 and in 2017.

the – direct or indirect – creation of job opportunities and the enjoyment of fundamental human rights, including Trade Union freedom, throughout the world'.[6]

Despite the intent to raise awareness among companies operating at a global level by encouraging them to contribute positively not only to economic progress but also to social progress, a more explicit reference to the concept of Sustainable Development is contained in the 1998 Declaration on Fundamental Principles and Rights in labour. Although this Declaration is mainly known for recognizing the *ILO Core Conventions*, that is to say eight 'fundamental' conventions,[7] concerning freedom of association, the right to collective bargaining, the elimination of child labour, forced labour and discrimination at work, this document has further merit of having clearly stated, among the objectives of the ILO, also the promotion of large-scale Sustainable Development.

The task of the ILO, as it emerges from the opening recitals, is to '*mobilize the whole of its capacity for regulatory action, technical cooperation and research in all the fields of its competence, with particular regard to employment, professional training and working conditions, to ensure that, in the context of a global strategy of economic and social development, economic and social policies are mutually reinforcing in order to promote large-scale Sustainable Development*'.[8]

The objective of Sustainable Development is further reaffirmed in the subsequent ILO Declaration on social justice for a fair globalization of 2008,[9] which '*offers to managers and decision makers a balanced approach that relates to individuals and productive solutions on a national level, while providing a common international governance platform. A text that contributes to political coherence in favour of Sustainable Development within national strategies, between international organizations and in the context of development cooperation, incorporating social, economic and environmental objectives*'. Hence, the Organization's commitment '*to strengthening the institutional capacity of Member States, as well as that of representative organizations of entrepreneurs and workers, to favour the development of an adequate and coherent social policy as well as Sustainable Development*'.

---

6. Point n. 7 of the Tripartite Declaration (First Edition).
7. The Core Labour Standards are considered as binding for all Member States, regardless the ratification of the eight Conventions: as a matter of fact, the obligation is related directly to the belonging to the Organization, of which the Declaration constitutes a fundamental act. G. Casale, *Il diritto internazionale del lavoro e il ruolo dell'OIL*, in F. Carinci, A. Pizzoferrato (a cura di), *Diritto del lavoro dell'Unione Europea*, UTET, Torino, 2010.
8. ILO, Declaration of the International Labour Organization on Principles and Fundamental Rights in the Work and Its Followings adopted by the International Labour Conference in its Eighty-Sixth Session Geneva, 18 June 1998. This is the third solemn statement of principles and policies adopted by the Conference International Labour since 1919, year of the constitution of the ILO. The document is based on the 1944 Philadelphia Declaration and the 1998 Declaration on Fundamental Principles and Rights.
9. ILO, ILO's Declaration on Social Justice for a fair globalization, adopted by the International Labour Conference, within its Ninety-Seventh session, Geneva, 10 June 2008.

The same Declaration then identifies a concrete instrument for the realization of Sustainable Development, that is to say decent work,[10,11] '*placing it at the heart of the Organization's policies for the achievement of its constitutional objectives*' and promoting it as a '*priority objective of the national and international policies*'. *Decent work.*[12] that is 'work sufficient to ensure a free and dignified existence',[13] is a concept developed by the ILO in 1999,[14] but only in this Declaration is it institutionalized and defined in terms of strategic objective articulated in four different sub-objectives: (i) employment (*creating jobs*): an economy that generates investment opportunities, entrepreneurship, knowledge development, job creation and sustainable livelihoods; (ii) the promotion and guarantee of social rights (*guaranteeing rights at work*): the recognition and respect of workers' rights, in particular of poor and disadvantaged workers, who need representation, participation, and laws that protect their interests; (iii) protection and social security (*extending social protection*): the promotion of both social inclusion and productivity by ensuring safe working conditions that go along with family needs, providing adequate compensation in the event of loss or reduction of income from work and access to an adequate health system; (iv) the promotion of social dialogue (*promoting social dialogue*): a strong involvement of employers' organizations and workers is central to the increase in productivity, to avoid disputes in the workplace and to create cohesive societies.[15]

---

10. To deepen this topic, we invite you to refer to the 2013 ILO Report 'Sustainable Development, decent work and green jobs'.
11. The concept was also promoted during the 2012 United Nations Conference (Rio + 20) where the essential role of decent work was established for the achievement of Sustainable Development, emphasizing the importance of social inclusion, employment creation and the provision of decent work for anybody: '*... we consider green economy in the context of sustainable development and poverty eradication as one of the important tools available for achieving sustainable development and that it could provide options for policy-making but should not be a rigid set of rules. ... We emphasize that it should contribute to eradicating poverty as well as sustained economic growth, enhancing social inclusion, improving human welfare and creating opportunities for employment and decent work for all, while maintaining the healthy functioning of the Earth's ecosystems.' Vedi* UNCSD, *The Future We Want*, New York, 2012, para. 56.
12. Pope John Paul II, already on 1 May 2000, on the occasion of the Workers' Jubilee, launched an appeal for 'a global coalition in favour of decent work' by encouraging the strategy of ILO (Speech at the end of the Eucharistic celebration on the occasion of the Workers' Jubilee (1 May 2000): *Teachings* XXIII, 1 (2000), 720). Benedict XVI explained the concept by answering the question: 'What does the word "decent" mean if applied to work? It means a job that, in every society, is the expression of the essential dignity of every man and every woman: a freely chosen work, which effectively associates workers, men and women, with the development of their community; a job that, in this way, allows workers to be respected outside of any discrimination; a job that allows to satisfy the needs of families and to educate their children, without these being forced to work themselves; a job that allows workers to organize themselves freely and make their voices heard; a job that leaves enough space to rediscover one's roots on a personal, family and spiritual level; a job that ensures dignified conditions for workers who have retired.' See Caritas in veritate by Benedict XVI, 2009, n. 63.
13. S. La Forgia, *Il lavoro dignitoso, il lavoro decente e il lavoro purchessia, in Liber amicorum. Spunti di diritto del lavoro in dialogo con Bruno Veneziani*, Cacucci, Bari, 2012, pp. 165-170.
14. International Labour Office, Decent Work, Report of the Director General, International Labour Conference, 87th Session, Geneva, 1999.
15. Concerning Decent Work: International Institute for Labour Studies, *Decent Work: Objectives and Strategies*, International Labour Office, Geneva, 2006; United Nations, *Full and Productive Employment and Decent Work: Dialogues at the Economic and Social Council*, United Nation,

The ILO provides its support for the realization of decent work through the Decent Work Country Programmes, developed in collaboration with the constituents of the Organization, which define priorities and objectives within the plans of national development, with the aim of reducing the major deficits in social standards, through efficient programmes that embrace all four strategic objectives.[16] Moreover, the concept of decent work has been implemented also in Europe:[17] despite the community legislation on employment, social policy and gender equality go beyond the international norms and the initiatives on decent work incorporating its most important principles,[18] the action of ILO has quickly reached a general consensus among governments, workers, employers and European civil society.

Decent work is considered the prerequisite for equitable globalization, to reduce poverty and to achieve inclusive and *sustainable* development. In fact, it can represent, to all effects, in a logic of adopting a Sustainable Development perspective, both a new paradigm of reference for the labour law discipline and a concrete tool for the realization of a development considered as such: it represents a *paradigm of reference*, in the sense that the legislators should elect decent work as an objective to be pursued, based on the indications provided by ILO, trying to develop policies on economic, social and employment matters that guarantee the conditions for the realization of a 'decent' job; it represents a *tool*, in the sense that decent work is functional to the achievement of Sustainable Development, as shown in the UN Agenda 2030 (especially pursuant to the Objective 8, see below).[19]

New York, 2006; C. Massimiani, *La qualità del lavoro nell'esperienza dell'OIL e nelle politiche sociali europee*, Lulu Press, Raleigh, 2010.

16. For details: https://www.ilo.org/budapest/what-we-do/decent-work-country-programmes/lang--en/index.htm.
17. Communication of European Commission: 'Promoting the Possibility of Decent Work for Anyone: Contribution of the Union to the Realization of the Agenda for Decent Work in the World', adopted on 25 May 2015, COM(2006) 249.
18. M. Esposito, L. Gaeta, R. Santucci, A. Viscomi, A. Zoppoli, L. Zoppoli, *Istituzioni di diritto del lavoro e sindacale. Mercato, contratto e rapporti di lavoro*, Giappichelli, Torino, 2014, p. 8.
19. For detailed analysis on ILO and Core Labour Standards, we invite you to refer to: P. Alston, *Core Labour Standards and the Transformation of the International Labour Rights Regime*, in *European Journal of International Law*, 2004, vol. 15, nn. 3, 457–521; R. Blanpain, M. Colucci (a cura di), *L'Organizzazione Internazionale del Lavoro*, Jovene, Napoli, 2007; A. Bronstein, *International and Comparative Labour Law: Current Challenges*, Palgrave Macmillan, London, 2009; G. Casale, *Il diritto internazionale del lavoro ed il ruolo della Organizzazione internazionale del lavoro*, in *Diritto del lavoro dell'Unione europea*, Commentario diretto da F. Carinci, Vol. IX, *Diritto del lavoro e dell'Unione europea*, a cura di F. Carinci, A. Pizzoferrato, UTET, Torino, 2010; M. Louis, *L'Organisation Internationaledu Travail et le travaildécent. Un agenda social pour le multilateralisme*, l'Harmattan, Paris, 2011; S. Kott, J. Droux (eds), *Globalizing Social Rights: The International Labour Organization and Beyond*, Palgrave Macmillan, London, 2013; M. Weiss, *International Labour Standards: A Complex Public-Private Policy Mix*, in *International Journal of Comparative Labour Law and Industrial Relations* 2013, vol. 29, n. 1; B. Langille, *'Hard Law Makes Bad Cases': The International Labour Organization (Nervously) Confronts New Governance Institutions*, in *International Journal of Comparative Labour Law and Industrial Relations*, 2016, vol. 32, n. 4, pp. 407-423.

[B] United Nations: Global Compact, Millennium Development Goals and Agenda 2030

The UN, starting from the new millennium, has attributed considerable importance to the value of Sustainable Development, by integrating it into its internal and external policies.

The first recognition of such a theme can be found in the context of the *Global Compact*, commonly considered to be the world's largest corporate citizenship and sustainability initiative, founded on the desire to promote a more inclusive and sustainable global economy, respectful of human rights and labour, environmental protection and the fight against corruption. The Global Compact,[20] adopted in an attempt to face the most critical aspects of globalization in a logic of collaboration, is an initiative aimed at voluntary adherence to a set of principles that promote long-term sustainability values through political actions, business practices, responsible social and civil behaviours, taking into account future generations: over 18,000 companies from 157 countries worldwide have joined it.[21]

It is a sort of *network* that unites governments, businesses, UN agencies, trade unions and civil society, with the aim of promoting the culture of corporate citizenship on a global scale, developing (and implementing) policies and guidelines to manage sustainable economies and policies starting from the ten principles[22] that it promotes in terms of human rights, labour standards, environmental protection and the fight against corruption: they are universally shared as they derive from the Universal Declaration of Human Rights, from the Rio Declaration and the UN Convention against Corruption.

Subsequently, the UN developed the Millennium Development Goals, or MDGs: a list of eight objectives that all 193 UN Member States undertook in 2000 to be achieved in fifteen years: (i) eradicate the extreme poverty and world hunger; (ii) make primary education universal; (iii) promote gender equality and women's autonomy; (iv) reduce child mortality; (v) reduce maternal mortality; (vi) fight HIV/AIDS, malaria and other diseases; (vii) guarantee environmental sustainability; (viii) develop a global partnership for development.[23]

These objectives, which expressly include the interest in sustainability, although limited to its environmental dimension, were immediately integrated into the *Global Compact*, receiving strong media and operational approval. Although important milestones have been reached thanks to the *MDGs*, the progress made has not been equally distributed among the countries and regions,[24] leaving significant steps and strong

20. The Global Compact was presented by the UN Secretary-General Kofi Annan in 1999, during the Davos World Economic Forum on 31 January 1999, proposing to start with the business leaders gathered in Davos 'a Global Pact of shared principles and values, which will give a human face to the global market'.
21. http://www.globalcompactnetwork.org/.
22. *See* Annex 2: The Ten Principles of the UN Global Compact.
23. *See* Annex 3: The UN Millennium Development Goals (MDGs).
24. According to the Report *Global Wealth Report 2017: Where Are We Ten Years after the Crisis?*, elaborated by Credit Suisse, 1% of the World population possesses half of the World's Wealth.

differentiations in terms of sex, age, disability, ethnicity or geographical position.[25] Hence, the idea of following up on these objectives through the 2030 Agenda of the UN and its seventeen Sustainable Development Goals (SDGs),[26] of which the Global Compact itself is now promoter.[27]

This is an action programme for the people, the planet and prosperity, signed in September 2015 by the governments of the 193 UN Member States, which incorporates seventeen different objectives for achieving sustainable development (divided into 169 targets and more 240 indicators[28]) by 2030.

Each objective is considered as *stand-alone*, that is a self-referent objective, with independent meaning and value; as *enabler* for the achievement of other objectives; as *accelerator* of the achievement of other objectives. These are universal and global objectives, which can be applied to all countries in the world, both developed and developing (while the Millennium Goals were conceived in the context of donor/beneficiary relations, for which, for example, Italy was excluded or involved only as a UN donor country) and, if the previous objectives aimed to halve or reduce – in comparison to the levels of the 1990s – most of the problems faced, the SDGs, in a more optimistic view, use the language of 'uprooting' extreme poverty, hunger and child deaths for preventable diseases, aiming to permanently eliminate these social problems.

As for the issue of sustainability, if in the original version Sustainable Development was dealt with in a purely environmental profile and only within a single objective,[29] the SDGs propose to deal in an integrated manner with the three dimensions of sustainability, as defined in the Rio + Conference 20 (economic, social and environmental), adopting socially based themes that had not been addressed by the previous objectives, such as the issue of inequalities, peace, well-being, justice, employment and decent work.[30]

The Objective 8 of the 2030 Agenda bears particular importance for the purposes of this research, as it reads: '*To promote lasting, inclusive and sustainable economic*

25. The results reached thanks to MDGs are summarized in the UN Report: United Nations, *The Millennium Development Goals Report 2015*.
26. *See* Annex 4: The UN Sustainable Development Goals (SDGs).
27. ONU, *United Nations Global Compact Progress Report: Business Solutions to Sustainable Development*, 2017.
28. The quality, quantity and availability of open and accessible data (Big Data) is a notable difference between the ecosystems of the UN objectives, given the fifteen years that divide them: while the MDGs did not deepen the monitoring, evaluation and accountability, Objective 17 of the SDGs deals with them explicitly.
29. MDG n. 7: Guarantee Environmental Sustainability.
30. SDG n. 3 (Guarantee health conditions and well-being for all at all ages), n. 4 (Offer quality, inclusive and equal education and promote lifelong learning opportunities for all), n. 5 (Realizing gender equality and improving women's living conditions), n. 8 (Promote lasting, inclusive and sustainable economic growth, full and productive employment and decent work for all), n. 10 (Reduction of inequalities between countries), n. 16 (Promote peaceful and inclusive societies for Sustainable Development, guarantee access to justice for all, create effective, responsible and inclusive institutions at all levels), n. 17 (Reinforce the meanings of implementation and revitalize global collaborations for Sustainable Development).

growth, full and productive employment and decent work for all.'[31] If decent work is the main tool to achieve sustainable growth, labour law plays a predominant role in achieving the goals of the 2030 Agenda both to contribute to the creation of quality jobs, in decent working conditions (an estimated 470 million jobs are needed for those entering the labour market between 2016 and 2030[32]) and to eliminate poverty through stable and adequately paid jobs (almost 2.2 billion people, or about half the world's population, live on less than USD 2 a day[33]).

The importance of the document involved lies on the signing of the objectives by both the Member States, which undertake to work 'so that the Agenda is applied within its own country and at a regional and global level, taking into consideration the different national realities, the capacities and levels of development and respecting national policies and priorities'[34] and by all the specialized agencies headed by the UN, among which the ILO, the UN Education, Science and Culture Organization (UNESCO), the World Health Organization (WHO), the International Monetary Fund (IMF) and the World Bank (WB). The 2030 Agenda is in fact the first instrument in history to have been negotiated between all the specialized agencies of the UN, engaged in the implementation of the 2030 Agenda within their policies. Moreover, such implementation is constantly monitored in terms of distance from the SDGs and the related sub-objectives, through the work of the High Level Political Forum (HLPF) of the UN and the strong involvement of civil society.[35]

31. The objective set, as well as the other objectives, is further clarified in a series of sub-objectives, or rather targets, to be achieved by 2030 and a series of precise indicators to measure progress and delays in the pursuit of objective, for example, in terms of gross domestic product (GDP) growth, or employment rate by gender, disabled and age. *See* Annex 5: Goal n. 8 of the UN Sustainable Development Goals 'Promote Lasting, Inclusive and Sustainable Economic Growth, Full and Productive Employment and Decent Work for All': Targets, Indicators and Progress in 2019
32. *Source:* ENGIM, Civil Society Organization and other non-profit organizations established at the Italian Development Cooperation Agency.
33. Word Bank, *Poverty and Shared Prosperity 2016, Taking on Inequality Report*, 2017.
34. Agenda 2030, Point 21.
35. The HLPF of the UN meets annually under the auspices of the Economic and Social Committee (ECOSOC), while every four years the meeting takes place under the auspices of the General Assembly. The task of the HLPF is to evaluate the progress, the results and the important challenges for all countries, as well as to ensure that the Agenda remains 'relevant and ambitious'. In order to do this, various tools will be used, such as the 'Global Report on Sustainable Development', which assesses progress towards SDGs and national practices, to be conducted on a voluntary basis and a set of statistical indicators (240), approved in March 2017 by the UN, relating to Goals and Targets (UN, A/RES/71/313 Work of the Statistical Commission for the 2030 Agenda for Sustainable Development). The analysis of problems, challenges and progress will also be carried out at regional level, through the UN regional economic commissions or other relevant bodies. The monitoring process involves a strong role of stakeholders and civil society, called to analyse and evaluate policies and progress towards SDGs. In this perspective, the HLPF promotes the most interesting national experiences of civil society involvement, especially in order to design and implement sectorial policies in an integrated way. This participation should also take place in the context of other UN bodies of intergovernmental nature. However, civil society organizations are invited to explicitly announce their commitments to the implementation of the Agenda and the achievement of the SDGs, indicating concrete and measurable objectives. According to UN data (March 2017 Report, 'Progress towards the Sustainable Development Goals'), with reference, for example, to Objective 8, the data show that the path to reach the targets set is still long and difficult. For example, the average

[C] The OECD and the Guidelines for Multinationals

The Organisation for Economic Co-operation and Development (OECD) as well has had, and still has, a fundamental role in the affirmation and diffusion of the principle of Sustainable Development,[36] preparing a series of practical documents, such as the guidelines for multinational companies and governments for the promotion of a development that reconciles environmental, economic and social needs. The creation of a Round Table on Sustainable Development (RTSD) dates back to 1998: this is an informal meeting place where international businesses and civil society leaders can negotiate some issues, without any prejudice: a sort of forum for international dialogue in order to create a consensus for action, aimed at achieving the Sustainable Development objectives.

In 2010 the Sustainability Impact Assessment (SIA)[37] is promulgated, containing guidelines to explore the economic, environmental and social impact with a series of policies, programmes, strategies and action plans proposed by the OECD as a document for the choices of government authorities at different levels (national, regional, local).The following year, the OECD instead developed the famous Guidelines[38] for multinational companies, which contain '*principles and voluntary standards for responsible business behaviour, in compliance with applicable laws*'. Already in the Foreword of this document, which is soft-law[39] oriented, '*the objective of enhancing the*

---

annual growth rate of GDP per capita in the world is equal to 1.6%, for the period 2010-2015 (compared to 0.9% in the previous five-year period 2005-2009). In less-developed countries, the growth rate has increased from 3.5% (2000-2004) to 4.6% (2005-2009), to then drop to 2.5% in 2010-2015. The average GDP growth in the developing countries followed a similar trend, decreasing from 7.1% (2005-2009) to 4.9% (2010-2015), therefore below the 7% Sustainable Development Target. As for labour productivity (annual growth rate of real GDP per worker), globally this has dropped from an annual average of 2.9% (2000-2008) to 1.9% (2009-2016). This decrease represents a negative development for the global economy, with an adverse effect in terms of standards of living and real wages. Again, the global unemployment rate remains at 5.7% in 2016, with a preponderance of female unemployment compared to men for all age groups: young people are three times more unemployed than adults, with unemployment rates of 12.8% and of 4.4%, respectively, in 2016. Moreover, in more than 76% of the cases of the countries surveyed, more than one young person out of ten is part of the NEET category, that is outside of both the school system and the work system (neither in the educational system nor working), and in 70% of cases they are women. With reference instead to child labour, despite the number of working children aged 5 to 17 having decreased from 246 million in 2000 to 168 million in 2012, the issue remains a great concern: more than half of working children (85 million) perform dangerous jobs, 59% in the agriculture sector, although the number of girls involved in child labour has decreased by 40% from 2000 to 2012 and that of children by 25%.

36. T. Strage, A. Bayley, *Sustainable Development, Linking Economy, Society, Environment*, OECD Insights, OECD, 2008; OECD, *Perspectives on Global Development 2017: International Migration in a Shifting World*, OECD Publishing, Paris, 2016.
37. OECD, *Guidance on Sustainability Impact Assessment*, OECD Publishing, Paris, 2010.
38. The 'OECD Guidelines for multinational Enterprises: The Company's Responsible Conduct in a Global Context' date back to 1976 but have been reconsidered in 2000 and in 2011.
39. The governments adhering to the Guidelines undertake to implement them and promote their diffusion through the establishment of National Contact Points, which can report any violations committed by national companies outside their own territory, in addition to acting as linking mechanisms between governments and businesses.

contribution made by multinational companies to Sustainable Development'[40] is explained. According to the Organization, multinational companies '*have the opportunity to implement exemplary policies in the field of Sustainable Development*' and the duty to '*contribute to economic, social and environmental progress to achieve Sustainable Development*', while governments, at the same time, are required to stimulate the positive contribution that multinational companies can make to economic, environmental and social progress '*by adopting norms and policies supporting Sustainable Development and promoting their adoption*'. Companies are then urged to '*take full account of the policies in place in the countries in which they operate and take into consideration the points of view of the other stakeholders*', and they are invited to assess the consequences of their entrepreneurial action on the other stakeholders, that is to say workers, environment, consumers, customers, suppliers, competitors, the community, etc.[41] It is important to highlight how these Guidelines are addressed to the main market players, such as national governments and companies: both are elected recipients and actors of the Sustainable Development paradigm. If, as a matter of fact, at macro-legislative level Sustainable Development should be taken as a guiding criterion in the definition of the legislative policies in economic, social and environmental matters, at the same time companies, at the micro-regulatory level, are invited to evaluate in the relationship with the parties and in the performance of their entrepreneurial activity, the impact of their actions on their stakeholders. Further, significant is the collaboration of the OECD with the UN for the achievement of the Agenda 2030[42] Sustainable Development objectives, and the commitment to four distinct areas of intervention: applying the objectives to the strategies and policies of the OECD; increasing the production of data that can help in the progress of the analysis of their implementation;[43] improving OECD support for planning and political decisions at national level; and providing a space for governments to share experiences and best practices for the objectives, as well as reflect on the implications of the SDGs for external relations of the OECD.

[D] WTO and Sustainable Development

A decisive reference to Sustainable Development is contained in the Preamble of the institutional agreement of the WTO of 1994, the most important negotiating forum for multilateral trade relations at international level. This Preamble states the need to allow 'optimal use of global resources in accordance with the objective of Sustainable

40. OECD, *Guidelines for Multinational Enterprises*, OECD Publishing, 2011 edition.
41. The list of stakeholders is potentially infinite. Cfr. R. Del Punta, *Responsabilità Sociale dell'Impresa e Diritto del Lavoro*, in *Lav. dir.*, 2006, 1, p. 60.
42. OECD, *Better Policies for 2030: An OECD Action Plan on the Sustainable Development Goals*, 2016.
43. In the implementation of commitment ii), the interesting June 2016 Report, '*Measuring Distance to the SDG Targets: An Assessment of Where OECD Countries Stand*', according to which Italy has already reached 11 of the 17 objectives set, to the exclusion of objectives 2 (Zero Hunger), 5 (Gender Equality), 8 (Decent Work and Economic Growth), 9 (Industry, Innovation and Infrastructures), 10 (Reduce Inequalities), 12 (Responsible Consumption and Production), 17 (Partnership for Objectives).

Development': '*Recognizing that their relations in the field of trade and economic endeavor should be conducted with a view to raising standards of living, ensuring full employment and a large and steadily growing volume of real income and effective demand, and expanding the production and trade of goods and services, while allowing for the optimal use of the world's resources in accordance with the objective of sustainable development, seeking both to protect and preserve the environment and to enhance the means for doing so in a manner consistent with their respective needs and concerns at different levels of economic development.*'[44]

The reference to the principle involved is punctual, since the WTO imposes on its Member States a real balance between the social dimension[45] (the promotion of full employment and living standards), the environmental dimension (environmental protection) and the economic dimension (increase in incomes, demand and production), keeping into account the development levels and priorities of each country.

The inclusion of Sustainable Development[46] in the field of the WTO founding agreement in such terms entails a necessary interpretation of the latter in the light of the objective of a development that combines different axiological values, expressly providing a duty for the interested parties (that is to say for its current 157 members, representing more than 97% of world trade) to integrate the extra-economic (social and environmental) issues into their trade relations.[47]

Such an explicit reference to Sustainable Development as founding objective of WTO helps an evolutionary interpretation of the agreements and the exceptions to free trade.[48] More specifically, it is precisely this Preamble that can legitimize the inclusion of the theme of Sustainable Development in the so-called new generation[49] commercial

---

44. WTO Agreement, Preamble.
45. In the agreement establishing the WTO, as well as in the Preamble, the Contracting Parties recognize an emphasis on the social rights of workers within the GATT/OMC system, in Arts II, n. 1 (Scope of the WTO) and III, n. 1 (Functions of the WTO) 22, and n. 2, which establishes that the WTO: '... *shall provide the forum for negotiations among its Members... in matters dealt with under the Annexes ... (and) also provide a forum for further negotiations among its Members concerning their multilateral trade relations ...*'.
46. The reference to Sustainable Development was introduced in the Preamble of the WTO agreement with the Marrakech Ministerial Conference in 1995.
47. As in the Preamble of the 1947 GATT, these objectives should have been achieved through the '... *reciprocal and mutually-advantageous resolution decisions to ... the elimination of discriminatory treatment in international commerce*'. The differences with the Havana Charter that set the explicit goals of the newcoming ITO (International Trade Organization) and the achievement of conditions of full employment of the labour force and of economic and social progress are therefore evident (Chapter 1, *Purpose and Objectives*, Art. 1), for which the Contracting Parties recognized the commitment to undertake the most appropriate actions to support employment (Chapter II, *Employment and Economic Activity*, Art. 3, para. 1) as well as economic and industrial growth, in particular of developing countries (Chapter III, *Economic Development and Reconstruction*, Art. 10) which can be reached through a close collaboration with the UN (Chapter II, Art. 2, para. 2) to ITO. In this sense, *see* C. Di Turi, *Globalizzazione dell'economia e diritti fondamentali in materia di lavoro: il ruolo dell'OIL e dell'OMC*, Giuffrè, Milano, 2007, p. 140.
48. E. Radighieri, *I diritti fondamentali dei lavoratori nel commercio internazionale*, in L. S. Rossi (a cura di), *Commercio internazionale sostenibile? WTO e Unione europea*, il Mulino, Bologna, 2003, pp. 110-111.
49. An example of a new generation agreement is the Comprehensive Economic and Trade Agreement, the commercial and economic agreement concluded between Canada and the

agreements, that is to say in all those bilateral or multilateral agreements that provide not only for the removal of tariff barriers to trade (in terms of duties on imports and exports among the signatory countries) but also on those so-called 'non-tariff' barriers, that is to say all those bureaucratic and legislative obligations that slow down and make trade among the parties less advantageous, precisely because of the diversity of regulations planned on the same subject by the legal systems involved.

The demolition of these last barriers is taking place through a long and difficult negotiation process, aimed at achieving regulatory harmonization on a series of issues of national importance such as the environment, privacy, safety, transport, health, industry, small- and medium-sized enterprises, public procurement, energy and, in particular, social rights. This harmonization could, however, dangerously lead, with a view to simplifying trade and exchanges, to a decrease of national standards, or to a process of deregulation of the labour law discipline, in an attempt to level-off the less-guaranteed legislation (and therefore less expensive for trade) of the countries involved in the negotiations.

In detail, the integration of the principle of Sustainable Development in these agreements, as well as in the terms promoted by the WTO Preamble, could therefore constitute a valid guarantee for a constructive process of regulatory harmonization, since the principle involved would impose on the parties the obligation to ensure that economic growth, social development and environmental protection go hand in hand, preventing that increasing trade and investment deriving from the agreement result as detrimental to environmental protection and labour rights.

§2.03 THE EUROPEAN CONTEXT

[A] The Regulatory Framework

If, as we will see, Sustainable Development today can legitimately be considered a principle based on European law, it is necessary to point out that its realization has gone through a slow path, which lasted about half a century.

A first partial reference to Sustainable Development is in fact only[50] to be found in the updated version of the Maastricht Treaty of 1992 in the terms proposed by Article 2: '*The Community shall have as its task, by establishing a common market and an economic and monetary union and by implementing the common policies or activities referred to in Articles 3 and 4, to promote throughout the Community a harmonious and balanced development of economic activities, the equality among men and women, a sustainable and non-inflactionary growth respecting the environment, a high degree of convergence of economic performance, a high level of employment and of social*

European Union, whose Title 4 is entirely dedicated to Sustainable Development. The agreement entered into force provisionally on 21 September 2017, meaning most of the agreement now applies.

50. Consider that community action in the environmental field is regulated only from 1987, thanks to the Single European Act, Part II, Title VII, Environment.

protection, the raising of the standard of living and quality of life, economic and social cohesion and solidarity among Member States.'

Although there is no express reference to the term 'Sustainable Development', it can be deduced from the combined reading of the expressions 'sustainable growth' and 'balanced development' and from the dual interest for 'environmental protection' and 'social protection'.

It is with the Amsterdam Treaty of 1997 that Sustainable Development expressly became part of the Union's objectives, providing for the inclusion in the TEU of the following Preamble: '*... determined to promote economic and social progress for their peoples, taking into account the principle of sustainable development and within the context of the accomplishment of the internal market and of reinforced cohesion and environmental protection, and to implement policies ensuring that advances in economic integration are accompanied by parallel progress in other fields ...*'.[51] The treaty then provided for among the Community goals the one '*to promote economic and social progress and a high level of employment and to achieve balanced and sustainable development, in particular through the creation of an area without internal frontiers, through the strengthening of economic and social cohesion and through the establishment of economic and monetary union ...*'.[52] The legislative text then reformulated Article 2 of the Treaty on EU, adding the adjective 'sustainable' to the objective of a 'harmonious and balanced development' mentioned above[53] and inserting a new Article 3, letter c): 'Environmental protection requirements must be integrated into the definition and implementation of the Community policies and activities referred to in Article 3, in particular with a view to promoting Sustainable Development.'[54] With the revision of the EU treaties by the Treaty of Lisbon of 13 December 2007, the principle of Sustainable Development achieved a broader connotation at the level of primary law. In addition to reiterating the general objective of Sustainable Development[55] in various points, Article 2 TEU[56] was further modified, entering two new paragraphs: paragraph 3: ('*The Union establishes an internal market. It works for Europe's Sustainable Development, based on balanced economic growth and price stability, on a highly competitive social market economy, aiming at full employment and progress and a high level of protection and improvement of the quality of the environment. It promotes scientific and technological progress*') and paragraph 5 ('*Within the relations with the rest of the world, the Union affirms and promotes its values and interests, contributing to the protection of its citizens. It contributes to peace, security, sustainable development*

51. Article 1.2 of the Treaty of Amsterdam which modifies point 7 of the Preamble of the TEU.
52. Article 1.5 of the Amsterdam Treaty which modifies the letter b) of the TEU.
53. Article 2.2 of the Amsterdam Treaty which modifies Art. 2) of the TEU.
54. Article 2.4 of the Amsterdam Treaty which modifies the TEU, by inserting the new Art. 3 c), corresponding to Art. 11 of the TFEU (former Art. 6 of ECT).
55. Article 10 A, para. 2.) ('*favouring the Sustainable Development of developing countries in economic, social and environmental terms, with the primary objective of eliminating poverty*'); *and f) ('contributing to the development of international measures aimed at preserving and improving the quality of the environment and the sustainable management of global natural resources, in order to ensure Sustainable Development*'), today Art. 21, letters d) and f), relating to Chapter 1 on the general provisions on the Union's external action.
56. Today Art. 3 of TEU.

of the Earth, solidarity and mutual respect among people, free and fair trade, the elimination of poverty and the protection of human rights ...').[57]

Thus, in Article 11 it is provided that the needs connected with environmental protection '*should be integrated into the definition and implementation of Union policies and actions, in particular with a view to promoting Sustainable Development*'.[58] Further, the Lisbon Treaty guaranteed the annexation to the TEU of the Charter of Fundamental Rights of the EU signed in Nice in 2000, containing important references to Sustainable Development.

The first can already be found in the Preamble of the Charter: '*The Union contributes to the preservation and to the development of these common values while respecting the diversity of the cultures and traditions of the peoples of Europe as well as the national identities of the Member States and the organisation of their public authorities at national, regional and local levels; it seeks to promote balanced and sustainable development and ensures free movement of persons, goods, services and capital, and the freedom of establishment.*' The second reference is to be found in Article 37, pursuant to which, the principle of Sustainable Development is elected as Programmatic Principle: '*a high level of environmental protection and the improvement of the quality of the environment must be integrated into the policies of the Union and ensured in accordance with the principle of Sustainable Development.*' Both references are of particular importance for the normative value of the Nice Charter[59] and because Sustainable Development, for the first time, is evoked in the field of protection of fundamental social rights, and no longer only in economic and environmental matters.

Finally, an important boost to Sustainable Development was given on the occasion of the recent proclamation by the EU leaders of the *European Pillar of Social Rights* at the Göteborg social summit (Sweden):[60] conceived mainly for the European area but applicable to all EU Member States that wish to join it, the non-binding document establishes twenty fundamental principles and rights to support the smooth functioning and fairness of labour markets and social protection systems. It is the joint responsibility of Member States, EU institutions, social partners and other stakeholders to build a more inclusive and fairer EU and an economic and monetary union more deeply rooted not only in economic, but above all in social, shared values.

The pillar is structured in three main categories, each dealing with different themes: (i) *Equal opportunities and access to the labour market*: education, training and lifelong learning, gender equality and equal opportunities, as well as active support for employment; (ii) *Fair working conditions*: flexible and secure employment, fair wages, information on working conditions and protection in the event of dismissal, social dialogue, involvement of workers, balance between professional activity and family life, the importance of a healthy, safe and adequate work environment and data protection; (iii) *Social protection and inclusion*: childcare and child support, social

57. Point 4 of Lisbon Treaty's General Provisions, which modifies the TEU.
58. Article 11 TFEU, former Art. 6 of ECT.
59. The Lisbon Treaty inserts the Nice Charter among the primary law European Sources.
60. The text was presented on 17 November 2017 by the president of the European Commission, Juncker, the president of the European Parliament, Tajani and the current president of the European Council, Ratas during the social summit for employment and fair growth.

protection, unemployment benefits, minimum income, income and old-age pensions, healthcare, inclusion of people with disabilities, long-term care, housing and assistance for the homeless and access to essential services.[61]

Despite the fact that the effectiveness of the Pillar remains dubious at present, as it has no legal force, it is important to point out that this initiative is in line with the recent European[62] initiatives (increasing the upward convergence of the Member States on social benefits), as well as with the Sustainable Development objectives, integrating both the provisions of the 2030 Agenda and the ILO, as well as the UN and the OECD.

In light of the many normative references found among the primary law sources of the EU, the principle of Sustainable Development can be considered fully a European regulatory principle, promoted and protected both by EU[63] and by its Member States.[64]

---

61. *See* Annex 6, The European Pillar of Social Rights in 20 Principles.
62. This is the case of the recent proposal for a Directive on work-life balance: Brussels, 26.4.2017 COM(2017) 253 final, 2017/0085 (COD), Proposal for a Directive of the European Parliament and of the Council on the balance between activities, professional and family life for parents and carers and abrogating Council Directive 2010/18/EU.
63. Hence the explicit reference to Sustainable Development in multiple European Directives and Regulations on environmental issues: Directive 2000/60/EC (Directive 2000/60/EC of the European Parliament and of the Council, of 23 October 2000, which establishes a framework for Community action in the field of water, Recital 41), Directive 2001/42/EC (Directive 2001/42/EC of the European Parliament and of the Council of 27 June 2001 concerning the assessment of the effects of certain plans and programs on the environment (Recital 1); Directive 2001/77/EC (Directive 2001/77/EC of the European Parliament and of the Council of 27 September 2001 on the promotion of electrical energy produced from renewable energy sources in the electricity internal market (Recital 1) (repealed by Directive 2009/28/EC of the European Parliament and of the Council of 23 April 2009 on the promotion of the use of energy from renewable sources, amending and subsequently repealing and Directives 2001/77/EC and 2003/30/EC), Directive 2004/35/EC (Directive 2004/35/EC of the European Parliament and of the Council of 21 April 2004 on environmental liability with regard to the prevention and repair of environmental damage, according to the 2nd recital '*The prevention and repair of environmental damage should be implemented by applying the "polluter pays principle", as established in the treaty and coherently with the principle of "Sustainable Development". The fundamental principle of this directive should therefore be that the operator whose activity has caused environmental damage or the imminent threat of such damage will be considered financially responsible in order to induce operators to take measures and develop practices to reduce to minimum risks of environmental damage*') or the most recent Regulation 834/2007 (Regulation (EC) No. 834/2007 of the Council of 28 June 2007 concerning organic production and labelling of organic products and repealing the regulation (EEC) No. 2092/91).
64. Sustainable Development is also widely recognized in European soft-law sources, particularly in the draft of the European Constitution whose Preamble refers to inter- and intra-generational responsibility: 'The enjoyment of these rights gives rise to responsibilities and duties towards others as well as the human community and future generations.' Again, in Art. 3, the well-being of people will be achievable only if the Union strives 'for a Europe of Sustainable Development based on balanced economic growth, a highly competitive social market economy aiming at full employment and social progress, a high level of protection and improvement of the quality of the environment'. Sustainable Development is then developed in various statements by the Council, the European Commission and Parliament. On this point, refer to the Declaration of 26 June 1990 of the European Council of Dublin, to the Decision of the European Council of Göteborg in June 2001, and to the Declaration on the guiding principles of the Sustainable Council Development of 16-17 June 2005. Among the most significant interventions of the European Commission, it is important to recall the 2001 Communication on 'Sustainable Development in Europe for a better world. European Union Strategy for Sustainable Development', the '2002 Co-Communication Towards a global partnership for Sustainable Development', or the October 2010 Green Paper on EU development policy in support of Sustainable Development, where it is called the 'new

In fact it already finds important and concrete applications, with reference, for example, to the System of Generalized Tariff Preferences, to the Horizontal Social Clause referred to in Article 9 TFEU and to the activity of promoting Corporate Social Responsibility (CSR) policies.

[B] The Special Incentive Scheme for Sustainable Development and Good Governance (GSP +)

In Europe, a concrete application of Sustainable Development can be found in the Generalized System of Preferences (GSP) of the EU under Regulation 978/2012, which provides for a (total or partial) reduction of duties on imports into Europe from developing countries, to facilitate their access to the European market provided that they ensure compliance with a series of international social and environmental standards.[65]

Among the different regimes provided for by the preferential system,[66] in Article 9, a special incentive regime 'for Sustainable Development and Good Governance' (GSP +) is provided for. This regime provides for the total or partial removal of customs tariffs for a series of product categories, regarding developing countries that are considered vulnerable by virtue of the lack of diversification and insufficient integration into the international trading system. The latter, however, are obliged to assume a series of obligations and responsibilities deriving from the ratification and effective implementation of essential international conventions for human rights and workers, environmental protection and good governance.

The Regulation refers in fact to an attachment containing as many as fifteen essential UN and ILO conventions on human rights and labour law,[67] and to seven

---

engine of global growth', and the Europe 2020 Communication, which provides for the development of a strategy for smart, sustainable and inclusive growth. Last but not least, the Resolution of the European Parliament of 8 June 2011, on the external dimension of social policy, the promotion of social labour standards and CSR, in which the EU sets itself the 'goal of becoming a pole of excellence in the field of CSR ... in order to support the transition to a sustainable economy', and calls on the Commission to include a chapter on Sustainable Development in the free trade agreements negotiated with third countries, containing a legally binding CSR clause.

65. V. Cagnin, *L'Unione Europea e il Sistema di preferenze tariffarie generalizzate*, in *Riv. giur. lav.*, 2015, 4.

66. Regulation 978/2012 provides for three different agreements: (i) a general regime that provides for the total or partial removal of customs tariffs for developing countries; (ii) a special incentive scheme for Sustainable Development and good governance (GSP +); (iii) a special regime in favour of the least developed countries, EBA – Everything But Arms, which guarantees the total abatement of customs tariffs for all products, with the exception of weapons trade.

67. The following are the essential UN/ILO Conventions on human rights and labour law: Convention for the Prevention and Repression of Genocide (1948); International Convention on the Elimination of All Forms of Racial Discrimination (1965); International Convention on Civil and Political Rights (1966); International Covenant on Economic, Social and Cultural Rights (1966); Convention on the Elimination of All Forms of Discrimination Against Women (1979); Convention Against Torture and Other Cruel, Inhuman or Degrading Treatment or Punishment (1984); Convention on the Rights of the Child (1989); Convention concerning Forced Labour, n. 29 (1930); Convention concerning Trade Union Freedom and the Protection of Trade Union Law, n. 87 (1948); Convention concerning the Application of the Principles of the Right to Organize

conventions relating to environmental principles and good governance. Among these, the ILO Core Conventions stand out in terms of the abolition of forced labour (n. 29/1930 and n. 105/1957), trade union freedom (n. 87/1948), the right to organize and collective negotiation (n. 98/1949), the minimum working age (n. 138/1973) and the prohibition of discrimination in employment and occupation (n. 111/1958 and n. 100/1951).

In this regard, the choice of the EU to subordinate preferential customs treatment to the respect of international conventions promoting fundamental social rights indicates, on the one hand, the close collaboration between the EU and the ILO in the policy of balancing the needs of international competitiveness (granting subsidized tariffs to stimulate the exports of the beneficiary countries) and the demands of job protection; on the other hand, an important promotional activity in the process of potential diffusion of the ILO's *core labour standards* also among countries currently not included in the audience of the beneficiaries of the GSP, being an essential condition for obtaining (and maintaining in the time) of preferential tariffs for exports to Europe.[68]

Therefore, through the GSP + regime, the principles developed within the ILO can be transformed into binding projects, that is to say concretely justifiable through international law, with the relative, robust, incentives and sanctions apparatus:[69] it is essentially the attempt of the EU to contribute to achieving Sustainable Development through the exercise of its economic power. Otherwise, the regime presents itself as a commercial policy tool aimed at fostering international cooperation as well as a mechanism of distributive justice in the international trade system with a general scope,[70] functional to promote the integration of developing countries into the system of commercial exchanges, stimulating their economies and accelerating their development, as long as this can be defined as 'sustainable'.

The system of tariff preferences for Sustainable Development and Good Governance can therefore be considered a concrete application of the principle of Sustainable Development, that is to say a positive model of linkage between international trade and social rights, in order to implement production processes that respect the Core Labour Standards, and, more generally, human rights. The attempt is in fact that of using international trade as a means to promote economic growth in countries in difficulty (still not economically self-sufficient) and to respond, at the same time, positively to

and Collective Bargaining, n. 98 (1949); Convention concerning Equal Pay for Male Labour and Female Labour for Work of Equal Value, n. 100 (1951); Convention on the Abolition of Forced Labour, n. 105 (1957); Convention concerning Discrimination in Employment and Professions, n. 111 (1958); Convention concerning the Mminimum Age for Admission to Employment, n. 138 (1973); Prohibition of the Worst Forms of Child Labour and Immediate Actions in View of Their Elimination, n. 182 (1999).

68. EU hopes to increase the list of beneficiary countries, currently reduced to ten countries: Cape Verde, Georgia, Armenia, Kyrgyzstan, Mongolia, Pakistan, the Philippines, Sri Lanka, Bolivia and Paraguay (data updated to March 2018).
69. R. Salomone, *Preferenze tariffarie generalizzate e core labour standards*, in *Lav. dir.*, 2011, pp. 105-117.
70. A. Perulli, V. Brino, *Manuale di Diritto internazionale del lavoro*, Giappichelli, Torino, 2015, p. 99.

the need for Sustainable Development, by targeting developing countries to a model of growth that can reconcile economic needs with social-environmental needs.

[C] The Horizontal Social Clause (Article 9 TFEU) and Evaluations on Sustainability of European Policies

A further practical application of the paradigm involved in Europe can be identified in the Horizontal Social Clause referred to in Article 9 TFEU. This clause provides for the obligation for the EU and the Member States to '*take into account*', in the definition and implementation of its policies and actions, '*the needs connected with the promotion of a high level of employment, the guarantee of adequate social protection, the fight against social exclusion and a high level of education, training and protection of human health*'.[71]

The importance of the clause involved was immediately called into question because of the 'soft' formula of the expression '*shall take in account*' (incorrectly translated into Italian as simple present tense).The doubt about the precept value of this clause arose from the comparison with the '*harder*' formulas adopted for the other Horizontal Clauses contained in the Treaty.[72] It should be noted, in fact, that for these clauses, the legislator had chosen more imperative verbal forms: the needs connected with the protection of the environment '*must be integrated*' into the definition and implementation of Union policies and actions (Article 11), and those related to consumer protection '*are taken into consideration*' (Article 12), or even, the Union and the Member States '*take full account*' of the needs in terms of animal well-being (Article 13).

In response to this doctrinal criticism, we can see how Article 9 is not the only Horizontal Social Clause to have a formulation of doubtful direct preceptive value since, in similar terms, the Union 'aims' to eliminate inequalities (Article 8) and, still

71. The social clause involved represents a legal basis for the Social Impact Assessment envisaged already in the Commission Communication of 2002, with which it was intended '*to start the impact assessment as a tool to improve the quality and consistency of the development process of strategies. It will contribute to the realization of an effective and efficient regulatory environment and to a more coherent implementation of the European strategy for Sustainable Development. Thanks to the impact assessment, the probable favourable and unfavourable effects of the proposed strategic actions are identified, thus offering the possibility of informed political judgments about the proposal and identification of the compromises necessary for the achievement of mutually incompatible objectives*'. *See* Point 1.1, Opinion 2012 / C 24/06, Opinion of the European Economic and Social Committee on the theme '*Strengthening the cohesion and the coordination of the EU in the social field thanks to the new Social Horizontal Clause pursuant to the article 9 of the TFEU*' (own-initiative opinion), (2012 / C 24/06) of 26 October 2011, Lecturer: LECHNER.
72. Article 8 TFEU: '*In its actions the Union aims to eliminate inequalities, as well as to promote equality, between men and women*'; Art. 10 TFEU: '*In defining and implementing its policies and actions, the Union aims to combat discrimination based on sex, racial or ethnic origin, religion or belief, disability, age or sexual orientation*'; Art. 11 TFEU: '*The needs connected with environmental protection must be integrated into the definition and implementation of Union policies and actions, in particular with a view to promoting Sustainable Development*'; Art. 12 TFEU: '*In the definition and implementation of other policies or activities of the Union, the requirements concerning consumer protection are taken into consideration.*'

'*aims*' to promote equality between men and women and to combat discrimination (Article 10). However, considering the established commitment of the EU to promote, for example, gender equality or the principle of non-discrimination, the choice of the verb '*aims*' does not seem to give less importance to the issue of social concerns with respect to environmental concerns, despite the verb '*aims*' (like the conditional expression 'should consider' in Article 9) is undoubtedly less preceptive than the statements 'take into account' or 'take full account' contained in Articles 11, 12, 13.[73]

Having established the binding nature of the commitments within the horizontal social clause involved, it should be noted that the obligation imposed on the EU, as well as on its Member States, to take into account the social impact of its policies and actions, constitutes a precise and concrete application of the principle of Sustainable Development.

This application can be found under two profiles (or obligations): first, in having to consider not only the economic dimension of one's own policies and actions but also the social dimension (and specifically the effects on employment, social protection, social exclusion, education and human health), in the same way as Sustainable Development suggests a reconciliation between the social and economic dimensions (together with the environmental one); second, in having to adopt a long-term perspective imposed on political choices: EU and Member States are obliged to project the consequences of their own decisions by adopting a long-term logic, thus considering also the effects for future generations of their own choices, in the same way as Sustainable Development imposes a solidarity among the different generations.

Article 9 can legitimately be considered a veritable litmus test in order to verify whether the choices and policies implemented by the EU and its Member States are acceptable from a social point of view.[74] This is a provision clearly aimed at giving a certain coherence to the actions of supranational bodies, so as to combine economic and social reasons, without the former prevailing over the latter, in the light of the objectives of solidarity and social cohesion of which the EU has long been a promoter.[75]

---

73. The horizontal social clause referred to in Art. 9 TFEU should not be assigned a merely political nature but the same binding force attributed to the Horizontal Clause intended to combat discrimination pursuant to Art. 10 TFEU, which has long been present in the legal order and is recognized as having a specific scope. *See*, in this sense, G. Bronzini, *Il modello sociale europeo nel Trattato di Lisbona*, in F. Bassanini, G. Tiberi (a cura di), *Le nuove istituzioni europee*, il Mulino, Bologna, 2008, pp. 109 ss; G. Bronzini, *Tutela dei disoccupati, lotta alla povertà e contrasto dell'esclusione sociale nell'Europa del 'dopo-Lisbona'*, in *Relazione rivista per il Convegno organizzato dal Consiglio nazionale forense sul tema 'La salvaguardia dei diritti dell'uomo e delle libertà fondamentali', Celebrazione dei LX anni della firma della Convenzione Europea*, Roma, 17-19 Giugno 2010; Cfr. G. Bronzini, *Il Trattato di Lisbona: funzionerà il 'compromesso dilatorio'?*, in *Questgiust.*, 2008, p. 143.
74. Cfr. U. Villani, *La politica sociale nel Trattato di Lisbona*, in *Riv. giur. lav.*, 2012, 1, p. 47.
75. G. Bronzini, *Tutela dei disoccupati, lotta alla povertà e contrasto dell'esclusione sociale nell'Europa del 'dopo Lisbona'*, in *Relazione rivista per il Convegno organizzato dal Consiglio nazionale forense sul tema 'La salvaguardia dei diritti dell'uomo e delle libertà fondamentali', Celebrazione dei LX anni della firma della Convenzione Europea*, Roma, 17-19 Giugno 2010, p. 3.

For this reason it has been defined as 'a fundamental novelty of the Treaty'[76] which, if well applied, can represent an important step forward towards a more socially-oriented Europe[77] in the necessary reconciliation between the economic and social objectives of the Union,[78] legitimizing *'another new future of the Lisbon Treaty'*.[79]

Finally, it is worth recalling that the themes chosen by the legislator are in line with some objectives promoted by the UN 2030 Agenda, with particular reference to objectives 8 (employment, social protection, social inclusion), 3 (health and well-being) and 4 (quality education): such a coincidence reflects the close collaboration between the UN and Europe in the objective of guaranteeing a development that can be defined as 'sustainable'.

[D] The Promotion of CSR

A further concrete application of Sustainable Development at European level, which is also reflected at national level, can be found in the phenomenon of CSR, widely promoted by the EU since the beginning of the new millennium.[80] As it is known, CSR is commonly described by taking the definition contained in the 2001 Green Paper, in terms of *'voluntary integration of social and ecological concerns of companies in their*

76. On the novelty introduced by the Lisbon Treaty, please refer to: B. Caruso, *I diritti sociali fondamentali dopo il Trattato di Lisbona (tanto tuonò che piovve)*, in *WP C.S.D.L.E. 'Massimo D'Antona'.INT – 81/2010*; F. Bassanini, G. Tiberi (a cura di), *Le nuove istituzioni europee. Commento al Trattato di Lisbona*, il Mulino, Bologna, 2010; S. Giubboni, *I diritti sociali nell'Unione europea dopo il Trattato di Lisbona. Paradossi, rischi e opportunità*, in *Relazione al convegno Diritto civile e principi costituzionali europei e italiani*, held in Perugia on 25 and 26 March 2011.
77. Point 1.1, Opinion 2012 / C 24/06. Opinion of the European Economic and Social Committee on the theme 'Strengthening EU cohesion and coordination in the social field thanks to the new Horizontal Social Clause referred to in Article 9 of the TFEU' (opinion of initiative), (2012 / C 24/06) of 26 October 2011, Rapporteur: LECHNER.
78. Belgian Presidency of the EU, '*The horizontal social clause and social mainstreaming in the EU. The Horizontal Social Clause as a call for intensified cooperation and exchange of knowledge through the Commission's Impact Assessment*', ed. Federal Public Service and Social Security, Brussels, 2010, p. 19.
79. Cfr. P. Pochet, C. Degryse, *Social Policies of the European Union*, in *Global Social Policy*, 2010, vol. 10, n. 2, p. 249.
80. About this matter: R. Salomone, *La responsabilità sociale dell'impresa: riflessioni a margine di una strategia europea sullo Sviluppo Sostenibile*, in *Dir. relaz. ind.*, 2004, 2, p. 379; M. Ferraresi, *Responsabilità sociale dell'impresa e diritto del lavoro*, Cedam, Padova, 2012; A. Perulli (a cura di), *La responsabilità sociale dell'impresa: idee e prassi*, il Mulino, Bologna, 2013; M. Napoli (a cura di), *La responsabilità sociale delle imprese*, Vita e Pensiero, Milano, 2005; L. Montuschi, P. Tullini (a cura di), *Lavoro e responsabilità sociale dell'impresa*, Zanichelli, Bologna, 2006; R. Del Punta,*Responsabilità sociale dell'impresa e diritto del lavoro*, in *Lav. dir.*, 2006, 1; A. Tursi, *Responsabilità sociale dell'impresa, «etica d'impresa» e diritto del lavoro*, ivi, p. 65; S. Scarponi, *Globalizzazione e responsabilità sociale delle imprese transnazionali*, ivi, p. 149; V. Ferrante, *Responsabilità sociale dell'impresa e lavoro subordinato*, ivi, p. 83.

commercial operations and in their relations with the interested parties'[81] or, more recently, as '*the responsibility of companies for their impact on society*'.[82]

The concept involved has found new life and legitimacy in recent years thanks to the affirmation, in the national, European and international panorama, of Sustainable Development: hence the new definition of CSR, in terms of '*application of the principles of Sustainable Development to corporate governance*'[83] or, in other words, of '*un concept qui doit permettre aux entreprises de prendre en compte le développement durable dans leur stratégie*'.[84]

In fact, if Sustainable Development concerns, at a macro level, '*the simultaneous pursuit of economic prosperity, environmental quality and social equity*', at the micro dimension, that is, at the entrepreneurial level, '*companies aiming for sustainability need to perform but against the triple bottom line*'.[85]

CSR, as well as Sustainable Development, is therefore delineated in the simultaneous and parallel pursuit of the objectives of the so-called *Triple Bottom Line*,[86] that is to say a system for evaluating company performance based on three different indicators or parameters: environmental, social and economic. The first measures the compatibility between entrepreneurial activity and the protection of ecosystems (analysis of the impacts of activity and products, in terms of resource consumption, waste production and polluting emissions). The second (social parameter) investigates not only the social consequences of business activity on the totality of *stakeholders* (working conditions, level of remuneration, non-discrimination practices and social dialogue for what concerns the workers but also the relationships with suppliers, customers and the local community). Finally, the third (*economic* parameter) is not limited to the economic performance as traditionally understood but it is also related to the ability to contribute to the economic development of the business settlement area, in compliance with the principles of *fair competition*.

Companies, following this approach, should evaluate every policy and action starting from the base (*bottom*) and pursuing three objectives simultaneously (*triple line*): economic prosperity, environmental quality and social equity. In this sense, therefore, the Triple Bottom Line approach can be considered as the full implementation of the three pillars of Sustainable Development. The companies that decide to undertake a CSR path prove to be aware of the considerable impact of their actions, policies and decisions on the surrounding environmental and social reality and can facilitate the realization of Sustainable Development by combining their business

81. Commissione Europea, *Libro Verde, Promuovere un quadro europeo per la responsabilità sociale delle imprese*, Bruxelles, 18.7.2001 COM(2001) 366 definitivo, p. 20.
82. Communication from the Commission to the European Parliament, the Council, the European Economic and Social Committee and the Committee of the Regions, A renewed EU strategy for the 2011-14 period on corporate social responsibility, Brussels, 25.10.2011 COM(2011) 681 final.
83. J. P. Robé, E. Mazuyer, *Faut-il faire une évaluation sociale des entreprises?*, in *Revue de droit du travail*, 2010, pp. 413 ss.
84. See the definition given by ORSE (Observatory on CSR in Paris), www.orse.org.
85. *See* the definition of Sustainable Development given by the *Global Development Research Center*, www.gdrc.org.
86. Cfr. J. Elkingtonm, *Cannibals with Forks: The Triple Bottom Line of 21st Century Business*, Capstone, Oxford, 1997.

assessments linked to logic of profit, with the necessary considerations on social and environmental impact.

The adoption, in fact, of the principles promoted by CSR, understood not as an alternative to current economic practices, but rather as an indispensable complement in order to internalize the external costs of production, should lead the entrepreneur to take reasoned and sustainable choices in several fields: from the economic (investment in research, development of new production methods) to the environmental (more correct and efficient management of waste, rationalization of the use of energy) to reach the social (attention to human resources, transparency in company policies, protection of health, safety and well-being in the workplace, respect for work-life balance, promotion of lifelong learning, consideration of workers' interests, involvement of trade unions, society and all enterprises placed along the value chain of the good produced).[87] In other words, the entrepreneur should weigh his choices in light of the interests of each *stakeholder*. In fact, the close connection between CSR and Sustainable Development is also clear from the common '*multi-stakeholder*' approach: if Sustainable Development proposes taking into consideration the needs of present and near and far future generations, in the same way, CSR proposes to the entrepreneur to consider the effects of his actions on stakeholders, that is to say the '*interested parties*' within the entrepreneurial activity.

There are different definitions of *stakeholder*: from the most restrictive, according to which it is '*a member of a group whose support is necessary for the company to*

87. In accordance with the provisions of Art. 24 of the d. m. of 12 December 2000, a reduction of 5% in the INAIL (*National institute for insurance against industrial injuries*) rate is provided for (for companies with more than 500 employees) of 10% (for companies up to 500 employees) after the first two years of activity if the company has implemented or maintained an SA 8000 certified Social Responsibility system, has created models of Social Responsibility reporting (sustainability report, social report, integrated report) sworn by a third party, or has adopted principles, fundamental themes, specific aspects of social responsibility, specific to UNI ISO 26000: 2010, implementing and maintaining Integrated Prevention models, implemented through policies, practices, integrated procedures of Social Responsibility models based on UNI ISO 26000: 2010 and OSH management systems (OHSAS 18001 and UNI INAIL Guidelines), in addition to other management systems (ISO 9001: 2015, ISO 14001: 2015, EMAS: 2009). The advantage is also granted to the company that has implemented or maintained principles, fundamental themes, specific aspects of social responsibility, specific to UNI ISO 26000: 2010, and has consequently adopted measures to reduce risk levels following forms of prevention with a view to gender, through the following activities: (1) reports of near-accidents and/or missed incidents distinguished by cause, age, origin and gender; (2) working history and differentiated medical-health assessments; (3) special medical and health assessments in the event of pregnancy, breastfeeding, etc.; (4) specific differential training; (5) dedicated food education programmes; (6) initiatives agreed with the Regional and/or Provincial Equality Counsellor; (7) secondary welfare measures (set of concessions granted to female workers by the single company, such as, for example, facilities for nurseries or nurseries within the company itself, with contributions on the fee to be paid, specific health services, etc.), also adopted in mutual form by means of equal bodies. This tax cut is also granted for companies that have privileged, in the selection of suppliers and/or contractors and subcontractors, also with regard to the protection of health and safety at work, those that: (i) have followed criteria of Sustainable Public Procurement; (ii) have followed Green Public Procurement criteria; (iii) have signed the corporate code of ethics; (iv) have acquired the 'Legality Rating' of the AGCM – Antitrust; (v) have employed workers belonging to disadvantaged categories, in addition to legal obligations; (vi) have signed anti-corruption company procedures and/or clauses; (vii) belong to the 'Third Sector'.

continue to exist',[88] or '*an individual, a community or an organization that influences the operations of a company or suffers from the repercussions. The interested parties can be internal (for example: employees) or external (for example: consumers, suppliers, shareholders, financiers, the local community)'*,[89] to the widest, that consider as stakeholders '*any individual or group that can influence or be influenced by the company's actions*'.[90] Stakeholders can then be defined in relation to business risk, that is to say as voluntary and involuntary '*risk bearers*' and as entities that are necessary for the survival of the company: '*voluntary stakeholders bear a form of risk as a result of having invested some form of human or financial capital, something of value, in a company. Involuntary stakeholders are at risk due to the company's activities. But without the element of risk there is no interest at stake.*'[91]

Beyond the scale of the definition adopted, what I want to emphasize is the passage, proposed by the CSR, from a traditional *mono-stakeholder* approach, where the company operates in the interest of creating profit for the shareholder, to a multi-stakeholders approach, where all the different stakeholders are considered in the definition and implementation of corporate decisions. This fully reflects the principles of Sustainable Development, which suggests taking into account the needs, the expectations and the environmental, economic and social patrimony of present and future generations: in other words, the broadest definition of *stakeholders* ever.

The significant interdependence between Sustainable Development and CSR, in addition to the multi-stakeholder approach, emerges from multiple institutional documents, including the Resolution of 8 June 2011 of the European Parliament,[92] which states that CSR should more and more involve in the organization of work and the definition of corporate strategies 'in order to support the transition to a sustainable economy', and the Commission is invited to 'systematically' include in the free trade agreements negotiated with third countries 'a chapter on Sustainable Development, containing a legally binding CSR clause' which 'provides for not only the compliance with the eight fundamental conventions[93] and the four ILO[94] priority conventions but also specific incentives to encourage companies to undertake CSR commitments and a

88. '*Those groups without whose support the organization would cease to exist*', Stanford Research Institute.
89. *See* annex to the 2001 Green Book.
90. R. E. Freeman, *Strategic Management: A Stakeholder Approach*, Pitman, Boston, 1984, p. 46.
91. Cfr. M. B. E. Clarkson, *A Risk Based Model of Stakeholder Theory*, in Proceedings of the 2nd Toronto Conference on Stakeholder Theory, Centre for Corporate Social Performance and Ethics, University of Toronto, Toronto, 1994.
92. Resolution of 8 June 2011 of the European Parliament 'on the external dimension of social policy, the promotion of social and labour standards and corporate social responsibility'.
93. We refer to the Convention on forced labour, n. 29 of 1930, to the Convention on freedom of association and the protection of trade union law, n. 87 of 1948, to the Convention on the right of organization and collective negotiation, n. 98 of 1949, to the Convention on equal pay, n. 100 of 1951, to the Convention on the abolition of forced labour, n. 105 of 1957, to the Convention on discrimination (employment and profession), n. 111 of 1958, to the Convention on the abolition of forced labour, n. 105 of 1957, to the Convention on discrimination (employment and profession), n. 111 of 1958 and the one on the minimum age, n. 138 of 1973.
94. The four priority conventions of the ILO are those dedicated to labour inspection (C-81/1947), employment policy (C-122/1964), inspection of agricultural work (C-129-1969) and to the tripartite consultation (C-144/1976).

duty of diligence on the part of companies and groups of companies (for example, providing for measures aimed at identifying and preventing any violations of human or environmental rights as well as cases of corruption and tax evasion, even at the level of the subsidiaries).

Furthermore, the link between the two concepts involved also emerges clearly from the Communication of the European Commission of 25 October 2011,[95] according to which companies, 'through CSR, can contribute significantly to achieving the objectives of the Treaty on the European Union for Sustainable Development and for a highly competitive social market economy', and in the recent ISO 26000[96] guidelines, which define CSR as 'the behaviour that contributes to Sustainable Development'.[97]

§2.04 AN OVERLOOK AT NATIONAL EXPERIENCES

As already mentioned in the part of this book related to the doctrinal debate on the value of the concept under investigation, Sustainable Development has been elevated over time to a Constitutional principle, mostly in the context of recent constitutional revisions or in the more recent newly proclaimed Constitutions. In some cases (Portugal, Switzerland and France), the reference to Sustainable Development in the constitutional charter is declared and unequivocal; in others, however, (including Italy) although there is no explicit reference to the concept involved, it is easily deducible from reading one or more articles.

[A] The Election of Sustainable Development to a Constitutional Principle

Starting from the Constitutions of the most virtuous countries, it is interesting to observe how Sustainable Development is specifically based on the Constitution of three different European countries: Portugal, Switzerland and France.

Portugal, on the occasion of the constitutional revision of 1997, was the first country in Europe to expressly insert two specific references to Sustainable Development: one in Article 66, on the subject of environment and quality of life – where a series of duties are provided to the State, '*in order to ensure the right to the environment*

95. Communication from the Commission to the European Parliament, to the Council, to the European Economic and Social Committee and to the Committee of the Regions, Renewed EU Strategy for 2011-14 on Corporate Social Responsibility, Brussels, 25.10.2011 COM(2011) 681 final.
96. The ISO 26000 standard is the guideline that is proposed as the international reference on CSR. The standard aims to help organizations in applying the principles underlying CSR and identifying the issues that must be taken into consideration in the management of economic, environmental and social impacts.
97. CSR is the behaviour that '*contribue au développement durable, à la santé et au bien-être de la société, respecte les lois en vigueur et qui est en accord avec les normes internationales de comportement; et qui est intégré dans l'ensemble de l'organisation et mis en œuvre dans ses relations*' (ISO 26000: 2010, point 4).

within an overall framework of sustainable development'.[98] The other in Article 81, on the subject of the primary duties of the State, where it is provided that the State – in the economic and social sphere – is appointed, '*within the overall framework of a Sustainable Development strategy*', to promoting and improving the social-economic well-being of people and their quality of life, especially with regard to disadvantaged people.[99]

Sustainable Development represents a clear constitutional principle also for Switzerland, whose Constitution, reformed in 2000, provides in Article 73 ('Sustainable Development'), on the subject of environment and territorial planning, that 'the Confederation and the Cantons operate in favour of a lastingly balanced relationship among nature, its capacity for renewal and its use on the part of man'. Thereafter, Article 104 provides, in terms of agriculture, for an 'ecologically sustainable and market-oriented production' as a means of guaranteeing the supply of the population, safeguarding the natural vital bases and the rural landscape, and, more importantly, the guarantee of a decentralized occupation of the territory.

With a few years of delay – even if it is inappropriate to speak about delay, having seen the vanguard of the initiative compared to the other countries of the world – also France, in 2005, has constitutionalized the principle of *développement durable*, already widely present in the system,[100] annexing to the Constitution the *Charte de l'environnement*, (Environmental Charter),[101] according to which, in order to '*ensure*

98. Article 66 of Portuguese Constitution: '*Environment and quality of life*': '*1. Everyone has the right to a healthy and ecologically balanced human living environment and the duty to defend it. 2. In order to ensure the right to the environment within an overall framework of sustainable development, the state, acting via appropriate bodies and with the involvement and participation of citizens, is charged with: a) Preventing and controlling pollution and its effects and the harmful forms of erosion; b) Conducting and promoting town and country planning with a view to a correct location of activities, balanced social and economic development and the enhancement of the landscape; c) Creating and developing natural and recreational reserves and parks and classifying and protecting landscapes and places, in such a way as to guarantee the conservation of nature and the preservation of cultural values and assets that are of historic or artistic interest; d) Promoting the rational use of natural resources, while safeguarding their ability to renew themselves and ecological stability, with respect for the principle of inter-generational solidarity; e) In cooperation with local authorities, promoting the environmental quality of rural settlements and urban life, particularly on the architectural level and as regards the protection of historic zones; f) Promoting the integration of environmental objectives into the various policies with a sectoral scope; g) Promoting environmental education and respect for environmental values and assets; h) Ensuring that the fiscal policy renders development compatible with the protection of the environment and the quality of life.*'
99. Article 81 of Portuguese Constitution: '*Priority duties of the state*': '*1. In the economic and social field the state is under a priority duty: a) Within the overall framework of a sustainable development strategy, to promote an increase in people's social and economic well-being and quality of life, especially those of the most disadvantaged persons; ...* .'
100. In France there are several laws on Sustainable Development: the law on air, Loi No. 96-1236 of 30 December 1996 published in the Official Journal, n. 1, 1 January 1997, the law of orientation for the management of the territory and Sustainable Development, Loi No. 99-533 of 25 June 1999, published in the Official Journal, n. 148, 29 June 1999; the law on solidarity and urban development, Loi No. 2000-1208 of 13 December 2000, published in the Official Journal, n. 289, 14 December 2000.
101. The Environmental Charter was incorporated into the French Constitution with the Constitutional Law n. 2005-205 of 1 March 2005. The text of the French Constitution can be consulted at: http://www.assemblee-nationale.fr/connaissance/constitution_11-2011.pdf.

Sustainable Development, the choices intended to meet the needs of the present must not compromise the ability of future generations and other people to satisfy their needs'[102] (taking up almost literally the definition of Sustainable Development proposed by the Brundtland Report).

Thus, four different principles are introduced at the constitutional level: (i) the precautionary principle, which specifies the need to adopt measures if there are not sufficient reasons to believe that an activity or product is a risk for serious damage to health and environment, ensuring a high level of protection of the environment and human, animal or plant health, in the event that the scientific data related to the problem do not allow a complete risk assessment; (ii) the *pollueur-payeur* principle (the polluter pays principle), which aims to prevent and repair damage to nature caused by an industrial plant or activity; (iii) the principle of preventive action and correction, which concerns the attention to the environment and the objective of using the best possible techniques at an acceptable economic cost; (iv) the principle of participation-information, which gives the right to every citizen to have access to information relating to the environment, including those relating to substances and dangerous activities: the citizen must be involved in the processes of elaboration of projects that have a significant impact on the environment or on land management.

The importance of sustainability for the French system is further reaffirmed in Article 6 of the Charter in question, which considers Sustainable Development as a fundamental programmatic principle for future national policies: '*public policies must promote sustainable development. To this end, they combine protection and enhancement of the environment, economic development and social progress.*'[103]

In addition to the examples of these virtuous and precursor countries in the constitutionalization of the principle under investigation, in many other countries the constitutional texts contain a reference that is not explicitly named, but is clearly underlying, and intuitively inferable from reading one or more articles. In some cases, the reference to Sustainable Development underlies the concept of intergenerational balance protecting the interests of future generations: this is the example of the 1988 Constitution of Brazil where in Article 225[104] the universal right '*to an ecologically balanced*[105] *environment, and, as a common good for the people, indispensable for a healthy quality of life; the public authority and the community are obliged to defend it and preserve it for present and future generations*' is provided for.

---

102. Original text, taken from the Preamble of the Environment Charter: '*Qu'afin d'assurer un développement durable, les choix destinés à répondre aux besoins du présent ne doivent pas compromettre la capacité des générations futures et des autres peuples à satisfaire leurs propres besoins.*'
103. Original text of Art. 6: '*Les politiques publiques doivent promouvoir un développement durable. A cet effet, elles concilient la protection et la mise en valeur de l'environnement, le développement économique et le progrès social.*'
104. Article 225 of the 1988 Costitution of Brasil: '*Todos têm direito ao meio ambiente ecologicamente equilibrado, bem de uso comum do povo e essencial à sadia qualidade de vida, impondo-se ao poder público e à coletividade o dever de defendê-lo e preservá-lo para as presentes e futuras gerações.*'
105. The Constitutions of El Salvador (2000), Costa Rica (2001) and Guatemala (1993) also refer to an 'ecologically balanced environment'.

Along similar lines Article 41 of the Argentine[106] Constitution promotes the right '*to a healthy, balanced environment, suitable for human development and for productive activities to meet the needs of the present without compromising the needs of future generations, with the duty to protect them. Environmental damage will primarily generate the obligation to restore the previous situation, in compliance with the law*'.

Furthermore, Article 97 of the Constitution of Japan states that '*The fundamental human rights guaranteed by the present Constitution to the people of Japan are the result of the struggle that man has been leading for freedom since ancient times. They have survived to numerous and strenuous ordeals and are given to this and future generations, with the mandate to guarantee their inviolability forever.*'

On the contrary, in other countries, the principle of Sustainable Development is conceived in terms of safeguarding their natural heritage: it is the case, for example, of the constitutional text of Colombia (1991), where the reference to Sustainable Development is in relation to the exploitation of natural resources (Article 80).[107] Differently, in many other countries of Central and South America, Africa and Asia the link to Sustainable Development is aimed to contrast phenomena not only of environmental degradation but also of corruption and environmental crime that can increase the depletion and exploitation of their resources. The common trait of these Constitutions is the concern about the State having to guarantee the protection and rational exploitation of its resources and to take the necessary measures to preserve and improve the environment. In this sense, the constitutional text of Angola (1992) is exemplary where it speaks of a 'right to environmental protection', and it aims to guide development by guaranteeing a rational and efficient use of national productive capacities and resources. It also emphasizes that all natural resources belong to the State that determines the limits of their exploitation. The constitutional texts of Sudan (1998) and Cambodia (1993 and 1999) also speak of the role and duties of the State towards environmental protection.

However, if we take the European framework as a reference, the principle of Sustainable Development can be deduced in Constitutional texts, although without explicit mentions, in the Constitutions, for example, of Germany (1994 revision) and Finland (1999 revision) where there is a reference to the 'Natural conditions of life' that must also be protected against 'future generations', while the constitutional text of Greece (1986 reform), under Article 24, states that 'the protection of the natural and cultural environment constitutes a State duty'. In the Constitution of Spain, instead, the universal right to 'enjoy an adequate environment for the development of the person' is reaffirmed.

The above-mentioned framework highlights how Sustainable Development, elected as a constitutional principle, even though more or less explicitly, finds a certain

106. '*Todos los habitantes gozan del derecho a un ambiente sano, equilibrado, apto para el desarrollo humano y para quelas actividades productivas satisfagan las necesidades presentes sin comprometerlas de las generaciones futuras; y tienen el deber de preservarlo. El daño ambiental generará prioritariamente la obligación de recomponer, según lo establezca la ley.*'

107. The same reference is done in other Constitutions: Uruguay (1996), Bolivia (1967), Guyana (1970), Nepal (1990), Burundi (1992), Burkina-Faso (1991).

legitimacy and normative value. Therefore, if contemporary Constitutions '*have become an instrument of dynamic composition of conflicts between tables of values that are coexistent, but that must be concretely reconciled, if the legal system wants to maintain coherence and legitimacy*',[108] it is legitimate to assume that Sustainable Development found over time an important space within the values to be promoted and protected at national level.

[B] Italy and Sustainable Development Goals: Delays and Progress

Italy is one of the countries where the concept of Sustainable Development has not (yet) found a space defined in the Constitutional text, despite the growing awareness of the projection of public policies on the rights of future generations. At present, only the interpretation of a combined set of constitutional provisions (Articles 2, 9, 32, 41 and 42)[109] may lead to infer the implicit existence of the principle in the Constitution, especially in light of its intrinsic search for compatibility among economic development, protection of the environment and health, promoted expressly in Article 41.

Such a delay in incorporating a principle that is by now established within the EU, however, is not surprising if we consider that the issue of environmental protection has only entered the lexicon of the Constitution, following the reform of Title V of the Constitution with the Constitutional law n. 3 of 18 October 2001. However, some constitutional reform projects are proposing changes to the Article 9 concerning the fundamental right of the environment, and to the Article 41, introducing the principle of Sustainable Development, as recognized in the ambit of international and community law.

As for the first, a series of projects about reconsidering Article 9[110] have been presented since 1990, with the aim of including environmental protection among the

108. M. D'Antona, *Diritto del Lavoro di fine secolo, una crisi d'identità*, in *Riv. giur. lav.*, 1998, 1, p. 324.

109. Article 2: '*The Republic recognizes and guarantees the inviolable rights of man, as an individual, and in the social groups where he expresses his personality, and demands the fulfilment of the intransgressible duties of political, economic, and social solidarity.*'; Art. 9: '*The Republic promotes the development of culture and scientific and technical research. It protects the landscape and the historical and artistic heritage of the Nation.*'; Art. 32: '*The Republic safeguards health as a fundamental right of the individual and as a collective interest, and guarantees free medical care to the indigent. No one may be obliged to undergo particular health treatment except under the provisions of the law. The law cannot under any circumstances violate the limits imposed by respect for the human person.*'; Art. 41: '*Private economic initiative is free. It cannot be conducted in conflict with public weal or in such manner that could damage safety, liberty, and human dignity. The law determines appropriate planning and controls so that public and private economic activity is given direction and coordinated to social objectives.*'; Art. 42: '*Property is public or private. Economic goods belong to the State, to entities or to private persons. Private property is recognized and guaranteed by law, which prescribes the ways it is acquired, enjoyed and its limits in order to ensure its social function and to make it accessible to all. Private property can, in such cases provided for by law and with provisions for compensation, be expropriated for reasons of the public weal. The law establishes the regulations and limits of legitimate and testamentary inheritance and the rights of the State in questions of inheritance.*'

110. On the Constitutional Reform of Art. 9, P. Mantini, *Per una nozione costituzionalmente rilevante di ambiente*, in *Riv. giur. amb.*, 2006, 2, pp. 207 ss. On this topic, *see also*: A. Venturi, *Costituzione, ambiente e Sviluppo Sostenibile. Elementi di comparazione giuridica per una*

fundamental principles of the Republic. In particular, the constitutional proposal law n. 101/2006,[111] entitled *'amendment to article 9 of the Constitution on the protection of ecosystems and the promotion of Sustainable Development'*, proposes, precisely, to add the promotion of Sustainable Development among the fundamental principles of the Republic, adding to the Article 9 the following paragraphs: *'(it) recognizes and guarantees the environment and ecosystems as inviolable assets and fundamental values of the planet. It promotes sustainable development and respect for animals. It protects biodiversity. It protects access to water as a public common good'*.

As for the second project, there has been a proposal[112] to integrate, with the reference 'to the environment', the list of limits that the economic initiative can meet: *'private economic initiative is free. It cannot take place in contrast with social utility or in such a way as to damage the environment, security, freedom, human dignity.'* Such an amendment to Article 41 of the Constitution may be in line with what is proposed by Sustainable Development in terms of balancing economic (economic initiative), social (safety, freedom and human dignity) and environmental (without causing damage to the environment) interests.

Italy should therefore follow the example of European countries and expressly incorporate the principle of Sustainable Development among the ones that are constitutionally protected, so as to guide judges in decisions, anytime economic development is in contrast with the protection of environment or with social rights: *'just as in Europe Sustainable Development has definitively become a parameter of guarantee of environmental protection policies, in the same way its inclusion in our Constitutional Charter can be represented as a balancing parameter, inextricably linked to the environmental value, and therefore of guaranteeing conflicting constitutional values.'*[113]

Beyond the constitutional text, if we look at the normative data, important recent references to Sustainable Development can be found, especially in the environmental field, in the interest of safeguarding the rights to a healthy environment of future generations. Proceeding in chronological order, we must mention Article 1 of the law 36/1994 (so-called Galli law), according to which *'all surface and underground waters, even if not extracted from the subsoil, are public and constitute a resource that is safeguarded and used according to solidarity criteria'* (paragraph 1) and *'any use of water is carried out safeguarding the expectations and rights of future generations to enjoy an integral environmental heritage'* (paragraph 2).

Still on the subject of the environment, it is worth recalling the reference to Article 1 of the law 152/1999,[114] pursuant to which *'this decree defines the general*

---

revisione costituzionale, in G. Cordini, A. Venturi (curated by), *Lo Sviluppo Sostenibile nelle aree protette del Mediterraneo*, Aracne, Roma, 2011, pp. 177 ss.

111. Proposal of Constitutional Law Mussi: *amendment to Article 9 of the Constitution on the protection of ecosystems and the promotion of Sustainable Development.*
112. Proposal of revision of Arts 9 and 41 of the Constitution on the part of 'Fare Ambiente', on 5 May 2011.
113. V. Pepe, *Riforma dell'art. 41 della Costituzione per uno Sviluppo Sostenibile: la sostenibilità come etica pubblica*, in *L'Italia Forestale e Montana / Italian Journal of Forest and Mountain Environments*, 2012, vol. 67, n. 1, pp. 44-54.
114. Legislative Decree 11 May 1999, n. 152, Updated text of the Legislative Decree 11 May 1999, n. 152, containing: 'Provisions on the protection of water from pollution and transposition of

discipline for the protection of surface, marine and underground waters, pursuing the following objectives: ... c) pursuing sustainable and durable uses of water resources, with priority for potable water' (paragraph 1) and '*the achievement of the objectives indicated in paragraph 1 is realized through the following tools: ... f) the identification of measures aimed at the conservation, saving, re-use and recycling of water resources*' (paragraph 2).

If these (albeit timid) references to Sustainable Development are strictly confined to environmental protection standards, it's been since the start of the new millennium that Sustainable Development has begun to be delineated, even in Italy, in its triple dimension, thanks above all to the *Strategy of Environmental Action for Sustainable Development in Italy,*[115] elaborated by the Ministry of the Environment and the Protection of the Territory for the period 2002–2010 (then renewed in 2017), through which there is the commitment to develop a national strategy for Sustainable Development in the field of full employment, social cohesion and environmental protection.

The first concrete reference in the legislative sphere to the principle of Sustainable Development is instead found only in 2006, with Law n. 152, of 3 April 2006,[116] '*Environmental law*'. The decree is particularly significant in the process of affirmation of the principle of Sustainable Development in the Italian legal system, since it defines the principle involved in its triple (environmental, social and economic) dimension, in Article 3 quater, matter-of-factly entitled '*Principle of Sustainable Development*': '*1. Every legally relevant human activity pursuant this code must comply with the principle of Sustainable Development, in order to guarantee to humanity that the satisfaction of the needs of current generations cannot compromise the quality of life and the possibilities of future generations; 2. Also the activity of the public administration must be aimed at allowing the best possible implementation of the principle of Sustainable Development, therefore, in the context of the comparative choice of public and private interests characterized by discretion, the interests of environmental protection and cultural heritage must be the object of priority consideration; 3. Given the complexity of the relationships and the interference between nature and human activities, the principle of Sustainable Development must allow to identify a balanced relationship, within the inherited resources, between those to be saved and those to be transmitted, so that in the field of the dynamics of production and consumption, the principle of solidarity is also included to safeguard and improve the quality of the (future) environment; 4. The resolution of the issues that involve environmental aspects must be sought and found in the perspective of guaranteeing Sustainable Development, in order*

Directive 91/271/EEC concerning the treatment of urban waste water and of Directive 91/676/EEC concerning the protection of water from pollution caused by nitrates from agricultural sources', following the corrective and supplementary provisions referred to in the Legislative Decree 18 August 2000, n. 258 published in the Official Journal, n. 246, 20 October 2000 – Ordinary Supplement n. 172.

115. Strategy of Environmental Action for Sustainable Development in Italy, Ministry of Environment and Territory Protection, Department for Sustainable Development and Personnel Policies and General Affairs Directorate for Sustainable Development, 07.15.02 / Rev. 38.
116. Just as it was modified by the law 16 January 2008, n. 4.

to protect the correct functioning and evolution of natural ecosystems from the negative modifications that can be produced by human activities'.

Along the same lines, the law of 28 December 2015, n. 221[117] on Green economy provides, in implementation of the National Strategy for Sustainable Development, several (among other) innovations, the provision of a sustainable mobility programme (initiatives of walking bus, *car-pooling* or *car-sharing* in the home-work and home-school route) and the establishment of ENEA, the National Agency for new technologies, energy and sustainable economic development: a body governed by public law aimed at research, technological innovation and the provision of advanced services to businesses, public administration and citizens in the energy, environment and sustainable economic development sectors.

The following year, on 28 July 2016, the Senate then definitively approved the reform of the budget law, providing that in a specific annex to the Economic and Financial Document (EFD) the trend of the past three years of the Fair and Sustainable Well-Being indicators as well as the forecasts on their evolution in the reference period should be reported: (1) the average available income adjusted per capita; (2) the index of inequality of disposable income; (3) the absolute poverty index; (4) healthy life expectancy at birth; (5) weight excess; (6) early leaving of education and training system; (7) the rate of non-participation in labour, with relative distinction by gender; (8) the relationship between the employment rate of women aged 25–49 with children of preschool age and women without children; (9) the predatory crime rate; (10) the efficiency index of civil justice; (11) the emissions of CO_2 and other climate-altering gases; (12) the index of illegal construction.

We should observe that one-third of the proposed indexes (nos 1, 2, 7, 8) are relevant to the Objective 8 of Agenda 2030: this underlines the decisive role of labour and more specifically, of labour law, in determining the achievement of a general well-being and a fair and Sustainable Development.[118]

The new rules also provide that, by 15 February of each year, the Parliament will receive from the Minister of Economy and Finance a report on the evolution of the performance of fair and sustainable welfare indicators based on the effects determined by the budget law for the current three-year period, as well as a forecast assessment of the future trend as well as the impact of the policies.[119]

A similar reporting obligation is also imposed on large companies (over 500 employees), considered, by virtue of their importance and visibility, as public-interest entities.[120] These companies, according to the provisions of D. lgs. 30 December

117. Law of 28 December 2015, n. 221: Environmental provisions to promote green economy measures and to contain the excessive use of natural resources (16G00006) (GU General Series n. 13, 18 January 2016).
118. About the difficulties on the measurement of Sustainable Development, refer to: S. Bell, S. Morse, *Sustainability Indicators: Measuring the Immeasurable?*, 2nd edition, Earthscan, London – Washington D.C., 2008.
119. For the EFD 2019, please *see* Ministry of Economics and Finance, Economic and Finance Document, April 2019, available at http://www.dt.mef.gov.it/modules/documenti_it/analisi_progammazione/documenti_programmatici/def_2019/01_-_PdS_2019.pdf.
120. According to the Art. 16, para. 1, Legislative Decree 27 January 2010, n. 39/2010, are Entities of Public Interest: 'a) the Italian companies issuing securities admitted to trading on Italian and

2016,[121] transposing EU Directive 95/2014,[122] are obliged, starting from 2018, to elaborate an 'Individual declaration of a non-financial nature' in environmental and social terms, containing information that is suitable to ensure 'the understanding of the business activity, its performance, its results and the impact produced by it'.

The Declaration involved must 'at least' describe: (a) the business model of management and organization of the company's activities; (b) the policies applied by the company, including those of due diligence, the results achieved through them and the relevant non-financial performance indicators; (c) the main risks, generated or suffered, connected to the aforementioned topics and deriving from the company's activities, its products, services or commercial relationships, including, where relevant, supply chains and subcontracting. The Declaration must then contain information regarding: (a) the use of energy resources, distinguishing between those produced from renewable and non-renewable sources, and the use of water resources; (b) greenhouse gas emissions and polluting emissions into the atmosphere; (c) the impact, where possible, on the basis of hypotheses or realistic scenarios also in the medium term, on the environment and on health and safety or other relevant environmental and health risk factors; (d) the social and aspects linked to the management of employees, including the actions put in place to ensure gender equality, the measures aimed at implementing the conventions of international and supranational organizations on the subject, how the dialogue with the social partners is carried out; (e) respect for human rights, the measures adopted to prevent violations, as well as actions taken to prevent discriminatory attitudes and actions; (f) the fight against both active and passive corruption, with indication of the instruments adopted for this purpose.

Finally, the new National Strategy for Sustainable Development,[123] with which Italy is committed to declare the strategic objectives of the UN 2030 Agenda for Sustainable Development in the context of economic, social and environmental planning. This Strategy mainly aims at evaluating the Italian 'positioning' with respect

---

European Union regulated markets and those that have requested such admission to trading; b) banks; c) the insurance companies referred to in Article 1, paragraph 1, letter u) of the private insurance code; d) the reinsurance companies referred to in article 1, paragraph 1, letter cc) of the private insurance code, with registered office in Italy, and the secondary offices in Italy of the non-EU reinsurance companies referred to in Article 1, paragraph 1, letter cc-ter), of the private insurance code; e) the companies issuing financial instruments, which, although not listed on regulated markets, are widely spread among the public; f) companies that manage regulated markets; g) the companies that manage the clearing and guarantee systems; h) central depositories of financial instruments; i) securities brokerage companies; l) asset management companies; m) investment companies with variable capital; n) payment institutions pursuant to Directive 2009/64/EC; o) electronic money institutions; p) the financial intermediaries referred to in Article 107 of the TUB.'

121. Legislative Decree 30 December 2016, n. 254, Implementation of Directive 2014/95/EU of the European Parliament and of the Council of 22 October 2014, amending the Directive 2013/34/EU as regards the communication of non-financial information and information on the diversity by some companies and certain large groups (Official Gazette No. 7, 10 January 2017).

122. Directive 2014/95/EU of the European Parliament and of the Council of 22 October 2014 amending Directive 2013/34/EU with regard to the communication of non-financial information and information on the diversity of certain companies and large groups.

123. Ministry of Environment and Land and Sea Protection, National Strategy for Sustainable Development, October 2017.

to the seventeen Goals and the 169 Targets of the 2030[124] Agenda and to identify both a system of strengths and weaknesses on which to build the objectives to be pursued, starting from the positioning analysis, and a system of national strategic objectives organized around the areas (5P) of Agenda 2030 – People, Planet, Prosperity, Peace and Partnership (formulation that fully shows all the dimensions of the development's sustainability).

The most recent regulatory changes are therefore significant to determine a substantial change in the content of economic and financial planning documents, pushing the Government and Parliament to consider the *SDGs* and the contents of the 2030 Agenda in the definition of policies and helping to shift the focus of the economic policy from mere growth in terms of gross domestic product to the improvement of collective well-being, without precluding the possibilities of future generations.

The proposed regulatory framework shows how even in Italy the concept of Sustainable Development has entered the legislator's vocabulary in its most correct triple meaning, despite the fact that the first references were limited to protecting the environment, so as to result as the future 'target' at which to aim.[125] This awareness shows how the objective of Sustainable Development can reasonably constitute a new paradigm of reference for national legislation, and in particular, for the forthcoming reforms in the field of labour law.

---

124. The document highlights some interesting data with reference to the Objective 8 of the 2030 Agenda: in 2016, in Italy, the unemployment rate is 11.7%, the percentage of employed people on the total of the population 37.7%, the rate of non-participation at work 21.6%, the percentage of people aged 15-24, neither employed nor included in an education or training course is at 19.9% and the percentage of NEETs at 24.3%.

125. Speech by the President of the Republic, Sergio Mattarella, at the ceremony for the delivery of the insignia of the Knight of the Order 'to the Merit of Work', Palazzo del Quirinale, 30 November 2017: 'Sustainable Development is the goal we must aim at. Sustainability is not just about the necessary environmental balances: sustainable is a growth that includes, that strengthens cohesion in society, that reduces inequalities; and that broadens the network of integration and international cooperation.'

CHAPTER 3

Labour Law and Sustainable Development: Value Analogies and Application Profiles in the National Context

§3.01 VALUE AND METHODOLOGICAL ANALOGIES BETWEEN THE OBJECTS OF INVESTIGATION

The idea of investigating the possible interconnections between labour law and Sustainable Development arises from the observation of the analogies found between the axiological paradigm of Sustainable Development and the aims and values underlying the labour law discipline.

As a matter of fact, by pondering on the founding concepts of Sustainable Development, it is possible to find a double, significant commonality with the fundamental principles of labour law. The first similarity is expressed in terms of value, with explicit reference to the common values of solidarity among generations (§3.02) and the interest in the elimination of inequalities (or the guarantee of an equality of possibilities) (§3.03).

The second is to be considered in methodological terms, with reference to the reconciliation - promoted by both paradigms - of conflicting axiological interests, specifically social and economic ones (§3.04).

§3.02 GENERATIONAL SOLIDARITY IN THE LABOUR MARKET AND IN THE ENTERPRISE

With reference to the first axiological consonance, both Sustainable Development and labour law are based on the value of intergenerational and intra-generational solidarity, which is defended and promoted at the same time.

As already illustrated, the solidarity among current and distant – in space and time – generations is the defining key element of the concept of *sustainable development*, meaning a development able to reconcile the needs of current generations without precluding the same possibilities for future generations, the labour law discipline guarantees and promotes a principle of social solidarity contemplated by the Italian Constitution.

The value of solidarity is matter-of-factly constitutionally protected, pursuant to Article 2,[1] which states that '*the Republic recognizes and guarantees the inviolable rights of man, both as an individual and in the social formations where his/her personality is expressed, and requires the fulfilment of the mandatory duties of political, economic and social solidarity.*' The article involved must be read in the constitutional context, therefore considering its location between Article 1 which founds the Republic on labour and Article 3, where dignity appears with an explicit social connotation and the reference to the '*obstacles of economic and social order*' literally refers to the duties of '*economic and social solidarity*'.[2] From this point of view the connotation of labour is seen as a fulfilment of the duty of solidarity and at the same time as a title to demand solidarity on the part of the Republic.[3]

Solidarity can therefore be understood legitimately as that *fil rouge* that holds together the various forms of labour and social protection, that is to say, a unifying principle of the law of employed people (labour relations and employment protection) and the law of the excluded (labour market law, edict of social inclusion, that is the right of those affected by old and new poverty).[4]

The issue of solidarity in the field of labour law is in fact delineated in different perspectives in the labour market, that is to say in terms of welfare, trade union coverage, employment and employability, both at an intra-generational level (among current generations) and at an intergenerational level (among successive generations).

[A] Solidarity Tools for Generational Turnover

The labour law discipline provides a wide range of tools to relaunch youth employment[5] or to provide retirement incentives for older

1. M. Barbera, *Sub Art. 2 Costituzione,* in G. Branca (curated by), *Commentario alla Costituzione,* Zanichelli-Il Foro Italiano, Bologna-Roma,1975; P. Barcellona, *La solidarietà come fatto e come diritto,* in *Lav. dir.,* 1996, pp. 4-5; F. Giuffrè, *La solidarietà nell'ordinamento costituzionale,* Giuffrè, Milano, 2002; G. Zagrebelsky, *Fondata sul lavoro. La solitudine dell'articolo 1,* Einaudi, Torino, 2013.
2. S. Rodotà, *Solidarietà. Un'utopia necessaria,* Laterza, Roma, 2014, p. 46.
3. M. G. Garofalo, *Solidarietà e lavoro,* in M. Napoli (curated by), *La solidarietà,* Vita e Pensiero, Milano, 2009, p. 8.
4. M. Napoli, *Prefazione. La solidarietà da riscoprire,* in M. Napoli (curated by), *La solidarietà,* Vita e Pensiero, Milano, 2009, p. IX.
5. An example of this is the 'Garanzia Giovani' project, which aims to ensure an opportunity for work or training within four months from the start of unemployment or from leaving the formal education system, or the provision, pursuant to Law 107/2015 of a mandatory guidance service for young people attending the second two-year period and the last school year, in order to create a link between the school system and the external world, transforming the concept of learning into that of permanent activity and giving equal dignity to both school and work training. In this

workers,[6] aiming at a better functioning of the labour market and at greater employment. Some of these tools are based expressly on the value of occupational solidarity among workers of the same company and between workers and unemployed of different generations, in line with what is proposed by the paradigm of Sustainable Development. In particular, two institutes are highlighted, strongly characterized by the values of solidarity: the 'generational pacts' and 'solidarity contracts'.

The first, introduced by the Ministerial Decree of the Ministry of Labour and Social Policies n. 807/2012,[7] are essentially trade union agreements that provide for a sort of 'generational changeover', that is the reduction of working hours for workers close to retirement, from full-time to part-time in the view of employing young people with contract of apprenticeship or permanent contract, in order to promote youth employment and accompany older workers towards retirement, guaranteeing, at the

regard, the most recent decree n. 3 of 2 January 2018 of the ANPAL (National Agency for Active Labour Policies), governing the NEET Employment Incentive entitled to private employers who, from 1 January 2018 to 31 December 2018, hire young people between 16 and 29 years of age adhering to the 'Garanzia Giovani' programme, for an indefinite period (also for administrative purposes) or professionalizing apprenticeship, also in part-time mode. The incentive is equal to the social security contribution paid by the employer, with the exclusion of the INAIL premiums, for twelve months within a maximum limit of EUR 8,060 on a monthly basis, re-proportioned in the case of part-time work.

6. The retirement incentive measures for workers that are close to meeting the requirements for retirement are governed by Art. 4, paras 1-7 of the Law 92/2012. The legislation involved authorizes, in the case of staff surplus, the employer with more than fifteen employees, subject to agreement with the most representative trade unions at company level, to pay workers a benefit equal to the pension treatment that would be due according to the rules in force, and to pay to INPS (*social security body*) a contribution up to the minimum retirement requirements, provided that these workers reach the minimum requirements for retirement, of old age or early retirement, in the four years following the end of the relationship of work. Another tool recognized by the employer to facilitate workers to retirement is the facilitated part-time: pursuant to Art. 1, para. 284, Law 208/2015 (the so-called 2016 Stability Law), employees of the private sector enrolled in compulsory general insurance and the substitutional and exclusive forms of the latter with a full-time and open-ended employment contract that accrue by 31 December 2018 the right to retirement pension treatment, pursuant to Art. 24, para. 6 of the Legislative Decree 201/2011, may – provided that they have completed the minimum contribution requirements for the right to retirement pension, in agreement with the employer, for a period not exceeding the period elapsing between the date of access to the benefit and the maturity date of the registry requirement pursuant to the aforementioned Art. 24, para. 6, – reduce the time of the employment relationship to between 40% and 60%, obtaining a monthly sum from the employer corresponding to the social security contribution for pension purposes to be paid by the employer, relative to the service performance not carried out. This amount does not contribute to the formation of employment income and is not subject to social security contributions. For periods of reduction in work performance, the notional contribution commensurate with the remuneration corresponding to work not performed is recognized. Therefore, for the purpose of identifying the remuneration to be assumed as the basis for calculating the retirement shares of workers who have worked part-time, applying Art. 41, para. 6 of the D. lgs. 148/2015 (relating to expansive solidarity contracts) the number of weeks of work performed part-time is neutralized, where this entails a more favourable pension treatment.
7. Law n. 2, 28 January 2009, Conversion into Law, with amendments, of the Law Decree of 29 November 2008, n. 185, containing urgent measures to support families, work, employment and business and to redesign the National Strategic Framework in an anti-crisis perspective.

same time, a transfer of knowledge and experience among generations and thus safeguarding a transfer of skills.[8]

Although more than EUR 40 million have been allocated in funds,[9] the generational pacts have not had a significant following, except in some cases.[10]

The causes of this failure can be found both in the lack of publicity of the initiative, and in the confused procedure, and, above all, in the insufficient income support of the elderly worker who accepts the reduction in working hours and, consequently, suffers the deduction of remuneration: in essence, it does not seem sufficient, especially in the current negative economic situation, to guarantee the contribution coverage of hours not worked for the purpose of preserving the pension treatment calculated on the basis of the originally scheduled working time.[11]

A further instrument with vast potential in terms of occupational solidarity is undoubtedly the solidarity contract, in its dual 'defensive' (expression of solidarity in the company) and 'expansive' (solidarity in the market) version, introduced in Articles 1 and 2 of the l. 863/84[12] and recently re-proposed by D. lgs. 148/2015, in Articles 21 (paragraphs 1 and 5) and 41.

8. In the event of hiring young people with an apprenticeship and/or permanent contract, the Regions and the Autonomous Provinces pay to INPS (*social security body*) a contribution-based integration, by way of voluntary contribution, for older workers who voluntarily consent to a part-time contract. From the simultaneous employment of the young person and reduction of the working hours of the elderly worker, a positive company employment balance must be achieved. The Regions and the Autonomous Provinces sign agreements with INPS aimed at determining, within the limits of the resources already assigned with the Directorial Decrees, the financial amount and transfer the necessary resources to the Institute. The Regions and the Autonomous Provinces communicate to the Ministry of Labour and to Italia Lavoro S.p.A. the sum they intend to attribute to the intervention in order to allow payments if they have not already been made with regard to the other interventions: 50% after the communication of the total amount indicated; 50% following a request, with the enclosed declaration relating to the agreement with the INPS, the list of older workers hired part-time with the indication of the monthly payments for which the voluntary contribution is provided and the list of young people hired in connection with the voluntary acceptance of part-time by older workers.
9. The Ministry of Labour, with directorial decree n. 481/2012, assigned to the regions the resources to be used – in the form of incentives to workers for reintegration, also for self-employment, and hiring bonuses for companies – as part of the 'welfare to work system action for re-employment policies 2012–2014 ', for a total of EUR 40,285,961.61.
10. The best and consistent generational pacts are those in the credit sector that have led to 48,000 retirements and 13,000 young people hired in ten years. Another significant pact is that of Luxottica (July 2016) (according to which 100 workers, within three or five years from retirement can request a 50% part-time, without this affecting their final pension, in exchange for the commitment of the 'company to hire 100 young people on permanent contracts) and that of Enel (of November 2015, containing a plan that provides for about six thousand retirements between 2016 and 2020, against the recruitment of three thousand young people).
11. Cfr. G. Canavesi, E. Ales, *Il sistema previdenziale italiano. Principi, struttura ed evoluzione*, Giappichelli, Torino, 2017.
12. Law n. 863/1984, Urgent Measures to Support and Increase Occupational Levels. On the subject of solidarity contracts, *see*, among others: G. Pera, *I contratti di solidarietà*, in *Giorn. dir. lav. rel. ind.*, 1984, p. 69; R. Pessi, *Funzione e disciplina dei contratti di solidarietà*, in *Giorn. dir. lav. rel. ind.*, 1985, p. 335; T. Treu, *La disciplina legale dei contratti di solidarietà*, in *Dir. lav.*, 1985, 1, p. 14; G. Arrigo, *I contratti di solidarietà*, in AA.VV. (curated by), *Il diritto del lavoro negli anni ottanta*, vol. II, Editoriale Scientifica, Napoli, 1988, p. 139; M. Brollo, *I contratti di solidarietà*, in F. Neri (curated by), *Le politiche del lavoro negli anni '80*, Franco Angeli, Milano, 1989, pp. 189-203; G. Ferraro, *Politiche dell'impiego e crisi occupazionale nella legge n. 236*, in *Lav. Inf.*,

'Defensive' solidarity contracts are agreements, stipulated between the company (falling within the scope of the CIGS (*Extraordinary Temporary Unemployment Compensation*)) and trade union representatives, concerning the reduction of working hours[13] in order to maintain employment in the event of a company crisis[14] and therefore to avoid the declaration of the redundancy of personnel, also through its more rational use, thus promoting an internal solidarity within the company, among the same community of workers.[15]

On the contrary, 'expansive' solidarity contracts, originally governed by Article 2, l. 863/94, and re-proposed, almost in an identical manner by Article 41 of the D. lgs. 148/2015, favour new permanent contracts through a simultaneous and planned reduction in working hours and the remuneration of workers already present in the company, promoting intergenerational solidarity between employed and unemployed. In fact, in the face of a stable reduction in working hours, with a reduction in pay and the concurrent hiring of new staff on an open-ended basis, employers are granted, for each worker and for each salary, a social security contribution for three years.[16] The workers affected by the reduction in working hours (and, consequently, of salary), who decide to take advantage of the part-time to enjoy a better balancing of life reconciliation times, to dedicate themselves to parental role, or to domestic work or to a new training course, however, are guaranteed the payment of contributions for pension purposes correlated to the amount of the lost remuneration (paragraph 2-bis).

The INPS (*National Institute for Social Security*) also provides for a further support in the event that the solidarity contract favours the employment of young people in the company: if the hiring involves workers aged between 15 and 29, for the first three years and in any case no later than the twenty-ninth year of age of the hired worker, the employer's contribution fee is due at an amount corresponding to that provided for apprentices, without prejudice to the remuneration paid by the worker to the extent established for the generality of workers. This greater advantage is a proof of

1993, 19; G. Santoro Passarelli, *I contratti di solidarietà: due esperienze a confronto*, in *Riv. it. dir. lav.*, 1994, 1, p. 263; S. Renga, *Mercato del lavoro e diritto*, Franco Angeli, Milano, 1996.

13. The average hourly reduction of the workers involved in the solidarity contract cannot exceed 60% of the daily, weekly or monthly schedule.
14. It is worth mentioning that the solidarity contract is a special case of intervention by the 'Cassa Integrazione Guadagni' (*Extraordinary Temporary Unemployment Compensation*), that is to say a temporary measure, a shock absorber designed to compensate for a short-term employment crisis. A. M. Ponzellini, *Solidarity Contracts: Costs and Benefits in Economic, Employment and Organizational Terms*, draft of the Final Report, CESOS, Turin, 17 November 2015, p. 26.
15. In detail, the rule provides for a reduction in hours for a salary supplement equal to 60% of the lost salary, increased for 2009 and 2010 to 80% only for workers involved in defensive solidarity contracts, for a maximum of twenty-four months, extendable for another twenty-four months. Art. 5, para. 5 Law 236/1993 also provided for the possibility of accessing the CIGS (*Extraordinary Temporary Unemployment Compensation*) through the stipulation of a defensive solidarity contract also for companies not falling within the scope of the CIGS, always with the aim of avoiding, through an agreement for the reduction of working hours, staff dismissal. The intervention of the CIGS is reduced and can be extended up to twenty-four months, extendable to thirty-six.
16. According to Art. 41, para. 1 of the D. lgs. 148/2015 for the employer that stipulates expansive solidarity contracts, a contribution is provided to be paid by the INPS (*social security body*) management of welfare interventions, equal to 15% of the gross remuneration in the first year and 10% and 5% for each of the two following years.

the incentive given to employers to achieve a generational change within the company, in a perspective of solidarity among different generations of workers.

If this has so far been a scarcely applied typology, given the high degree of solidarity assumed between employed and unemployed,[17] the Jobs Act (pursuant to 41, paragraph 3-bis of Legislative Decree No. 148/2015) was intended to re-evaluate this instrument, which had been neglected for almost thirty years,[18] linking, in a kind of changeover, the two types of solidarity contracts: defensive and expansive. In order to favour the increase in company staff and, at the same time, to facilitate a possible generational change, with a view to encouraging employment, companies are now granted the right to agree with trade unions[19] on the transformation of a contract for defensive solidarity already stipulated[20] in an expansive solidarity contract, on condition that the overall reduction in working time is not higher than the one already established.[21]

After the transformation of the contract, the workers involved in the hourly reduction will continue to receive the original salary supplement, which, however, is paid by the CIG (*Temporary Unemployment Compensation*), in the measure of 50%. The employer is entitled to integrate such treatment at least up to the extent of the original supplement, but this supplement is not taxable for social security purposes, as the notional contribution scheme is applied to the sum paid by the employer.

There is therefore no penalty for workers, either from an economic or retirement perspective.

At the same time, employers benefit from a 50% reduction in the additional contribution due in the case of CIGS (*Extraordinary Temporary Unemployment Compensation*), a non-repayable contribution on new employments for three years, and a contribution reduced to 10% for hiring people under 30 years of age, as well as the allocation of the portion of TFR (Trattamento di Fine Rapporto; *severance pay*) accrued on the salary supplement to be paid by the INPS.

Finally, it should be noted that Article 41, co. 5 of the D. lgs. 148/2015 introduced a sort of 'generational changeover', linking these solidarity contracts to a form of 'flexible early retirement'. The paragraph involved guarantees to companies the possibility of reducing, through these collective company agreements, the working hours of older workers who are nearing retirement, in order to expand employment for an indefinite period: this is a virtuous solution because it combines the partial advance

17. M. V. Ballestrero, G. De Simone (curated by), *Massimo Roccella, Manuale di Diritto del Lavoro*, Giappichelli, Torino, 2012, p. 238.
18. M. Russo, *Lavoratori anziani e giovani: tra tutele individuali e tentativi di solidarietà intergenerazionale*, in A. Perulli (curated by), *L'idea di diritto del lavoro, oggi. In ricordo di Giorgio Ghezzi*, Cedam, Padova, 2016, p. 431; G. Canavesi, E. Ales, *Il sistema previdenziale italiano. Principi, struttura ed evoluzione*, Giappichelli, Torino, 2017.
19. Such agreements can be signed by the trade unions identified by Art. 51 of the D. lgs. 81/2015, that is, indifferently, the most representative national or territorial organizations at national level, or their company Unions.
20. The new rule applies to defensive contracts in progress for at least thirteen months at the date of entry into force of the decree (8 October 2016) and for those stipulated before 1 January 2016.
21. For a deeper analysis, E. Massi, *Il ricambio generazionale. Il contratto di solidarietà espansiva*, in *Dir. prat. lav.*, 2017, 7.

of the pension to a generational changeover.[22] To incentivize this process, the system recognizes particular incentives both for the company, which can obtain an economic contribution for the first three years, and for the workers who join the part-time work, who will be entitled to receive the pension treatment, which can be combined with the remuneration, within the maximum limit of the remuneration treatment lost following the adoption of part-time work,[23] in the event that they 'have agreed to perform a work service lasting no longer than half of the working time before the reduction agreed in the collective agreement'.

Such legislative interventions demonstrate how the legislator intends to promote, in line with the philosophy of Sustainable Development, intra and intergenerational solidarity in the company and in the market: the opportunity for the workers in the company to recognize a sort of 'gradual retirement', opting for a part-time work that leaves room for young people, expresses a logic of constructive solidarity, which can reach a more even distribution of employment and employability, specifically of young people and NEETs,[24] guaranteeing the possibility of a gradual transfer of knowledge and skills from workers close to retirement to new employees.

However, reserving pension flexibility only for defensive-expansive solidarity contracts constitutes a limitation of the legislation under examination, since it refers to companies that, as users of CIGS treatments, are in a state of crisis. If, on the one hand, the ratio of such legislative intervention can be found in the offer to companies in difficulty of being able to have new life by hiring more qualified personnel or with more advanced skills in order to boost productivity, it would be important, on the other hand, to recognize such a possibility even outside the context of the company crisis, in a logic of wider employment solidarity, better functioning of the labour market and more efficient use of the part-time formula. Furthermore, it would certainly be appropriate to increase the tax advantages for the employer, as the other incentives currently available to increase employment are substantial.[25]

22. T. Treu, *Prove di staffetta generazionale*, in *Il Sole 24 ore*, 2 ottobre 2015.
23. Often, for the realization of the changeover a selective criterion is used on the basis of the relationship of kinship between the new employees and the senior employees who accept the transformation of the relationship from full-time to part-time. In this way, however, there is the risk of nullifying the spirit of 'generational' solidarity - not simply limited to the family environment - which characterizes these instruments. Cfr. G. Canavesi, E. Ales, *Il sistema previdenziale italiano. Principi, struttura ed evoluzione*, Giappichelli, Torino, 2017.
24. Otherwise, according to authoritative economists, the increase in youth employment, as well as that of the elderly and women, would occur more likely in case of reduction in the dualism on the labour market, of the fiscal pressure on labour and with an increase in productivity, compared to the choice to take away the work 'from the old' to give it 'to the young' (as regards this, *see* T. Boeri, V. Galasso, *Per una vera staffetta tra generazioni*, in *lavoceinfo*, 24 May 2013).
25. Consider, for example, the incentives in favour of the professionalizing apprenticeship now extended also to the unemployed, without age limits, earning an unemployment benefit (Art. 47, para. 4, Legislative Decree n. 81/2015).

§3.03 EQUALITY OF POSSIBILITIES: THE THEORY OF CAPABILITIES APPLIED TO LABOUR LAW

The second value coincidence that can be found between labour law and Sustainable Development concerns the equality of opportunity among all citizens and among present and future generations. In this regard, it is worth remembering that Sustainable Development suggests satisfying the needs of the present without compromising the ability of future generations to satisfy their own, and it requires 'to extend to everyone the possibility of implementing their aspirations for a better life'.[26] This objective, which seems to assume a relevant principle in the field of labour understood as a 'vocation' and instrument of social elevation, refers to the *Theory of Capabilities* of Amartya Sen[27] and Martha Nussbaum[28] and to its applicability in the field of labour law.

The *Capability Approach* is generating growing interest, above all in international doctrine but also among authoritative compatriot authors,[29] as a possible and new point of reference for a labour law system that is not only dedicated to safeguarding its own value tradition but also in search of renewed axiological foundations and new syntheses - still socially inspired but less paternalistic - among the values of freedom, equality and justice,[30] especially in the fields where the traditional approach is vulnerable to neoliberal criticism and inadequate to the current economic and social challenges.

The *capability* of an individual reflects the various combinations of functions (states of being and doing) and the freedom of the individual to choose his/her own lifestyle.[31] We are dealing with the individual and strictly personal capacity to achieve

26. Brundtland Report, *Our Common Future*, elaborated by the 1983 World Commission on the Environment and Development of the United Nations, chaired by Madame Gro Harlem Brundtland, Norwegian Prime Minister.
27. A. K. Sen, *The Idea of Justice*, Penguin Group, London, 2009, trad. it. *L'idea di giustizia*, Mondadori, Milano, 2010.
28. M. C. Nussbaum, *Diventare persone*, il Mulino, Bologna, 2001; M. C. Nussbaum, *Giustizia sociale e dignità umana. Da individui a persone*, il Mulino, Bologna, 2002; M. C. Nussbaum, *Capacità personale e democrazia sociale*, Diabasis, Reggio Emilia, 2003. For an interesting confrontation between Nussbaum and Sen's thought, refer to F. Magni, *Etica delle capacità. La filosofia pratica di Sen e Nussbaum*, il Mulino, Bologna, 2006, pp. 93 ss.
29. Refer to the following publications: B. Hepple, *Diritto del lavoro, diseguaglianza e commercio globale*, in *Giorn. dir. lav. rel. ind.*, 2003, 97, p. 32; B. Caruso, *Occupabilità, formazione e capability nei modelli giuridici di regolazione dei mercati del lavoro*, in *Giorn. dir. lav. rel. ind.*, 2007, pp. 1-99; S. Deakin, *Economic Approaches to the Evaluation of Labour Law: Comparing Coase, Hayek and Sen*, in A. Perulli (curated by), *Efficacia e diritto del lavoro*, Padova, Cedam, 2008, pp. 55-58; S. Deakin, A. Supiot (eds), *Capacitas: Contract Law, Capabilities and the Legal Foundations of the Market*, Hart Publishing, London, 2009; S. Deakin, *The Contribution of Labour Law to Economic and Human Development*, in G. Davidov, B. Langille (eds), *The Idea of Labour Law*, Oxford University Press, Oxford, 2011, pp. 179 ss; R. Del Punta, *Leggendo the Idea of Justice di Amartya Sen*, in *Giorn. dir. lav. rel. ind.*, 2013, 138, 2, pp. 197-219; T. Treu, *Labour Law and Sustainable Development, WP C.S.D.L.E. 'Massimo D'Antona'.INT – 130/2016;* R. Del Punta, *Labour Law and the Capability*, in *International Journal of Comparative Labour Law and Industrial Relations*, 2016, vol. 32, n. 4.
30. R. Del Punta, *Diritto del Lavoro*, 9th edition, Giuffrè, Milano, 2017, p. 127.
31. A. K. Sen, *Capability and Well-Being*, in M. Nussbaum, A. K. Sen (eds), *The Quality of Life*, Clarendon Press, Oxford, 1993, p. 31.

the desired 'functions' and thus to achieve the maximum possible of one's life aspirations, which give the subject an effective sovereignty of choice. This presupposes the attribution of a full responsibility to the individual on his/her own existence, that is to say in a principle of full and substantial freedom of the subject.[32]

The *Theory of Capabilities* is in fact the theory that concretizes the capacity and freedom of people (understood as '*positive power*') to be able to do or be what they wish to do or be.[33] And one of the purposes of labour law is precisely to help the worker to be the subject of his life.

In other words, the *capability* can be understood as the substantial freedom to enhance one's own resources to guarantee self-sufficiency as a person and economic agent with the related benefits in terms of wealth produced and social equity:[34] the reference is to the freedom that individuals need to survive and improve their position, including the freedom to get education, training and careers according to their aspirations, as well as the ability to get a decent job, in line with what the ILO promotes in terms of *decent work*.

There is therefore no reference to the subjects' assets or resources, but to their life opportunities and their freedom of choice between an indeterminate variety of combinations of functions, presuming the responsibility entrusted to each of them to consciously choose their own lifestyles and projects.[35]

Along the same lines, according to a more normative rather than economic approach, Nussbaum internalizes Sen's *Capability Approach* but he reconsiders it by integrating it with the Aristotelian vision of the human being as an animal with needs that political authorities should take into account to respect human dignity and whose main task should be to enable individuals to develop and fully express their potential to allow everyone to express their freedom of choice in different situations and to fully realize themselves as human beings. The request to the political authority could therefore be understood as the necessary intervention by the legislator, in terms of policies and instruments capable of achieving the desired equality in terms of possibilities and opportunities, in line with the role of the dimension of Sustainable Development.

By adopting the *Capability Approach*, the main task of labour law in the current phase of globalization is to facilitate the equality of *capabilities*.[36] The equality involved could be guaranteed by the labour law discipline, not in terms of resources or income,

32. '*The capability of a person reflects the alternative combinations of functionings the person can achieve, and from which he or she can choose on collection.*' Cfr. A. SEN, *Capability and Well-Being*, in M. Nussbaum, A. K. Sen (eds), *The Quality of Life*, Clarendon Press, Oxford, 1993, p. 31.
33. M. D'ANTONA, *La grande sfida delle trasformazioni del lavoro: ricentrare le tutele sulle esigenze del lavoratore come soggetto*, in F. AMATO (curated by), *I 'destini' del lavoro. Autonomie e subordinazione nella società post-fordista*, Franco Angeli, Milano, 1998, pp. 138 ss.
34. S. DEAKIN, F. WILKINSON, *'Capabilities', Ordine spontaneo del mercato e diritti sociali*, in *Dir. merc. lav.*, 2000, 2, pp. 317 ss.
35. B. CARUSO, *Occupabilità, formazione e capability nei modelli giuridici di regolazione dei mercati del lavoro*, in *Giorn. dir. lav. rel. ind.*, 2007, 1, p. 12.
36. B. HEPPLE, *Diritto del lavoro, diseguaglianza e commercio globale*, in *Giorn. dir. lav. rel. ind.*, 2003, 97, p. 32. Sulla teoria dell'uguaglianza in termini di *capabilities*, A. K. SEN, *Development and Freedom*, Oxford University, New York, 1999.

which depend on the level of social-economic development present in each region or country, but guaranteeing to each individual the possibility of seeking a job or a job career of one's choice, of freedom of association and collective action, the right to participate in economic and political decision-making processes that affect one's life, the right to benefit from social rights in general.[37]

The *capabilities* approach therefore seems able to contribute to the development of a more dynamic and sustainable labour law,[38] allowing the labour law discipline to be conceived as a force to balance the inequality existing in the world of labour, such as that existing between man and woman, reintroducing and legitimizing the Rawlsian side – in an egalitarian perspective – of labour law.

Such equality, moreover, cannot be separated from solidarity, since it should be intended as 'not so much a moral virtue ... but a complementary objective legal principle of the principle of equal treatment set forth in art. 3 of Constitution'.[39] Solidarity actually leads to equality and is a necessary prerequisite.[40] According to Mengoni's teaching, in fact, the equality of citizens before the law is not complete 'if it is not complemented by the solidarity duty of all people to take on, in proportion of their possibilities, the common weight constituted by the costs of being together in society'.[41] For this reason, equality and solidarity are the basis of labour law and Sustainable Development, since equality can only be achieved through a prior integration of the value of solidarity.

[A] 'Smart Work': A 'Double Win' for the Reconciliation of Work-Life Balance and the Increase in Productivity

The Capability Approach suggests a further reflection in terms of *work-life balance*, to the extent that the equality of capabilities implies a new conception of labour that includes both subordinate and self-employed workers, aimed at reconciling paid and family work.[42]

In fact, if the reconciliation between paid and family work is a prerequisite for achieving equality of opportunity, labour law is the greatest instrument delegated for the purpose under consideration. It is in fact a requirement that has long been internalized by the labour law discipline and recently taken in the context of the legislative intervention by the Jobs Act in terms of smart work ('lavoro agile') (Articles

37. R. Pessi, *Economia e Diritto del lavoro*, in *Arg. dir. lav.*, 2006, p. 441.
38. R. Del Punta, *Labour Law and the Capability*, in *International Journal of Comparative Labour Law and Industrial Relations*, 2016, vol. 32, n. 4, pp. 383-405.
39. L. Mengoni, *Fondata sul lavoro: la Repubblica tra diritti inviolabili e doveri inderogabili di solidarietà*, in M. Napoli (curated by), *Costituzione, lavoro e pluralismo sociale*, Vita e Pensiero, Milano, 1998, p. 3.
40. G. P. Cella, *Solidarietà e coesione sociale*, in M. Napoli (curated by), *La solidarietà*, Vita e Pensiero, Milano, 2009.
41. L. Mengoni, *Fondata sul lavoro: la Repubblica tra diritti inviolabili e doveri inderogabili di solidarietà*, in M. Napoli (curated by), *Costituzione, lavoro e pluralismo sociale*, Vita e Pensiero, Milano, 1998, p. 3.
42. B. Hepple, *Diritto del lavoro, diseguaglianza e commercio globale*, in *Giorn. dir. lav. rel. ind.*, 2003, 97, pp. 49 ss.

18-23, l. 81/2017): a novelty that derives from the need to adapt the rigid discipline of the employment relationship to the evolution of the ways of working and producing deriving from the technological progress of Industry 4.0.

Leaving aside a precise analysis of the normative novelty,[43] for the purposes of this reflection it is sufficient to recall how smart work, in the logic of accompanying the profound cultural change in the conception of labour,[44] concerns a particular and flexible modality of execution of the employment service, made partially outside the company premises, using IT tools, in the manner established by the individual agreement concluded between the employer and the worker (who is also required to provide for a right of disconnection).[45]

Focusing on the ratio of the intervention[46] - considered among the most responsive to the current needs of production and labour market[47] -, it is possible to understand the legislator's intention to regulate a new modality of execution of the performance, more in line with the peculiar needs of a globalized and highly computerized[48] market, with a dual purpose: to increase competitiveness and facilitate the reconciliation of life and work.[49]

For the company, the increase in competitiveness could be realized under different profiles: on the one hand, thanks to the increase in efficiency, productivity and flexibility of the new organization of work allowed by technology and the digital economy;[50] on the other hand, thanks to a corresponding and substantial reduction in business costs, such as structural costs (through the rationalization of physical spaces

---

43. About the discipline of smart work cfr. M. Tiraboschi, *Il lavoro agile tra legge e contrattazione collettiva: la tortuosa via italiana verso la modernizzazione del diritto del lavoro*, in *Dir. rel. ind.*, 2017, 4, pp. 921 ss; P. Rausei, *Tutto Jobs Act: Lavoro Autonomo e Smart Work*, Wolters Kluwer Italia, Milano, 2016; M. Lai, L. Ricciardi, *La nuova disciplina del lavoro agile*, in *Dir. prat. lav.*, 2016, pp. 707 ss; M. Lamberti, *L'accordo individuale e i diritti del lavoratore agile*, in L. Fiorillo, A. Perulli (curated by), *Il jobs act del lavoro autonomo e del lavoro agile*, Giappichelli, Torino, 2018; M. Lai, *Evoluzione tecnologica e tutela del lavoro: a proposito di smart working e di crowd working*, in *Dir. rel. ind.*, 2017, 4, pp. 985 ss; M. Corso, *Sfide e prospettive della rivoluzione digitale: lo smart working*, in *Dir. rel. ind.*, 2017, 4, pp. 978; L. M. Pelusi, *La disciplina di salute e sicurezza applicabile al lavoro agile*, in *Dir. rel. ind.*, 2017, 4, pp. 1041 ss.
44. 'This bill responds to the need to create a flexible mode of execution of the employment relationship, in order to increase its productivity and facilitate the reconciliation of life and work and to accompany the profound cultural change in the conception of work.' See Report on the Bill presented by the Minister of Labour and Social Policies (Poletti) communicated to the Presidency on 8 February 2016.
45. On the contrary, the Loi Travail of 8 August 2016, which came into force on 1 January 2017, establishes that the right to disconnect must be the subject of collective bargaining, and only in the absence of collective bargaining could it be regulated by an individual agreement, but there it is in any case the obligation to regulate the conditions of use through company agreements. About the French right to disconnection.
46. We should recall how the Delegated Law of 10 December 2014, n. 183, was '*with regard to the reform of social safety nets, labour services and active policies, as well as in the matter of reorganizing the discipline of labour relations and inspection activities and of protecting and reconciling care, life and work needs*'.
47. R. Pessi, R. Fabozzi, *Gli obblighi del datore di lavoro in materia di salute e sicurezza*, in L. Fiorillo, A. Perulli (curated by), *Il jobs act del lavoro autonomo e del lavoro agile*, Giappichelli, Torino, 2018, pp. 228-229.
48. *Ibid.*, p. 227.
49. Article 18, Law 81/2017.
50. Refer to the papers about the topic curated by P. Loi and V. Speziale in *Riv. giur. lav.*, 2017, 2.

and the sharing of workstations), or the costs related to the internal canteen service, or even, the overtime costs.[51]

Smart work would ensure that workers achieve greater balance between private life and professional life, greater flexibility in the performance of work, as well as the elimination (or at least reduction) of commuting time for journeys to and from work, since workers are free to place their own performance within the predefined time frame and are able to negotiate with the employer the procedures for such performance in full compliance with the limits of maximum duration of daily and weekly working hours that derive from the law and from collective bargaining.[52]

The logic underlying the recent legislative intervention in terms of smart work could therefore be traced back to the idea of Sustainable Development. Despite the opposition of interests between business and work, the respective objectives are not in this case opposed, but rather mutually connected, to the extent that a better working condition is reflected as an advantage also for the company in terms of a greater focus on the objectives, of an accountability on the results, of a reduction in absenteeism,[53] as well as in an increase in productivity deriving from the increase in the motivational aspect, with a consequent lower *turnover*.[54]

The interdependence and the reciprocal reinforcement between the advantages for the parts, typical of smart work, express the same virtuous circle of Sustainable Development in its social, environmental and economic pillars, where the different profiles, although apparently contrasting, are by definition mutually reinforcing.[55]

On closer investigation, smart work - matter-of-factly - achieves *economic* sustainability for both the worker and the employer. Smart work, first and foremost, benefits from a reduction in business costs, both in terms of fixed costs, with reference to the lower need for physical company spaces and equipment to be made available for workers (desks, chairs, PCs, printers, etc.), and in terms of variable costs if we consider the management expenses (electricity, heating, water, canteen service, ordinary consumables) and those related to the compensation of overtime (being able to agree on a distribution of working time with the worker on time slots normally dedicated to overtime work). Furthermore, the employer benefits from a considerable economic advantage in terms of greater worker's productivity (more motivated and empowered) and greater efficiency, guaranteed not only by technological evolution (generally observed also in other forms of self-employment and subordinate work) but also in terms of reducing non-work time (refer to the elimination of the coffee breaks of

51. For a recent and interesting mapping of company bargaining on the topic of smart work, cfr. E. Dagnino, M. Menegotto, L. M. Pelusi, M. Tiraboschi (curated by), *Guida pratica al lavoro agile dopo la legge n. 81/2017, Formule contrattuali – Schemi operativi – Mappatura della contrattazione collettiva*, ADAPT University Press, Modena, 2017, pp. 109-172.
52. Article 18, para. 2, Law 81/2017.
53. M. Tiraboschi, *Il lavoro agile tra legge e contrattazione collettiva: la tortuosa via italiana verso la modernizzazione del diritto del lavoro*, in *WP CSDLE 'Massimo D'Antona'.IT – 335/2017*, p. 25 e in *Dir. rel. ind.*, 2017, 4.
54. On the effects of technology on labour, ILO-Eurofound, *Working Anytime, Anywhere. The Effect on the World of Work*, 2017, https://www.eurofound.europa.eu/publications/report/2017/working-anytime-anywhere-the-effects-on-the-world-of-work.
55. On this issue, refer to the analysis of the topic in §3.05.

employees at the bar or at the automatic vending machines or the mutual distraction of colleagues caused by sharing the workplace) or in terms of more extensive management coverage achieved through a different fragmented temporal distribution of smart workers' performances (think of working mothers and their greater propensity to work in the evenings, nights or weekends, that otherwise would not count as working hours in a 'standard' work organization). An economic advantage, however, can be seen, as anticipated, also for the worker, both in terms of savings on transport costs and travel time, and for the board cost linked to living away from home the whole day: a lower cost that is inevitably translated into a greater net monthly gain and – consequently – also in a greater purchasing capacity (that is to say a greater propensity to consume and consequently, a relaunch of the company's production).

Second, smart work contributes to greater *environmental* sustainability, which can be expressed in terms of the ability to maintain the quality and reproducibility of natural resources over time and to preserve biological diversity while guaranteeing the integrity of ecosystems. In fact, the possibility for the worker to choose to carry out his own performance from home entails a reduction in CO2 emissions and traffic due to the employee's non-usage of means of (public or private) transport or in any case to reduce them, in the case the worker decides to carry out his own work performance in a different environment, choosing, for example, a space that is closer than the company headquarters (a park, a gym, a shopping centre, a bar or a co-working space). On the business side, this is reflected in a substantial reduction in the physical company locations necessary for the performance of the production activity or at least, in their better utilization, with a significant positive impact on the environment.

Third, this particular new articulation of subordination can also contribute to *social* sustainability for several reasons: first, by allowing strong support for parenting, facilitating return to work for working mothers at the end of parental leave or better management of work-family balance. In this regard, smart work was fully defined as an active policy tool, functional to gender equality, to break down the 'ceiling' and the 'crystal walls' that prevent women from accessing all sectors of the work and to the apical and super apical[56] positions. Second, smart work offers the possibility to workers to spend time on other interests, to take care of family members, and it allows a greater social inclusion, even towards disabled people with physical displacement difficulties, who could have access to more employment opportunities, working in areas other than the company. Smart work also allows for a reduction in the risk of isolation and alienation of workers, which can be found if they work exclusively at home or at a small or very small company in a context that is therefore devoid of social interactions: being able to choose to work in a *co-working* space, workers have the possibility to interact with other (agile or independent professionals) workers, to share knowledge and at the same time, to strengthen the sense of belonging to a community. Moreover, smart work, by virtue of the individual autonomy recognized to workers and their negotiating capacity, could contribute to the creation of decent jobs, which

56. V. Talamo, *Diversamente agile? Lo Smart Work nelle pubbliche amministrazioni*, in L. Fiorillo, A. Perulli (curated by), *Il jobs act del lavoro autonomo e del lavoro agile*, Giappichelli, Torino, 2018, p. 260.

facilitate the development of the individuals, their personal and family well-being and the dialogue with the employer, in line with what the ILO and the UN have suggested in terms of decent work, regarding MDGs (in particular with Objective 8).

The simultaneous and mutual achievement of full Sustainable Development through smart work therefore clearly reflects the possible implications of the adoption of a Sustainable Development logic in labour law and, at the same time, the functionality of the tools offered by the labour law discipline in achieving a development that is to be defined as such.

[B] The Enhancement of Individual Autonomy and the Problem of the Type

The underlying rationale for the new legislation, aimed at recognizing individual negotiating autonomy as a useful tool to pursue an advantage for both parties, justifies the choice of the legislator to delegate the discipline of the relationship to the individual contract and not to the heteronomous sources (law or collective bargaining[57]), according to the traditional labour law scheme. The individual agreement, pursuant to Article 19 paragraph 1 of the l. 81/2017, is matter-of-factly to regulate the '*performance carried out outside the company premises, also with regard to the forms of exercise of the employer's executive power and the tools used by the worker*'.

The novelty of the norm involved cannot be underestimated. Although the doctrine has authoritatively affirmed that, theoretically, the autonomy of the parties[58] dominates over the conformation of the due performance, it is common to note that the regulation of the employment relationship has been entrusted to the mandatory law and collective agreement, on the assumption of the inability of the individual contract to reflect a set of interests that are free from conditionings deriving from the imbalance of powers and social-economic status among the parties. Only recently, a part of the doctrine, valorizing the 'rediscovery of the individual' that in the world of labour derives from the de-standardization of the twentieth-century forms of Fordist and massified organization, has underlined how individual autonomy represents a much more penetrating and relevant source of regulation than what is commonly thought. In this perspective, when the relationship is constituted, much importance is given to the choice of the type of contract (independent or subordinate), as well as in the latter case, to the standard contract typology (full-time and open-ended) or flexible types (from fixed-term, or part-time or intermittent contract, etc.), as long as it complies with the

57. On this topic, P. Lambertucci, *Efficacia dispositiva del contratto collettivo e autonomia individuale*, Cedam, Padova, 1990; G. Pellacani, *Autonomia individuale e rapporto di lavoro*, Giappichelli, Torino, 2002; L. Mariucci, *Autonomia individuale e collettiva: l'attualità di un vecchio dilemma*, in *Lav. dir.*, 2008, 2, pp. 212-216; M. Novella, *Note sulle tecniche limitative dell'autonomia individuale nella disciplina del lavoro a progetto*, in *Lav. dir.*, 2004, 1, pp. 117-152, F. Scarpelli, *Autonomia collettiva e autonomia individuale nella regolazione del rapporto dei lavoratori parasubordinati*, in *Lav. dir.*, 1999, 4, pp. 553-570.
58. G. Giugni, *Mansioni e qualifica del rapporto di lavoro*, Napoli, Jovene, 1963, p. 102.

mandatory limits established by law.[59] The will of the parties plays an essential role also in the constancy of the relationship, which, thanks to individual autonomy, can deviate from the model provided by the collective agreement and the law, subject to the minimum standards of protection (think of the free determination of the time of work, intended both as an extension and as a distribution of the service throughout the day, week, month and year, to the freedom to identify the professional qualification, the contractual duties, the place where they are performed, the entity and the structure of remuneration, as well as any ancillary clauses such as the probationary period or non-compete clause).[60] Even in the case of dismissal, with reference, for example, to the choice of the worker to request the indemnity to replace the reinstatement in the workplace, or to negotiate at an individual level settlement agreements in the event of economic dismissal, there is no lack of regulatory spaces entrusted to the individual autonomy, although within the framework of a strict heteronomous discipline.

Despite these vast spaces of individual autonomy already covered by the legal system, the provision involved was perceived as an absolute novelty in the Italian tradition.[61] The element of discontinuity with respect to the past lies precisely in the wide range recognized to the power of individual will, concerning both the measures necessary to guarantee the right to disconnection of the worker, and, above all, the methods of exercising the powers of the employer, being the regulation of such aspects normally delegated to collective bargaining, certainly not to individual bargaining.[62]

The legislative provision effectively results to be a significant deviation from the type of subordination referred to in Article 2094 c.c., placing itself in clear disagreement with what happens in the normal discipline of the employment relationship.

Such a legislative choice, even if completely dystonic with respect to the more recent labour law tradition,[63] finds a double motivation.

The first justification lies in the impossibility of effectively regulating in the same way many new ways of working that are different from each other made possible by the technological evolution and by the productive changes of the past few years which, by definition, are constantly changing. In this sense, therefore, the intervention of the legislator is in line with the general tendency to the 'de-standardization' of the discipline[64] made necessary by the inadequacy of a single, rigid and mandatory discipline pertaining to the era of Fordist production and to the multiplication of work relationships, while reaffirming right from the beginning, how smart work is to be

59. R. Del Punta, *Verso l'individualizzazione dei diritti?*, in L. Corazza, R. Romei (curated by), *Diritto del lavoro in trasformazione*, il Mulino, Bologna, 2014, p. 28.
60. P. Ichino, *Il contratto di Lavoro II*, in A. Cicu, F. Messineo, L. Mengoni (diretto da), *Trattato di diritto civile e commerciale*, Giuffrè, Milano, 2003, pp. 198-199.
61. T. Treu, *Rimedi, tutele e fattispecie nella gig economy*, in *Lav. dir.*, 2017, 3-4, p. 393.
62. A. Perulli, *Il jobs act del lavoro autonomo e agile: come cambiano i concetti di subordinazione e autonomia nel diritto del lavoro*, in *WP C.S.D.L.E. 'Massimo D'Antona'.IT – 341/2017*, p. 15.
63. In fact, if we went back to the discipline of the origins, the recognition and relevance attributed to individual autonomy would be much wider, as demonstrated, on the other hand, by the explanation in terms of tacit acceptance by the worker of the discipline contained in the company regulation.
64. G. Proia, *Flessibilità e tutele 'nel' contratto di lavoro subordinato*, in *Giorn. dir. lav. rel. ind.*, 2002, pp. 423 ss.

understood as a 'modality of execution of the subordinate employment relationship' (not independent). Regarding the contractual qualification, part of the doctrine has already in part expressed a judgment: it is not a new subordinate[65] employment contract, but a way of performing the service that is part of a work contract,[66] that is to say a 'special' form of subordination, characterized by a very meagre legislative regulation that refers to individual autonomy.[67] On this point, without going into the details concerning the debate on the notion of special relationship, that is to say on the relationship between type and subtype[68] that reappears periodically as the legal system proposes schemes that are not completely attributable to the prototype of the employment relationship (full-time and open-ended),[69] given that the classification by type and subtype or by genus or species, has an exclusively descriptive and nominalistic[70] value in labour law, smart work does not seem to be able to be configured either as a type (like autonomy or subordination) or a subtype (that is configured according to the addition of one or more elements to those belonging to the type[71] or according to the alteration of the causal pattern of the type[72]), but rather as a 'special' (subordinate) relationship, since the specialty of the other types of subordination implies a certain degree of inapplicability of the standard discipline, and therefore it is negatively determined by reason of the absence of a typical element of the case provided for by Article 2094.

The prevailing doctrinal orientation tends in fact to characterize the 'special' labour contracts in relation to the applicable legal discipline, qualifying as such the contracts for which a particular discipline is provided for, which takes into account the peculiarities of the activity carried out by the worker or the employer, and the general

65. G. Santoro Passarelli, *Lavoro eterorganizzato, Lavoro eterorganizzato, coordinato, agile e il telelavoro: un puzzle non facile da comporre in un'impresa in via di trasformazione*, in *WP CSDLE 'Massimo D'Antona'.IT – 327/2017*, p. 9; G. Proia, *L'accordo individuale e le modalità di esecuzione e di cessazione della prestazione di lavoro agile*, in L. Fiorillo, A. Perulli (curated by), *Il jobs act del lavoro autonomo e del lavoro agile*, Giappichelli, Torino, 2018, p. 179.
66. L. Gaeta, *Appunti dal corso di diritto del lavoro*, Giappichelli, Torino, 2018, p. 244.
67. A. Perulli, *Il jobs act del lavoro autonomo e agile: come cambiano i concetti di subordinazione e autonomia nel diritto del lavoro*, in *WP C.S.D.L.E. 'Massimo D'Antona'.IT – 341/2017*, p. 14.
68. About typological diversification of labour relationships and specialty criterion, *see* G. Loy, *Riflessioni su specialità, tipo e sottotipo nel lavoro subordinato*, in M. Pedrazzoli (curated by), *Lavoro subordinato e dintorni*, il Mulino, Bologna, 1989, pp. 52 ss; G. Proia, *Rapporti di lavoro e tipo*, Milano, 1997; G. Santoro Passarelli, *Flessibilità e subordinazione: pluralità di fattispecie o di tutele?*, in AA.VV. (curated by), *Subordinazione e autonomia: vecchi e nuovi modelli*, in *Quad. dir. lav. rel. ind.*, UTET, Torino, 1998; G. Proia, *Metodo tipologico, contratto di lavoro subordinato e categorie definitorie*, in *Arg. dir. lav.*, 2002, p. 37; L. Nogler, *Ancora su 'tipo' e rapporto di lavoro subordinato nell'impresa*, in *Arg. dir. lav.*, 2002.
69. M. Magnani, *Diritto dei contratti di lavoro*, Giuffrè, Milano, 2009, p. 22.
70. M. D'Antona (curated by), *Politiche di flessibilità e mutamenti di diritto del lavoro: Italia e Spagna*, Editoriale Scientifica, Napoli, 1990, p. 538. Likewise, if the 'specialty' of labour relations was 'brought up only for the taxonomic anxieties of scholars, engaged in the perennial search for classifications and distinctions' (Cfr. L. Gaeta, *Appunti dal corso di diritto del lavoro*, Giappichelli, Torino, 2018, p. 358) it should be noted that classifications by types (or species) 'do not help, if not hinder, an understanding and a suitable arrangement of the most recent process of differentiation of the normative typologies of the employment relationship' (Cfr. M. Magnani, *Diritto dei contratti di lavoro*, Giuffrè, Milano, 2009, p. 24).
71. Cfr. A. Cataudella, *Spunti sulla tipologia dei rapporti di lavoro*, in *Dir. lav.*, 1983, 1, pp. 77 ss.
72. M. Magnani, *Diritto dei contratti di lavoro*, Giuffrè, Milano, 2009, p. 24.

law of the employment relationship is applied within the limits of compatibility. In this sense, smart work could be understood as a special subordinate contract, placed on the same level as the legal case of the subordinate work of the company,[73] in relation to the particularity of the position of the worker (like domestic work, the concierge relationship, the artistic work and sports work relationship[74]), where the element of particularity can be found both in the individual agreement and in the faculty to carry out the work partly within company premises and partly outside.[75]

A second justification for the novelty of smart work with respect to the classic scheme of subordination can be found in the enhancement of the centrality of the working person, 'because it is the organization of work that must adapt to the person and not vice versa'.[76] The election of bilateral bargaining as a suitable instrument to organize a discipline that is actually able to reconcile entrepreneurial reasons and individual, strictly personal - non-collective - interests of workers leads to a boost of (unexpected) trust in the intellectual abilities of the weak part of the employment contract and on his/her own autonomy and responsibility, demonstrating a strong revaluation of the individual autonomy and the proactive capacity of the worker. Distances have therefore been taken from the approach that wants the discipline of the relationship to be an apparatus of rules, for the most part mandatory, to defend a worker that is (always and in any case) weak,[77] thus becoming an interpreter of the new balances,[78] recognizing a central role to the autonomy of the worker, considered finally 'of age'.[79]

The tendency to rediscover the individual dimension seems in fact the dominant figure of the century that has just begun,[80] despite, for many jurists, the limitation of

73. G. Santoro Passarelli, *Diritto dei lavori. Diritto sindacale e rapporti di lavoro*, Giappichelli, Torino, 2013, p. 432.
74. Other 'special' contracts are considered as such in relation to the object of the performance (apprenticeship, training and trial work relationship) or due to the discipline, at least in part, of public sources (maritime and aeronautical recruitment relationship, or the port work relationship, the employment relationship of the public transport workers and inter-navigators and those of the tax collectors), or again based on the nature of the subject that uses the job performance. On the point, *see* R. Balzarini, *Contratti speciali di lavoro*, in U. Borsi, F. Pergolesi (diretto da), *Trattato di diritto del lavoro*, 3rd edition, Cedam, Padova, 1958, II, pp. 383 ss; R. Sconamiglio, *Lavoro subordinato: I) Diritto del lavoro*, in *Enc. giur. Treccani*, 1988, XVIII, pp. 1 ss; A. Tosi, *Rapporti speciali di lavoro*, in *Enc. giur. Treccani*, 1991, XXV, p. 1; V. Speziale, *L'articolazione della fattispecie*, in F. Carinci (curated by), *Il lavoro subordinato*, Tomo II, in M. Bessone (diretto da), *Trattato di diritto privato*, vol. XXIV, Giappichelli, Torino, 2007, pp. 119 ss.
75. Article 19, Law 22 May 2017 n. 81.
76. V. Talamo, *Diversamente agile? Lo Smart Work nelle pubbliche amministrazioni*, in L. Fiorillo, A. Perulli (curated by), *Il jobs act del lavoro autonomo e del lavoro agile*, Giappichelli, Torino, 2018, p. 259.
77. B. Hepple, *Diritto del lavoro e crisi economica. Lezioni dalla storia europea*, in *Dir. lav. rel. ind.*, 2009, p. 392; C. Barnand, *The Financial Crisis and the Euro Plus Act: A Labour Lawyer's Perspective*, in *International Law Journal*, 2012, p. 98; M. Rodriguez Pinero, *La grave crisi del diritto del lavoro*, in *Lav. dir.*, 2012, p. 3.
78. L. Fiorillo, *Il lavoro agile: continua il processo di ridefinizione del diritto del lavoro*, in L. Fiorillo, A. Perulli (curated by), *Il jobs act del lavoro autonomo e del lavoro agile*, Giappichelli, Torino, 2018, p. 170.
79. P. Ichino, *Il lavoro e il mercato. Per un diritto del lavoro maggiorenne*, Mondadori, Milano, 1996.
80. R. Del Punta, *L'economia e le ragioni del diritto del lavoro*, in *Giorn. dir. lav. rel. ind.*, 2001, 89, 1, p. 40.

individual autonomy through the binding regulation of the employment relationship, in consideration of the imbalance of the contractual power between the parties of the relationship itself, is a distinctive feature of labour law with respect to civil law.[81]

[C] Sustainable Development as a Source of Legitimacy of the Capability Approach in Subordination

The enhancement of individual autonomy, as a cornerstone of the Capability Approach, offers the opportunity to reflect, in broader terms, on the possible contribution of the Capability Approach to subordination, since smart work, as already mentioned, is a subordinate employment contract.

If, as it has been intended to be demonstrated, this approach is in line with what is suggested by Sustainable Development, in terms of achieving an equality of opportunity, also through a better work-life balance, finding important application and potential spaces in labour law, one cannot deny a certain difficulty in adopting such an approach also in order to ponder on the broader case of subordination.

The reflection involved starts from the consideration of the fundamental values of the very concept of *capability* (substantial freedom to enhance one's own resources to guarantee self-sufficiency as a person and economic agent with the related benefits in terms of wealth produced and social equity[82]) that can be summarized mainly in a strong valorizsation of the individual, his/her resources, his/her power and his/her freedom.

Starting from the concept of 'freedom' of the individual, there is immediately a certain criticality in applying the Theory of Capabilities to subordination,[83] since by definition labour law is based precisely on the limitation of individual freedom, that is to say on the provision of precise rights and obligations for both parties. When the worker signs an employment contract, he/she renounces his/her 'substantial freedom', being subject to the directive (as well as controlling and disciplinary) power of the employer, putting him/herself 'at disposal' of the company in the performance of the working activity. Specularly, even the employer's part is limited in its entrepreneurial 'freedom' manifesting itself in the exercise of the powers entrusted to it, since there are precise limiting provisions set by the code to guarantee the protection of the weak contractual party.

In the same terms, the Senian limit is observed with regard to the 'power' of the individual: the worker with a subordinate employment contract does not have contractual 'powers' but is historically subject to the power of the employer, not only by virtue of contractual weakness deriving from the substantial imbalance in the labour market in terms of excess of labour supply but also in view of the necessary labour management activity as 'head of the company'. We are actually referring to 'the powers

81. P. Ichino, *Il dialogo tra economia e diritto del lavoro*, in *Riv. it. dir. lav.*, 2001, I, p. 193.
82. S. Deakin, F. Wilkinson, *'Capabilities', Ordine spontaneo del mercato e diritti sociali*, in *Dir. merc. lav*, 2000, 2, pp. 317 ss.
83. R. Del Punta, *Labour Law and the Capability*, in *International Journal of Comparative Labour Law and Industrial Relations*, 2016, vol. 32, n. 4, p. 393.

of the employer' and not of a corresponding 'power' of the worker, but rather of 'rights' of the workers (and of the related obligations). In this sense, therefore, subordination does not seem to be the ideal place for the affirmation of one's individual power, neither on the part of the worker nor on the part of the employer, since there are still well-defined limits to employer powers (of procedure, of proportionality, in terms of *jus variandi*, transfer, control over work, employment of women workers in a state of maternity, etc.).

Furthermore, if one reflects on the valorization of one's resources, understood in terms of means, skills, manual and intellectual abilities, we would be pushed to relate this opportunity not to the sphere of subordination, but, more properly, to the ambit of a work relationship of an independent nature, as in the latter case there is greater freedom to enhance one's own resources.

The same reasoning is proposed again if we finally reflect in terms of equality, since subordination is by definition a relationship in which the parties are not placed in a situation of equality, but, as it has already been reaffirmed, there is an original imbalance in the internal part of the employment contract which justifies the very essence of labour law and its protective nature with respect to the employee.

These observations are inclined to considering the validity of the *Capability Approach* rather than for the sphere of subordination, for that of autonomy, where the parties are considered equal in principle, or placed on the same level (hence the 'collaboration' activity with the entrepreneur, not 'in the company'), in a situation of better balance of contractual powers and being able to better exploit their resources (or *capabilities*). Probably, in this sense, we might interpret the different approach of the bill 2229/2016[84] which originally allowed smart work, understood as the maximum expression of the *capabilities* of an individual and his/her individual autonomy, as well as his/her negotiating power, to be referred not only to forms of subordinate work but also to forms of self-employment. In the latter case, the provision to entrust the rules of the contract to the parties would certainly not have constituted as important a novelty as that which concerned subordinate work, since it would have been in line with what was already provided for in the classic collaboration relationships.

How, therefore, can the application of the *Capability Approach* be justified also within the sphere of subordination, in order to legitimize its valid use not only with regard to agile or self-employed work?

Sustainable Development could represent a new interpretation and at the same time a source of legitimization of the Capability Approach, that is, the necessary condition for its wider acceptance, even in the delineation of labour in subordinate mode.

Let us analyse the scope of this observation.

As Tiziano Treu said, the Theory of Capabilities would be useful in bringing the labour law discipline closer to the concrete needs of workers and in developing new

84. Bill S. 2229 'Negotiation adaptation of the modalities of smart work in the fourth industrial revolution', approved on 3 November 2016, then absorbed by the Bill S. 2233 'Measures for the protection of non-entrepreneurial self-employment and measures aimed at favouring the flexible articulation in times and places of subordinate work', definitively approved law on 10 May 2017.

protection techniques based on the active involvement of workers, able to widen their own margins of choice. However, the suggestion of this theory 'must be analyzed and developed in combination with the broader political approach necessary for the promotion of sustainable economic growth and development goals that allow for social and human progress,[85] 'based on the assumption that "the most challenging task of labour law is to prove that it can contribute to sustainable development and increase human *capabilities*'.[86]

Within the discipline of smart work, labour law has carried out this task to the letter: on the one hand, this particular form of subordination contributes, as we have seen, to the realization of a development in its environmental, social and economic dimension; on the other hand, it recognizes the possibility for the employee to take advantage of his/her own *capabilities*, enhancing his/her autonomy and capacity. It is precisely within the smart work that one can thus see the seeds of an evolution of subordination that is different from the past, as being bargained, leaving previously unthinkable spaces of autonomy, realizing an unprecedented co-responsibility of the subject who is in a state of subjection (the employee) in the definition of the ways in which the active dimension of the relationship is implemented (the exercise of employer powers).[87] We are facing a 'postmodern' or 'smart' subordination, to use a more fashionable term. It is more suited not only to the productive needs of companies but also to a new figure of worker: more aware, enterprising and independent, assuming a negotiated liability so far precluded, having both advantages and risks according to the case.

This is a legislative achievement that proves how labour law is slowly emerging from the shell that for years it has self-built to defend raging economic logics, demonstrating a fundamental awareness: the only way to survive and to put an end to this destructive dismantling process (in order not to use the already inflated term of 'crisis') is to accept the epochal change in progress and evolve accordingly.

Therefore, labour law should first of all adopt a 'development' logic, in the sense of adopting an evolutionary perspective, which takes into account the peculiarities of the economic, social and productive context of the new millennium, very far from the times –not only in temporal terms – where the relevant codes were considered as fully binding but also and above all in factual terms, being labour law required 'an exceptional effort to update itself to guarantee its stability within the new contexts'.[88]

Under no circumstances does such evolution imply a denial of its founding values, like solidarity, equity, social justice, health and safety, but, as a matter of fact, their necessary rediscovery, as well as the continuous processing of new rights that are

85. '*In this respect the suggestions of this theory need to be analyzed and developed in combination with the broader policy approach necessary to promote sustainable economic growth and development goals conducive to human and social progress.*' T. Treu, *Labour Law and Sustainable Development*, in *WP C.S.D.L.E. 'Massimo D'Antona'.INT – 130/2016*, p. 3.
86. *Ibid.*, p. 2.
87. A. Perulli, *Il jobs act del lavoro autonomo e agile: come cambiano i concetti di subordinazione e autonomia nel diritto del lavoro*, in *WP C.S.D.L.E. 'Massimo D'Antona'.IT – 341/2017*, p. 15.
88. V. Talamo, *Diversamente agile? Lo Smart Work nelle pubbliche amministrazioni*, in L. Fiorillo, A. Perulli (curated by), *Il jobs act del lavoro autonomo e del lavoro agile*, Giappichelli, Torino, 2018, p. 258.

more responsive to the needs of the workers of the new millennium, bearing in mind that 'with rights, the individual dimension of the employment relationship forcefully goes back in the game, since the law, which these rights sanctions and imputes, is aimed at workers as individuals, before as collective subjects'.[89]

On this point we should recall, as already argued by authoritative doctrine, that the relaunch of individual autonomy in terms of 'new frontier of labour law, does not mean overcoming the mandatory legal or contractual law'.[90] In fact, since smart work entails, together with the significant advantages already seen, a series of risks for the worker, both in terms of isolation, and, more often, linked to an overlapping of life and work,[91] the law provides that the agreement takes place in compliance with the '*limits of maximum duration of daily and weekly working hours, deriving from the law and from collective bargaining*',[92] and that the parties undertake to '*also identify the rest times of the worker as well as the technical and organizational measures necessary to ensure the disconnection of the worker from the technological equipment of the work*'. The objective is to protect the worker, thanks to this new generation's[93] right to disconnection, already provided for by the French legislation,[94] from the so-called risk of *burn-out*, or from a hyper-work stress caused by an excessive interference of work in private life, resulting as being - otherwise - always connected through the various technological tools of his/her own or provided by the employer to perform the work.

Therefore, without prejudice to the conservation, within the development, of the protective nature of the labour law discipline, its evolution should be able to be defined as 'sustainable', in the sense of the term, or in the necessary adoption of a dual logic, proposing a balance between the social interests of workers and the economic interests of the company, with the aim of reconciling them to obtain a maximization of both, as happened in the context of smart work. The discipline should therefore integrate the economic reasons and reconcile them with the social ones, without preferring an axiological category over the other.

With this interpretation it is possible to legitimize the *capabilities* approach also within the sphere of subordination, giving the same priority to economic reasons and to the recognition of the protection of workers, enhancing them as an active part of the employment contract and not only as recipients of protectionist measures.

---

89. R. Del Punta, *Verso l'individualizzazione dei diritti?*, in L. Corazza, R. Romei (curated by), *Diritto del lavoro in trasformazione*, il Mulino, Bologna, 2014, p. 18.
90. L. Zoppoli, *Flessibilità del diritto del lavoro e accumulazione di capitale*, in L. Mariucci (curated by), *Dopo la flessibilità, cosa? Le nuove politiche del lavoro*, il Mulino, Bologna, 2006, pp. 418-419.
91. A. R. Tinti, *A proposito di lavoro «agile» e work-life balance. La conciliazione ingannevole*, in *La rivista Il Mulino*, 27 maggio 2016.
92. Article 18, comma 2, l. n. 81/2017.
93. E. Dagnino, I. Moscaritolo, *Diritto alla disconnessione: un diritto di nuova generazione?*, in *Boll. Adapt*, 19 settembre 2016.
94. About the right to disconnect of the loi travail: J-E. Ray, *Naissance et avis de décès du droit à la déconnexion: le droit à la vie privée au XXIe siècle*, in *Droit Social*, 2002, pp. 939-944; L. Fauvarque-Gobin, *La conciliazione vita-lavoro nella Loi travail*, in L. Casano, G. Imperatori, C. Tourres (curated by), *Loi travail: prima analisi e lettura*, in *ADAPT Labour Studies e-Book Series*, 2016, p. 56; J-E. Ray, *Grande accélération et droit à la déconnexion*, in *Droit Social*, 2016, pp. 912-920.

Therefore, if Sustainable Development can reinforce the validity of the *capabilities* approach, it must be kept in mind that the latter can potentially constitute a significant contribution to the development of a more dynamic and sustainable labour law.[95] The relationship between the *Capability Approach* and Sustainable Development is therefore bidirectional, being two approaches, two normative theories that are mutually reinforcing.

The same interrelation can be observed between labour law and Sustainable Development: if labour law is one of the main instruments assigned to the realization of Sustainable Development, it can be elected as a reference paradigm in terms of values for labour law, for its reinterpretation and rewriting in the sustainable evolutionary logic mentioned above.

And again, between *Capability Approach* and labour law, the latter, in fact, has the task of promoting *capabilities* through the recognition of a series of rights for workers (*the primary goal of labour law should be that of safeguarding and developing workers' capabilities*[96]): (1) *capability for work* (that is the capacity to have a fairly paid job, in proportion to the quantity and quality of work performed and sufficiently to guarantee existential needs, corresponding as much as possible to individual preferences and expectations); (2) *capability for human respect and dignity* (that is the ability to obtain working conditions compatible with the health and safety of the worker and respect for his/her personal dignity as a human being; (3) *capability for professional skills* (that is the ability to have adequate employment training and to be included in an organizational production system that respects and increases the value of the knowledge and skills of the worker); (4) *capability for work-life balance* (that is the ability to have a sufficient amount of free time from work, *a fortiori* in case of needs linked to illness/accidents or in case of maternity/paternity or other personal needs); (5) *capability for voice* (or the ability to be part of a Union and participate in collective actions in defence of one's interests).[97] Note in this regard how the *capability for work* perfectly corresponds to the definition proposed by the ILO of *decent work* and how these *capabilities* are in line with the UN's Millennium SDGs.

And, at the same time, the very *capabilities* approach represents 'a cornerstone for a renewed labour law',[98] in the sense of a useful, innovative approach, to find new value foundations on which to base the development of the discipline.

To conclude this reflection, the evolution of subordination, triggered by the legislative intervention on the subject of smart work, in the broader context of transformation of labour law, is the tangible sign of a change in direction, which

95. '*The Capability Approach has the potential to make a significant contribution to the elaboration of a more dynamic and sustainable labour law*', Cfr. R. Del Punta, *Labour Law and the Capability*, in *International Journal of Comparative Labour Law and Industrial Relations*, 2016, vol. 32, n. 4, p. 385.

96. *Ibid.*, p. 388.

97. *Ibid.*, p. 392.

98. '*A cornerstone for a renewed labour law*'. Cfr. R. Del Punta, *Labour Law and the Capability*, in *International Journal of Comparative Labour Law and Industrial Relations*, 2016, vol. 32, n. 4, p. 383.

occurred in the logic of Sustainable Development, in line with what is suggested by the *Capability Approach.*

§3.04 THE BALANCE BETWEEN DIFFERENT AXIOLOGICAL PERSPECTIVES

In addition to the value similarities in terms of solidarity and equality of opportunity, a third methodological analogy can be found between Sustainable Development and labour law, regarding the balance of different axiological perspectives.

As we have seen, the Sustainable Development paradigm aims at mediating conflicting interests by promoting a continuous reconciliation between its three different dimensions (social, economic and environmental).

In the same terms, labour law is by definition a right in order to rebalance powers in the relationship: it was conceived and has been developed with the aim of mediating the entrepreneurial (economic) interests with those (social) of workers, in a continuous game of *check and balance* among the principle of freedom of economic initiative established by Article 41 paragraph 1 of the Italian Constitution, and the social clause of the following paragraph: (the private economic initiative) cannot take place '*in contrast with social utility or in such a way as to damage safety, freedom, human dignity*'. This is to say that labour law is not limited to assuming the task of reconciling the economic interests of the company with the rights of workers, but in broader terms, it proposes to protect the person and the fundamental social rights, by promoting absolute values such as justice, democracy, equity and equality, entrusting them to the same constitutional principles (Articles 1, 2, etc.), to the constitutionally bound legislator or to guaranteed existence (Articles 39 and 40) of a collective counterpower.[99]

[A] The Dismissal in the 'Flexicurity': An Idea of Sustainable Development

The institute of dismissal represents the ideal testing ground for the logic underlying the principle of Sustainable Development within the field of labour law. Such logic is related to the balancing between economic interests – the entrepreneurial and organizational needs – and the social interests, such as the worker protection, not only for the preservation of the workplace but also, in a more modern vision of the institution, to support income, social inclusion and reallocation in the labour market.

Leaving aside a precise and complete analysis of the Italian discipline of dismissal and its evolution, which goes beyond the scope of this survey, the attempt of this reflection is to investigate the rationale behind the main legislative interventions over the years concerning dismissal in order to assess its consistency in light of the principles of Sustainable Development.

99. R. Del Punta, *Responsabilità Sociale dell'Impresa e Diritto del Lavoro*, in *Lav. dir.*, 2006, 1, pp. 41-64.

The progressive increase in the protection of the worker during dismissals, which has taken place since when the relevant codes were put into force, underwent a U-turn with the 'Collegato Lavoro' (l. 183/2010) which introduced a reduction in the terms for appealing against dismissals,[100] and with the subsequent Fornero Law (l. 92/2012[101]), whose fundamental objective was to facilitate dismissals flexibility, in the wake of the (European) pushes towards a reduction in the regulatory rigidities put in place to protect the stability of the workplace.[102]

It is following the Fornero Reform that the field of application of the protections against illegitimate dismissal was completely redesigned through the partial modification of l. 604/66 and the complete rewriting of Article 18 of the Workers' Statute (l. 300/70), by reducing the scope of application of the reinstatement (degraded to a mere exception[103]) and generally lightening the sanctioning system, gradually decomposing the original real protection into a scale of diversified guarantees, favouring in any case a purely economic protection.

Such a legislative intervention is in line with the tendency, developed in those years, to understand labour law not only as an *employment relationship* law, but rather a *labour market* law. And in this different perspective, the labour law discipline is therefore entrusted with the task of tackling both the problems posed by unemployment (hence the idea of loosening the rigidity of the dismissal discipline to make the labour market more fluid and to favour the *turnover* of workforce) and those of productive transformations (and therefore allowing the company, by now far from the typical organization of Fordist or Taylorist work, greater flexibility in the management of the workforce that allows it to face an intermittent demand and an increasingly *on demand* production).

The dismissals flexibilization work initiated by the Fornero Law was finally completed by the Jobs Act (pursuant to Legislative Decree 23/2015, issued in the

---

100. G. Pellacani, *Il cosiddetto «Collegato Lavoro» e la disciplina dei licenziamenti: un quadro in chiaroscuro*, in *Riv. it. dir. lav.*, 2010, I, pp. 215 ss; C. Zoli, *La legge n. 183/2010: le novità in materia di licenziamento*, in *Arg. dir. lav.*, 2011, 4-5, pp. 833-851; M. T. Carinci, *Clausole generali, certificazione e limiti al sindacato del giudice. A proposito dell'art. 30, l. 183/2010*, in *WP C.S.D.L.E. 'Massimo D'Antona'.IT – 114/2011*; O. Mazzotta, *La giustizia del lavoro nella visione del 'collegato': la disciplina dei licenziamenti*, in M. Cinelli, G. Ferraro (curated by), *Il contenzioso del lavoro nella Legge 4 novembre 2010, n. 183 (Collegato lavoro)*, Giappichelli, Torino, 2011, pp. XXVII ss.; M. Tremolada, *Norme della l. n. 183/2010 in materia di certificazione e di limiti al potere di accertamento del giudice*, in M. Miscione, D. Garofalo (curated by), *Il Collegato lavoro 2010*, Ipsoa, Milano, 2011, pp. 158 ss; G. Benassi, *Clausole generali e giudice del lavoro: l'art. 30, primo comma, della legge n. 183 del 2010*, in *Arg. dir. lav.*, 2012, 1, pp. 91 ss.
101. L. Zoppoli, *Flex/insecurity. La riforma Fornero (l. 28 giugno 2012, n. 92) prima, durante e dopo*, Editoriale Scientifica, Napoli, 2012; M. Cinelli, G. Ferraro, O. Mazzotta (curated by), *Il nuovo mercato del lavoro dalla Riforma Fornero alla legge di stabilità 2013*, Giappichelli, Torino, 2013; L. Di Paola (curated by), *Il licenziamento. Dalla Legge Fornero al Jobs Act*, Giuffrè, Milano, 2016.
102. The logic underlying the legislative intervention is already evident in the heading of the Law: 'Provisions on labour market reform with a view to growth'.
103. The reintegration is applied only in cases of discriminatory or null dismissal and in the case of economic dismissal if the judge decrees the manifest non-existence of the fact that motivates it.

implementation of Law 183/2014[104]), with the drastic reduction of reintegration in the new contracts with increasing protections: completely excluded from economic dismissals, replaced by a growing monetary compensation according to the length of service and marginalized in the context of dismissals connected to the discriminatory or spurious dimension that the unilateral act of withdrawal conceals.[105]

The evolution of the discipline makes it possible to identify a clear change of route in the legislator's intervention in the first ten years of the new millennium.

If until then all legislative interventions in the field of dismissal were aimed at ensuring a better protection of the weaker part of the employment contract, introducing gradually stricter limits when withdrawing from the employment contract and widening the scope of the protections for the worker, it is clear that the subsequent reforms of the dismissal regulation from an indemnity perspective have shifted the balance towards the reconciling of the interests of the worker and the employer.

Such change is justified by the change of paradigm underlying the reference context: the value of job *stability*, previously promoted both with the principle of the necessary justification of dismissal, and with the remediation of reintegration, has given way to demands for flexibility in the labour market promoted by the progressive monetization of dismissal.

The Fornero reform and the Jobs Act were therefore placed in the context of the community debate developed around the idea of flexicurity.[106]

---

104. C. Cester, *I licenziamenti nel Jobs Act*, in *WP C.S.D.L.E. 'Massimo D'Antona'.IT – 273/2015*; R. Pessi, *Prime riflessioni sui decreti attuativi del Jobs Act*, in R. Pessi, C. Pisani, G. Proia, A. Vallebona (curated by), *Jobs Act e licenziamento*, Giappichelli, Torino, 2015; C. Zoli, *I licenziamenti per giustificato motivo oggettivo dalla legge n. 604 del 1966 al d. lgs. n. 23 del 2015*, in G. Ferraro (curated by), *Licenziamenti nel contratto a tutele crescenti*, Cedam, Padova, 2015, pp. 75-96; E. Ghera, D. Garofalo (curated by), *Le tutele per i licenziamenti e per la disoccupazione involontaria nel Jobs Act*, Cacucci, Bari, 2015; G. Vidiri, *Il licenziamento disciplinare nel primo decreto attuativo del* Jobs *Act tra luci e (non poche) ombre*, in *Arg. dir. lav.*, 2015, 2, pp. 353 ss; M. Marazza, *Il regime sanzionatorio dei licenziamenti nel Jobs Act*, in *Arg. dir. lav.*, 2015, 2, pp. 310 ss; M. Tiraboschi (curated by), *Le nuove regole del lavoro dopo il Jobs Act*, Giuffrè, Milano, 2016; F. Santoni, M. Ricci, R. Santucci (curated by), *Il diritto del lavoro all'epoca del* jobs act, Editoriale Scientifica, Napoli, 2016; R. De Luca Tamajo, *Jobs Act e cultura giuslavoristica*, in *Dir. lav. merc.*, 2016, 1, pp. 5 ss; R. De Luca Tamajo, *La (in)derogabilità della normativa lavoristica ai tempi del Jobs Act*, in *Labor*, 2016, 5-6, pp. 321 ss; P. Lambertucci, *Il lavoratore disabile tra disciplina dell'avviamento al lavoro e tutela contro i licenziamenti: brevi note a margine dei provvedimenti attuativi del c.d.* Jobs Act *alla 'prova' della disciplina antidiscriminatoria*, in *Arg. dir. lav.*, 2016, 6; G. Santoro Passarelli, *Appunti sulla funzione delle categorie civilistiche nel diritto del lavoro dopo il Jobs Act*, in *WP C.S.D.L.E. 'Massimo D'Antona'.IT – 290/2016*.
105. The reinstatement protection is considered too expensive for companies and uncertain as to its outcomes: the sentence of reinstatement can take place years after the dismissal, with unforeseeable costs for the company, since the sentence implies not only the onset of the right to reinstatement in the workplace but also of the right to compensation for damage suffered as a result of the illegitimate termination of the relationship, recognizing the wages owed to the worker by virtue of the employment relationship from the date of the judgment itself up to that of reinstatement, as well as the payment of welfare and social security contributions.
106. About flexicurity: L. Gallino, *Il lavoro non è una merce. Contro la flessibilità*, Laterza, Bari, 2007, p. 122; M. Brollo, *Il lavoro a tempo parziale tra flessibilità e sicurezza*, in F. Carinci, M. Miscione (a cura di), *Il collegato lavoro 2008. L. 24 dicembre 2007, n. 247*, vol. 11, Ipsoa, Milano, 2008, pp. 277-306; M. Delfino, *Diritti sociali e flexicurity*, in *Riv. it. dir. lav.*, 2009, 3, pp. 29-53; R. Del Punta, *La stabilità reale nell'epoca dell'instabilità*, in *Dir. lav. merc.*, 2010, pp. 753 ss;

This new reference paradigm of European origin,[107] born from the merger of the terms 'flexibility' and 'security', indicates the need to delineate the first part (flexibility) with regard to the employment relationship, and the second (security) with respect to the labour market, so as to give life to a sort of synallagmatic relationship between less rigidity in dismissing and hiring against greater passive and active assistance in the transition phase from one job to another.

Flexibility, at least in principle.[108] does not end in the employer's interest in greater freedom to recruit or dismiss, in order to organize work so as to respond effectively to the new needs and new skills required by production; it further has to do with the transitions that mark the life of an individual, in the transition from the world of school to that of work, from one job to another, from unemployment or inactivity to work and, again, from work to retirement.

Flexibility, in the wake of the *flexicurity* advocated by the European Commission, also means providing workers with better jobs, upward mobility and optimal development of talents and *capabilities*.

Security, however, means equipping workers with skills that allow them better adaptability and employability in the business (without having to resort to external flexibility) and in the market, through continuous training programmes. It therefore provides for the implementation of effective active labour market policies, which reduce periods of unemployment and facilitate the transition to new jobs, and for just as many policies of adequate income support (unemployment benefits) and coverage of social benefits (pensions and health care).

In this perspective, the idea of *flexicurity* is therefore in line with the principles proposed by Sustainable Development, since it induces to reconcile in a new way the need for flexibility in hiring and dismissing in the employment relationship, with the needs of protection of the worker in the labour market, in terms of security in employment, or by providing for adequate assistance tools for the worker both in terms

---

P. Auer, *La flexicurity nel tempo della crisi*, in *Dir. rel. ind.*, 2011, 21, 1, pp. 37-58; F. Valdes Dal Re, *Il dibattito sulla flessicurezza all'interno dell'Unione Europea*, in G. Loy (a cura di), *Diritto del lavoro e crisi economica*, Ediesse, Roma, 2011; A. Perulli, *Il diritto del lavoro tra libertà e sicurezza*, in *Riv. it. dir. lav.*, 2012, 1, pp. 247 ss; L. Zoppoli, *Flex-insecurity, La riforma Fornero (l. 28 giugno 2012, n. 92) prima, durante e dopo*, Editoriale Scientifica, Napoli, 2012; M. Brollo, *Lavoro a tempo parziale dopo la l. n. 92/2012: meno flex, più security*, in *Lav. giur.*, 2012, 10; B. Gazier, *La strategia europea per l'occupazione nella tempesta: il ripristino di una prospettiva a lungo termine*, in *Dir. rel. ind.*, 2011, 1; P. Ichino, *Inchiesta sul lavoro. Perché non dobbiamo avere paura di una grande riforma*, Mondadori, Milano, 2011, pp. 116 ss; G. Loy, *Flessicurezza e precarietà*, in *Riv. giur. lav*, I, 2013, pp. 479 ss; T. Treu, *Flessibilità e tutele nella riforma del lavoro*, in *Giorn. dir. lav. rel. ind.*, 2013; L. Zoppoli, *Contratto a tutele crescenti e altre forme contrattuali*, in *Dir. merc. lav.*, 2015, 2; L. Zoppoli, *Il 'riordino' dei modelli di rapporto di lavoro tra articolazione tipologica e flessibilizzazione funzionale*, in *Dir. rel. ind.*, 2015, 1, p. 76; T. Treu, *Una seconda fase della flexicurity per l'occupabilità*, in *Dir. rel. ind.*, 2017, 27, 3, pp. 597-633; T. Treu, *Flessibilità e oltre*, in *WP CSDLE 'Massimo D'Antona'.INT – 135/2017*.

107. 2006 European Commission, Green Paper 'Modernizing labour law to meet the challenges of the 21st century' (COM(2006) 708 of 22 November 2006). After the genesis and a difficult first application phase strangled in the bud by the financial crisis of 2007-2008, today we are at the second phase of flexicurity, as it was called by the Communication of the European Commission of 3 March 2010 entitled Europe 2020 and aimed at supporting intelligent, sustainable and inclusive growth.

108. According to the documents mentioned in the previous note.

of income subsidies in periods of unemployment (passive assistance) and in terms of help in the search for a new employment (active assistance).

If, in principle, *flexicurity* and Sustainable Development are aligned in terms of method and objective, it is worth observing, however, how, in its practical implementation, the paradigm of European derivation does contribute to 'development', but not to its 'sustainable' delineation, resulting as acting more in terms of flexibility (less guarantees in the employment relationship), rather than security (greater protection of the worker on the market).

There were, in fact, many legislative interventions concerning flexibility, both in terms of 'external' flexibility in hiring (since they could resort to a wide range of flexible contracts already provided for by Law 196/1997 and by Legislative Decree 276/2003, as well as the progressive randomness and extension of fixed-term contracts), and with reference to 'internal' flexibility, guaranteeing both numerical flexibility (think of flexible working hour regimes) and functional flexibility (concerning, for example, the recent changes to the power of *jus variandi* of the employer regarding tasks, according to the new version of Article 2013 c.c. which raises this power).

The most recent interventions on the discipline of dismissals have also given ample space to layoffs flexibility,[109] determining the shift from a *Job Protection*[110] system to a *flexicurity*[111] system, according to the logic influenced by economic theories of neoclassical inspiration, to loosen the legislation of labour protection (above all that on dismissal) to overcome the rigidity of the labour market and therefore to create more employment.[112]

Therefore, if with reference to the first term of the binomial flexibility-security it is possible to identify a mass of targeted legislative interventions, on the contrary, with reference to the topic of security, to date, we cannot find as many interventions. The reasons for such an imbalance can mostly be found in the rigidity that has traditionally characterized our system, in which a series of uncoordinated measures took place (due

---

109. Among the interventions suggested by the European Commission for the implementation of the flexicurity paradigm, the revision of national constraints on dismissals flexibility are also included (*see* the Commission Communication 'Towards common principles of flexicurity: More and better jobs thanks to flexibility and to security) COM(2007) 359 of 27 June 2007. About the urgency of national level action in order to lighten the rules on dismissal; *see also* the Commission Communication on the results of the public consultation opened by the Green Book COM(2007) 627 of 24 October 2007.

110. Ichino expresses himself in terms of regime change with regard to dismissal, in the transition from a regime centred on the property rule (reintegration) to that centred on the liability rule (compensation). P. Ichino, *La riforma dei licenziamenti e i diritti fondamentali dei lavoratori*, in L. Nogler, L. Corazza (a cura di), *Risistemare il diritto del lavoro. Liber amicorum Marcello Pedrazzoli*, Franco Angeli, Milano, 2012, pp. 792-823.

111. A. Perulli, *Observations sur les réformes de la législation du travail en Europe*, in *Revue de Droit du Travail*, 2015, 3, p. 170; D. Gottardi, *Riforme strutturali e prospettiva Europea di Flexicurity: andata e ritorno*, in *Lav. dir.*, 2015, 2, p. 239; B. Caruso, *Verso il diritto del lavoro della responsabilità*, in *WP C.S.D.L.E. 'Massimo D'Antona'.IT – 283/2015*.

112. According to these theories, the reduction of the legislative protection of labour was compensated by *workfare* policies consisting in social safety nets, which, however, had a limited duration and scope, conditioned by the search for and acceptance of new jobs. Cfr. T. Treu, *Una seconda fase della Flexicurity per l'occupabilità*, in *Dir. rel. ind.*, 2017, 3, p. 507.

to the constant changes of government), which led to the realization of extreme flexibility, through the proliferation of atypical and flexible contracts.[113]

As regards security, however, despite the most recent attempts (of the Fornero Reform and of the subsequent Legislative Decree 22/2015, in the implementation of the Jobs Act) of a progressive universalization of unemployment benefits, which should have served as a counterweight to the lesser protection in the case of illegitimate dismissal, thanks to better income support in the event of involuntary termination of the employment relationship,[114] there are no real universal safety nets in the labour market, to date.[115] This situation is also attributable to the failure to implement part of the reforms introduced by the Jobs Act, related to the system of services and active policies, with particular reference to the failure to allocate the human and organizational resources necessary to perform the functions entrusted by the legislator to the ANPAL (*labour active policies national agency*).

In addition to the current unsuitability of the social safety nets provided for in order to give adequate support to the workers' employment discontinuity – in particular for temporary workers, due to the prevalence of access conditions still linked to the amount of tax paid and reserved mainly for employees – we may add above all the inadequacy of the public services related to the governance of the labour market in facing the necessities of an increasingly large number of unemployed people, through an efficient and timely support to the search of a new job.

It is no coincidence that within the doctrine, *flex-insecurity*[116] has long been mentioned, reflecting the prevalence of the first term in the binomial flexibility – security.

The constant of the legislative evolution briefly re-proposed is in fact inscribed in the model of flexibility tout court: from the 1997 Treu Law to the 2003 Biagi Law, from the 2012 Fornero law to the Jobs Act, a temporal dissociation of *flexicurity* is perpetuated, with a first phase on the immediate flexibility in hiring and dismissing, and a second one on the security in the labour market, anticipated, but always postponed to the near future.[117]

---

113. T. Treu, *Flessibilità e oltre*, in *WP CSDLE 'Massimo D'Antona'.INT – 135/2017*, p. 18.
114. *Ibid.*
115. The Jobs Act provided for the re-modulation and universalization of Aspi (the Social Insurance for Employment provided by the Fornero Law) to all workers, including the economically dependent self-employed. The D. lgs. 22/2015 introduces instead for the collaborations an indemnity that is different from the New Aspi (moreover with a greater progressive reduction compared to the Aspi), that is the Dis-coll (*monthly unemployment benefit*), different for requisite, duration and financing. About these topics, P. Bozzao, *I nuovi trattamenti di disoccupazione: a piccoli passi verso l'Europa*, in A. Perulli, L. Fiorillo (a cura di), *Contratto a tutele crescenti e Naspi, Decreti legislativi 4 marzo 2015, n. 22 e n. 23*, Giappichelli, Torino, 2015, pp. 201-217; F. Natalini, *La riforma dell'Aspi nell'ambito del Jobs Act; nasce la Naspi. Come cambia il sussidio di disoccupazione. Le ulteriori novità: la Dis-Coll e l'Asdi, ibid.*, pp. 219-245.
116. Cfr. F. Berton, M. Ricchiardi, S. Sacchi, *Flex-insecurity. Perché in Italia la flessibilità diventa precarietà*, il Mulino, Bologna, 2009; R. Del Punta, *La stabilità reale nell'epoca dell'instabilità*, in *Dir. lav. merc.*, 2010, pp. 753 ss; L. Zoppoli, *Flex/insecurity. La riforma Fornero (l. 28 giugno 2012, n. 92) prima durante e dopo*, Editoriale Scientifica, Napoli, 2012.
117. F. Carinci, *Il diritto del lavoro che verrà (in occasione del congedo di un amico)*, in *Arg. Dir. Lav*, 2014, 3, p. 661.

Adopting the Sustainable Development model in the framework of the legislation under investigation may be useful to go back to the original spirit of *flexicurity*, fully realizing that second term of the binomial (*security*) in order to avoid flexibility being translated into precariousness. This is in the wake of the fact that the stability (or security) of the labour market will increasingly be characterized by a combination of employment contracts with one or more employers, different periods of 'non-employment' (such as unemployment, family or training commitments) and activities on a temporary basis (such as part-time work), during which remuneration and employability are, at least partially, maintained.[118]

In this sense, we should interpret the paradigm shift that places growing emphasis on measures of internal flexibility with respect both to those of external flexibility, widely used in past years, and to traditional measures of income support, services for employment and active policies.

The most significant measures in terms of *flexicurity* are those that modify the rules and conditions of use of flexibility for the purposes of '*retention*', aimed at strengthening the continuity and stability of the employment relationship, that is to say those measures aimed at achieving internal flexibility, related to flexible working hour regimes; functional flexibility, concerning the change of tasks and the adoption of flexible forms of work organization; wage and labour cost flexibility.[119]

In this perspective, the legislator should intervene by leveraging both the SDGs of the UN (Objective 3: guaranteeing the conditions of well-being for all at all ages; Objective 4: universally promoting learning opportunities during life; Objective. 8: promoting inclusive and sustainable growth, full and productive employment and decent work for every individual), and the principles of the European Pillar of Social Rights, in terms of education, training and lifelong learning, equal gender, equal opportunities, active employment support, flexible and secure employment, balance between professional and family life, social protection, unemployment benefits, minimum income and old-age pension.[120]

118. P. Auer, *La flexicurity nel tempo della crisi*, in *Dir. rel. ind.*, 2011, 21, 1, p. 54.
119. T. Treu, *Flessibilità e oltre*, in *WP CSDLE 'Massimo D'Antona'.INT – 135/2017.*
120. Principles (1) successfully guarantee transitions in the labour market; (2) guarantee equal treatment and opportunities and participation in the labour market; (3) guarantee equal treatment and opportunities in employment, social protection, education and access to goods and services available to the public; (4) right to timely and tailored assistance to improve employment and self-employment prospects, including the right to receive support for job search, training and requalification; right to transfer rights in the field of social protection and training during professional transitions; right of young people to pursue education, traineeship or apprenticeship or a qualitatively valid job offer within four months from loss of employment or exit from the education system; (5) the right to fair and equal treatment as regards working conditions and access to social protection and training, promotion of the transition to forms of permanent employment, of innovative forms of work that guarantee quality working conditions, of professional mobility, prohibition of abuse of atypical contracts; (9) guarantee the balance between professional activity and family life through flexible working methods; (13) right for the unemployed to adequately support the activation by the public employment services to (re) enter the labour market and adequate unemployment benefits of a reasonable duration, in line with contributions and national eligibility rules; (14) the right to a minimum income for anyone who does not have sufficient resources that can guarantee a dignified life in

The dismissal, from the perspective of Sustainable Development, must not in fact be considered as an event isolated from the context of the labour market and its transitional dynamics, but it should fit into the broader institutional design of adequate active and passive policies to guarantee the necessary support of protections in the market, so that remedial protection, by now predominantly indigent and not 'real', is accompanied by a social safety net so that the breach of the contract represents a more sustainable event for the worker and for the society in general.

Moreover, the internalization of the principle of Sustainable Development by individuals, with particular reference to responsibility towards others, could contribute to a fuller realization of flexicurity, given the importance and culture of the context in which this strategy is implemented.

§3.05 MUTUALLY REINFORCING AXIOLOGICAL PROFILES IN LABOUR LAW

Finally, it is possible to find a further similarity of values between Sustainable Development and labour law in terms of interdependence and mutual reinforcement of balanced interests.

However, the necessary precondition for such a reflection is the adoption of a different perspective, albeit less shared in the doctrinal sphere,[121] with regard to the origins of labour law, understood in terms of capitalist law and market regulation.

This theory underlines the ambivalence of labour law regulation, that is to say it being functional to the production system and at the same time antagonistic of its excesses, having a protective function of the fundamental social rights. This ambivalence is also represented through the idea of a demarcation between the area of 'generic incidence' of competition law, which is manifested in the more general drive towards harmonization of labour legislation with the aim of reducing differentials of national protection, which can affect the competitive position of companies, and the 'specific area of impact', where competition laws interfere with labour law.[122] In particular, according to this perspective, labour law was conceived as a branch of company law, being at the same time an instrument of legal rationalization of the economy and economic rationalization of law.[123] In this perspective, the objective of labour law is to ensure equality in the conditions of competition among companies, with the aim that none of the parties benefits from the other. In fact, Gerard Lyon-Caen believed that

---

all stages of life and access to goods and services; (15) right for employees and self-employed workers to a pension commensurate with their contributions, guaranteeing an adequate income.

121. The main promoters of such theory are Gérard Lyon-Caen, Antoine Jeammaud and Gaetano Vardaro.

122. G. Meliadò, *Concorrenza e politiche sociali*, in A. Baylos Grau, B. Caruso, M. D'Antona, S. Sciarra (a cura di), *Dizionario di diritto del lavoro comunitario*, Monduzzi, Milano, 1996, p. 282.

123. G. Vardaro, *Tecnica, Tecnologia e ideologia della tecnica nel diritto del lavoro*, in *Pol. dir.*, 1986, p. 85.

labour law was conceived as part of the competition law 'à son ombre':[124] according to this theory, the protection of the worker is 'a sub-product' (le sous-produit) of labour law, that is to say a direct consequence of its primary function of guaranteeing fair competition among companies.[125] In fact, since its inception, labour law, in its legislative and collective bargaining component, pursues, alongside the typically protective function of the employed, a task of regulating competition, in a triple direction: (a) to prevent downward competition[126] among workers who struggle - due to excess supply - to enter the world of labour; (b) to limit competition among companies, which, given their position on the market, could otherwise play on labour costs to take advantage of competitors; (c) to reduce, as far as possible, and above all with supranational remedies, competition between regulations or regulatory dumping, which has the effect of provoking capitalist migrations towards countries that are attractive for the lower cost and less labour protection.[127]

Thus adopting this different theory concerning the origins of the discipline, a further convergence between labour law and Sustainable Development could be found: labour law is complementary and functional to competition law in the same way as the social pillars of Sustainable and economic Development are among them complementary and functional to achieving Sustainable Development.

In this perspective, therefore, labour law would not hinder growth or development, but would make the divergent axiological perspectives, such as company growth and the protection of social rights, compatible and mutually reinforcing, making development 'sustainable', that is to say internalizing economic reasons, while maintaining the traditional role of safeguarding the social reasons. Labour law must in fact necessarily be compatible with the efficiency of the economic system because it is a precondition for the protection of the rights that involve a redistributive effect of wealth and for its sizing.[128]

---

124. '*La convention collective a pour fonction d'assurer l'égalisation de la concurrence entre entreprises du même secteur, de même son extension. La législation elle-même, celle sur la sécurité ou la durée du travail tend à éviter que telle entreprise ne s'assure des avantages par rapport aux autres en faisant travailler pour longtemps ou plus «dangereusement»'. Elle se veut éliminatrice du «dumping social». Le Droit du travail est né comme Droit organisant une concurrence équitable entre entreprises, donc comme complémentaire, et non comme d'esprit différent du Droit de la concurrence*». G. Lyon-Caen, *L'infiltration du Droit du travail par le Droit de la concurrence*, in *Droit Ouvrier*, 1992, p. 313.
125. For an interesting reconstruction of the capitalist function of labour law, *see* A. Jeammaud, *Le droit du travail dans le capitalisme, questions de fonctions et de fonctionnement*, in *WP C.S.D.L.E. 'Massimo D'Antona'.INT – 41/2005.*
126. The minimum levels of protection in fields such as wages, working hours and employment conditions are aimed at preventing destructive competition, setting a standard below which working conditions cannot go. S. Deakin, F. Wilkinson, *Il diritto del Lavoro e la teoria economica. Una rivisitazione*, in *Giorn. dir. lav. rel. ind.*, 1999, 84, 4, p. 617; A. Maresca, *Concorrenza tra ordinamenti e diritto del lavoro*, in A. Plaia (a cura di), *La competizione tra ordinamenti giuridici, Mutuo riconoscimento e scelta della norma più favorevole nello spazio giuridico europeo*, Giuffrè, Milano, 2007, p. 115.
127. R. De Luca Tamajo, *Concorrenza e diritto del lavoro*, in A. Perulli (ed.), *L'idea di diritto del lavoro, oggi. In ricordo di Giorgio Ghezzi*, Cedam, Padova, 2016, p. 14.
128. R. Pessi, *Economia e diritto del lavoro*, in *Arg. dir. lav.*, 2006, p. 979.

The balance achieved between the opposing axiological interests does not end in fact in an act of reciprocal limitation of a dimension because it does not prevail over the other: the realization of the single interests (or of the different dimensions of Sustainable Development) is advocate of a mutual interdependence, since a greater economic sustainability contributes to the achievement of social sustainability and vice versa.

The same applies to labour law and to its continuous search for mediation between the economic dimension (interest of the entrepreneur), the social dimension (interest of the worker) and the environmental dimension (interest of the worker in terms of health and safety and interest of the community).

If we consider, for example, the economic and social dimensions, labour law, as we have seen, is by definition a discipline that has appeared and developed precisely to counterbalance the disparities in power that can be found in the contractual employment relationship, in a continuous work of reconciling entrepreneurial economic interests and social interests of workers. However, Sustainable Development suggests considering the realization of an interest as functional to the realization of the convergent interest: in this sense, if the employer provides a company nursery for the employees, the cost incurred would turn into revenue, in terms of greater efficiency and greater productivity on the part of workers who, benefiting from the welfare provision, will feel more involved in corporate life and at the same time, more responsive and productive. The same reasoning also applies to the economic and environmental pillars, both for Sustainable Development and for labour law. Consider, for example, health and safety policies in the workplace: an intervention aimed at improving safety has an immediate advantage for the worker (less risk of accidents) but at the same time, it translates into an economic return for the company (in terms of lower social security costs and lower risk of reputational damage). Furthermore, the entrepreneurial initiatives to limit the release of gas and industrial waste into the environment are indeed adopted by the entrepreneur not only in the interests of the workers, and in a wider perspective, of the entire community and of the environment (social and environmental interests) but also to reduce waste, such as the production or consumption of plastic material, which translates into cost savings (economic interests).

It is in these terms of interdependence among the values protected by labour law that one must read what has been defined as the 'function of labour law of the new millennium': that of achieving a balanced reconciliation between human values and the efficiency needs of the production system that generates the resources to meet those values.[129]

129. *Ibid.*, p. 996.

CHAPTER 4

Sustainable Development: A New Paradigm for Labour Law

§4.01 SPACES OF SUSTAINABILITY

As I have tried to prove, the Sustainable Development paradigm has already found concrete applications in the field of labour law, at the level of European policies (the reference is to the Horizontal Social Clause referred to in Article 9 TFEU, to the European System of Generalized Preferences for Sustainable Development and Good Governance and CSR practices), as well as national legislation (about solidarity contracts and smart work).

However, the proposed research is not exhaustive, since the assumption of Sustainable Development as a reference paradigm in the current process of mutation of the discipline can find in labour law a fertile ground for a potentially boundless propagation and delineation. The reference to the values of solidarity, equality and reconciliation between different axiological levels can in fact be promoted in the context of the regulation of labour relations (from their genesis to their dissolution) and, more generally, in the construction of a labour market where economic growth coexists with social sustainability.

A change of paradigm in the terms advocated could in fact contribute to reversing, or at least to diverting, the deconstructive path of the subject, which has now been underway for a decade, bridging the significant gaps in the regulation of the labour market in social terms, providing, for example, sustainable responses to the issues of disparity between *insiders* and *outsiders*, gender differences, that is to say between pensioners of different ages, in order to achieve, in all these cases, full equality in terms of *capabilities* and opportunities, as called for by the Sustainable Development model. Let's analyse the extent of this scenario.

[A] The Insiders Versus Outsiders Conflict

Although solidarity (pursuant to Article 2 of the Constitution) constitutes one of the founding values of the entire juridical system, it appears to be a conflicting issue among generations, dramatically representing a constitutional problem of intergenerational justice.[1]

This problem of justice and solidarity in terms of employment is evident, for example, in the terms proposed by the *insiders-outsiders* theory developed by Lindbeck and Snower[2] and promoted in Italy by Pietro Ichino, which significantly identifies spaces of reform guided by the principle of Sustainable Development.

Labour law has in fact always been permeated by a twofold conflict: first, between the interests of workers and the rationality of production; second, between the interest of the employed and the people who are looking for a job and cannot find it.[3] With reference to this last conflict, Hugo Sinzheimer, in his fundamental essay on the crisis of labour law, wonders: 'what meaning does labour law have, if, at best, it is a right that is applied to an elite of workers, who are fortunate enough to retain employment, while an economic cemetery of structural unemployment is growing?'[4]

The question is extremely topical, in the light of a strong dualism that has been present for some time in the labour market, primarily in Italy, where there is a clear division in terms of opportunities, rights and resources, between the holders of an open-ended contract[5] (*insiders*) and those who oppose social exclusion and unemployment[6] by alternating flexible, precarious and black work (*outsiders*). A division that has become more acute over time and has manifested itself in what has been called 'the ocean storm of work', triggered by having deliberately put into competition half a billion workers in the world who have enjoyed for a few decades of good wages and

1. M. D'Antona, *Diritto del lavoro di fine secolo, una crisi d'identità?*, in *Riv. giur. lav.*, 1998, 1, p. 326.
2. A. Lindbeck, D. J. Snower, *The Insider-Outsider Theory of Employment and Unemployment*, MIT Press, Cambridge Mass., London, 1988.
3. M. Persiani, *Diritto del lavoro*, Cedam, Padova, 2004, p. 98.
4. H. Sinzheimer, *Arbeitsrechts und Rechtssoziologie*, Europ. Verl.-Anst, Frankfurt, 1976.
5. The Jobs Act actually created a further division among the Insiders themselves, even within the same company, that is to say among the holders of a fixed-term contract taken before 7 March 2015 (date of entry into force of Legislative Decree 4 March 2015, n. 23), and among those hired after, to whom the new discipline applies, that is an evident setback of workplace protections. The order of 26 July 2017 of the Court of Rome declared the question of the constitutional legitimacy to be relevant and not manifestly groundless concerning Art. 1, para. 7, lett. c) of the law n. 193/2014 and Artis 2.3.4 of the D. lgs. 23/2015. About this matter, V. Speziale, *Il contratto a tempo indeterminato a tutele crescenti tra law and economics e vincoli costituzionali*, in *WP C.S.D.L.E. 'Massimo D'Antona'.IT – 259/2015*; S. Giubboni, *Profili costituzionali del contratto di lavoro a tutele crescenti*, in *WP C.S.D.L.E. 'Massimo D'Antona'.IT – 246/2015*; M. V. Ballestrero, *La riforma del lavoro: questioni di costituzionalità*, in *Lav. dir.*, 2015, 1, pp. 39 ss; A. Perulli, *Una questione di 'valore': il Jobs Act alla prova di costituzionalità*, in *Dir. rel. ind.*, 2017, 4, pp. 1059 ss.
6. With reference to the OECD countries, the unemployment rate is less than 4% in the Czech Republic, Iceland, Japan, Korea and Mexico, while in Greece it is 23.4%, in Spain 18.7%, and it is over 10% in Italy, in Portugal and Turkey. OECD, *OECD Employment Outlook*, OECD Publishing, Paris, 2017.

working conditions, with a billion and a half new employees working in distressing conditions with miserable wages.[7]

The labour market can, in fact, be defined according to two levels, or, in more figurative terms, as a fortress that is inaccessible to a part of the workforce: that part which is excluded not only from the current benefits but also from a reasonable hope of benefitting from future of prosperity ensured to those who managed to enter into such a fortress.[8] The difficulty in entering the labour market for *outsiders* is due to the lack of convenience for companies to replace *insiders* because of replacement costs, given by the sum of dismissal costs (the limitation of dismissals can be considered as one of the most effective barriers protecting *insiders* against the *outsiders*' competition) and those of employment of *outsiders*, being such costs linked, for the most part, to the training of the latter and the selection of personnel.

Starting from these assumptions, the intensification of the protection against dismissal and the salary improvements obtained by the *insiders* may therefore constitute[9] an obstacle for the unemployed to access the protected fortress, having on the contrary the effect of pushing the system towards the *insider-outsider* model. On the basis of these premises, the *insiders* can achieve a positive salary difference with respect to the salary level to which the *outsiders* can aspire, corresponding to the cost of their replacement: the existence of this replacement cost prevents the *outsiders* from competing on equal terms with the insiders, and therefore from lowering wages to a level that guarantees full employment. The problem would therefore seem to be attributable mostly to wage rigidity: the *insiders* are able to have and maintain higher wage levels than those that *outsiders* would be willing to accept to enter the labour market, due to replacement costs that would weigh on the employer.[10]

It therefore appears evident that labour law plays a fundamental role in protecting the excluded from the fortress guarded by the labour law discipline and in the effective promotion of solidarity in the labour market, since the underlying dualism of the *insider-outsiders* theory can legitimately be applied also to other categories of

---

7. L. Gallino, *Il lavoro non è una merce. Contro la Flessibilità*, Laterza, Roma, 2007, Prefazione.
8. A. Ichino, P. Ichino, *A chi serve il diritto del lavoro*, in *Riv. it. dir. lav.*, 1994, 1, p. 500.
9. Using a conditional tense is mandatory since according to other authoritative doctrine, there is no empirical evidence that proves that the legislative protection of employment has a negative effect on unemployment rates. *See* Vedi L. M. Kahn, *The Impact of Employment Protection Mandates on Demographic Temporary Employment Patterns: International Microeconomic Evidence*, in *Economic Journal*, 2007, vol. 117 (521), F333–F356; R. Del Punta, *Economic Challenge to Labour Law*, in A. Lyon-Caen, A. Perulli, *Valutare il diritto del Lavoro, Evaluer le Droit du Travail, Evaluate Labour Law*, Cedam, Padova, 2010, p. 87.
10. On this point, remember the Shapiro-Stiglitz model (1984), according to which although the unemployed are offered lower salaries than the employed, companies should not substitute one with the other because it is believed that there is a direct relationship between levels of the salary and level of the work commitment, according to which if the salary is high enough to satisfy and gratify the workers, the latter feel responsible to commit themselves to perform their work. C. Shapiro, J. E. Stiglitz, *Equilibrium Unemployment as a Worker Discipline Device*, in *The American Economic Review*, 1984, 74, 3, pp. 433-444. Cfr. A. Ichino, P. Ichino, *A chi serve il diritto del lavoro*, in *Riv. it. dir. lav.*, 1994, p. 475.

individuals: unionized and non-unionized workers, permanent and temporary workers, public sector and private sector workers, workers in large or small companies, young people and adults, men and women, and so on.

In order to guarantee a fair distribution of unemployment risk and therefore a greater *turnover* between *insiders* and *outsiders* in a more fluid labour market, a double intervention would be necessary: (i) a decrease in costs of dismissals, (ii) and a simultaneous decrease in hiring costs.

On the merits, Sustainable Development could indeed guide the interventionist spirit of the legislator by promoting the adoption of some concrete reforms with a view to a more correct balancing of the entrepreneurial need (economic interest) with respect to the protection of the worker during dismissal (social interest).

This would not mean a tout-court decrease in the allowances recognized in the event of dismissal for economic, illegitimate or discriminatory reason, since the dismantling of the protections benefitted from by *insiders*, justified by the need to redistribute them in the area of *outsiders* in order to reconstruct the division between guaranteed and not guaranteed people, would achieve nothing but an equality within insecurity deriving from the re-emergence of the risk of expulsion from the labour market.[11] It is no coincidence that the theories of *law and economics*, which have imported in the labour policies the (hyper-liberal) hypothesis according to which the reduction of safeguards for employed workers automatically produces an increase in the chances for the unemployed, are fallacious, therefore any intervention of deregulation would be useful for occupational and productive expansion.[12]

The adoption of a Sustainable Development perspective in order to reduce dismissal costs (point i) is rather transformed into a more correct integration of the economic value (or entrepreneurial interest) in this delicate phase of the employment relationship, in the sense of guaranteeing the employer the *certainty* of his own choices. A certainty that could be realized by eliminating all secondary dismissal costs (secondary only in reference to the temporal occurrence following the event) linked precisely to the uncertainty of the outcome of a termination of the relationship, by reason of the uncertainty of the judgments and of the duration of the causes.[13]

This would guarantee the employer a greater propensity to hire (even for an indefinite period) without the fear of having to bear completely random consequences, thus eliminating the disproportionate use of flexible contract types even in the face of stable and lasting staffing needs, opening up therefore the doors of the famous

11. Cfr. L. Gaeta, *Verso un diritto diseguale senza diseguaglianze*, in L. Gaeta, L. Zoppoli (a cura di), *Il diritto diseguale: la legge sulle azioni positive*, Giappichelli, Torino, 1992; U. Romagnoli, *Il diritto del lavoro nel prisma del principio d'eguaglianza*, in *Riv. trim. dir. proc. civ.*, 1997, p. 544.
12. Cfr. L. Mariucci, *Le politiche del lavoro di fronte alla crisi*, in *Riv. it. dir. lav.*, 2009, 3, p. 129.
13. The reference is to the possibility of legitimately dismissing an employee without running the risk of being involved in a multi-year dispute for the possible (groundless) appeal of the dismissal involved and of having to eventually reintegrate the worker after years of dismissal (or, as it is often in the case of reinstatement, to recognize him a cumulative disproportionate allowance for procedural delays) in the face of an incontrovertible judicial error, which could compromise even the existence of the company because of the (unexpected) financial outlay asked.

fortress.[14] However, a better reconciliation of the social interest in the terms proposed by Sustainable Development could result in an adequate protection of the worker in the case of illegitimate or unjustified dismissals (in terms of a fair allowance commensurate with seniority and tasks carried out within the company, but without the employer being able to monetize the price of an illegitimate or unjustified dismissal downwards), as well as in the provision of adequate universal income support instruments in the phases in which the worker is unemployed.

The dismissal costs, since they are also determined by the costs related to the replacement of the staff incurred by the employer, could also be reduced by a more efficient match between the demand and the supply of labour, that is to say a better functioning of the labour market.

In this regard, Sustainable Development could act as a reference paradigm for the realization of greater social cohesion, pushing the legislator to provide efficient and free services in the labour market, not only in terms of a better mediation between labour supply and demand but also through continuous training programmes and professional requalification aimed at the employment opportunities actually existing in the market, so as to facilitate the worker previously dismissed to rapidly return into the labour market, without any loss of professionalism or *know-how* already acquired, or through the provision of appropriate professional guidance services for those wishing to enter the labour market. This could be achieved, for example, through a structural reform of the Employment Centres system - that are currently inefficient[15] - for example, by providing for the creation, on the part of these centres, of a digital platform that favours a real-time *matching* between job demand and supply, thus taking advantage of the new technologies of the fourth industrial revolution.

---

14. Such a reform of the rules on dismissals is, moreover, in line with what was proposed by the Jobs Act in terms of the contract with increasing protections, which has the merit of reducing and making the cost of the dismissal calculable *ex ante*, by proportioning it to the seniority of the worker involved.
15. For a deeper analysis on the issue of the inefficiency of Employment Centres: P. Ichino, *Il collocamento impossibile. Problemi e obiettivi della riforma del mercato del lavoro*, De Donato, Bari, 1982; M. Rusciano, *Il lavoro come diritto: servizi per l'impiego e decentramento amministrativo*, in *Riv. giur. lav.*, 1999, p. 25; P. Giannotti, *Gli orientamenti comunitari e internazionali in materia di collocamento*, in P. Olivelli (a cura di), *Il 'collocamento' tra pubblico e privato*, Giuffrè, Milano, 2003; M. Tiraboschi (a cura di), *La riforma del collocamento e i nuovi servizi per l'impiego*, Giuffrè, Milano, 2003; A. Alaimo, *I servizi all'impiego e l'art. 4 Cost. dopo le recenti riforme del mercato del lavoro*, in *Dir. lav. rel. ind.*, 2004, 2, pp. 249 ss; M. R. Freedland, N. Countouris, *Diritti e doveri nel rapporto tra disoccupati e servizi per l'impiego in Europa*, in *Dir. lav. rel. ind.*, 2005, 4, pp. 557 ss; G. Falasca, *I servizi privati per l'impiego*, Giuffrè, Milano, 2006; V. Filì, *Le deleghe per il riordino della normativa in materia di servizi per l'impiego e incentivi all'occupazione*, in F. Carinci, M. Miscione (a cura di), *Il Collegato lavoro 2008. L. n. 24 dicembre 2007, n. 247*, Ipsoa, Milano, 2008, pp. 19 e ss.; M. Napoli, A. Occhino, M. Corti, *I servizi per l'impiego. Art. 2098 c.c.*, Giuffrè, Milano, 2010; D. Garofalo, *Le novità in tema di servizi per l'impiego e di politica attiva del lavoro*, in F. Carinci (a cura di), *La politica del lavoro del Governo Renzi, Atti del X Seminario di Bertinoro-Bologna del 23-24 ottobre 2014*, Adapt University Press, Modena, 2015, p. 320; V. Cagnin, *Art. 10, L. 81 del 22 maggio 2017 ed il nuovo sportello di servizi al lavoro per i lavoratori autonomi: funzioni, soggetti coinvolti e criticità contestuali*, in A. Perulli, L. Fiorillo (a cura di), *Il Jobs act del lavoro autonomo e del lavoro agile*, Giappichelli, Torino, 2017; M. Ricci, *I servizi per l'impiego dopo le modifiche legislative tra luci e ombre*, in *Arg. dir. lav.*, 2017, 2, p. 326.

Moreover, a more fluid labour market would entail not only a reduction in dismissal costs, in the sense of facilitating the employer in the search for a new employee to replace the dismissed, but above all, a reduction in employment costs (point ii), guaranteeing equal opportunities for the access to the labour market, better employability in the labour market and an easier and faster reintegration of workers who have lost their jobs. If, moreover, the individual was able to have another job in a short time, the share of expenditure linked to social safety nets would also decrease, with a clear economic return for the overall public system.

The simultaneous realization of these reforms would guarantee the possibility of being able to see the dismissal as a natural moment of transition in the working life of an individual, being part of the normal evolution of a contractual relationship, which assures the worker a necessary indemnity while waiting for a new job.

Labour, in the light of the continuous policies of flexibility, should in fact now be considered not as a condition (the positioning inside or outside the fortress of labour law) but as a path (of continuous entry and exit from the walls). For this reason, it becomes essential to take care of the increase of the subjects' employability, through, for example, the continuous training of workers, so that the transition from one employer to another is experienced as an opportunity for the worker to better take advantage of his own cultural and experiential background, in a career-development perspective and no longer perceived in terms of a negative stigma of a subject's working life, which makes him/her less attractive in the labour market in a future reintegration.

This perspective would be consistent with what was recently suggested by the EU through the European Social Pillar, that is, in terms of equal opportunities for the access to the labour market, fair working conditions, security and social inclusion, and with what has been established internationally by Objective 8 of the *MDGs* ('*Promoting lasting, inclusive and sustainable economic growth, full and productive employment and decent work for all*').

Moreover, the realization of the interventions in the terms proposed here would be in line with a more correct application of the flexicurity policies, promoted for years but so far achieved, as already noted, only on the side of flexibility, rather than from that of security, since the transfer of protection from the employment relationship to the labour market[16] is not yet fully completed because of the malfunctions of the latter.

[B] The 'Unsustainability' of the Current Pension System

According to Article 38 of the Italian Constitution '*Every citizen unable to work and without the necessary means of subsistence shall be entitled to welfare support.*' (1st paragraph), and the '*workers shall be entitled to adequate means for their living requirements in case of accidents, illness, disability, old age and involuntary unemployment*' (2nd paragraph). Such provisions must be read together with Article 2 of the same Constitutional Charter, pursuant to which '*the Republic shall recognise and*

16. In this sense, *see* para. 3.4.1.

protect the inviolable rights of the person, both as an individual and in the social groups where human personality is expressed. The Republic expects that the fundamental duties of political, economic and social solidarity be fulfilled.'

Although pension assistance and solidarity among citizens are principles that are constitutionally protected, the current pension system is neither fair nor sustainable.[17]

Leaving aside an analysis of the functioning of the Italian pension system,[18] for the purposes of the present research it is sufficient to recall how it originally was salary-oriented, based on a sort of solidarity among generations, that is to say on the responsibility of the present social groups towards future ones, recognizing the existence of a subjective passive legal situation of the present generations towards future generations. This mechanism was balanced until, starting from the 1970s, the progressive demographic decline has shown a clear difficulty in financing the benefits of pensioners with the increasingly small contributions of fewer and fewer young people, pushing for the passage (happened in 1995 with the Dini reform) to a contribution-based calculation system, that is to say based on the contributions paid over the years by the worker, according to the logic of 'the more I pay, the more I receive'.

Although the solution adopted seems to be considered the only viable alternative available, the transition from a salary-based to a contribution-based system has given rise to a series of problems in terms of generational equity, in the sense that today there are pensioners who receive generous pensions, despite a low level of contributions paid, while the current generations of young workers, given the precariousness and the intermittence of their career,[19] risk to receive smaller pensions than those of previous generations precisely because of the discontinuity of contributions, reinforcing obvious discrimination among pensioners of different generations.

It is precisely on the basis of this premise that we highlight the need to go back to the values of solidarity and fairness (equality of possibilities) in terms of social security, as advocated by Sustainable Development. On this point, there are already two recent constitutional reform projects aimed at the formal recognition, within the Constitution, of the right of future generations to a decent pension, in order to ensure young people a fair pension by switching to the contribution-based system, in a logic of solidarity and equity among successive generations.

The first (*Mazziotti di Celso*[20]), aimed at '*ensuring intergenerational equity in social security and welfare treatments*', proposes replacing the fourth paragraph of Article 38 of the Constitution with the following: '*The tasks provided for in this article*

17. About the conflict among generations, pension-wise: T. Boeri, V. Galasso, *Contro i giovani: come l'Italia sta tradendo le nuove generazioni*, Mondadori, Milano, 2007.
18. P. Barcellona, *La solidarietà come fatto e come diritto*, in *Lav. dir.*, 1996, 4-5, p. 59; M. Napoli (a cura di), *La solidarietà*, Vita e Pensiero, Milano, 2009; S. Rodotà, *Solidarietà. Un'utopia necessaria*, Laterza, Roma, 2014; M. Fioravanti, *Costituzione italiana: articolo 2*, Carocci, Roma, 2017.
19. L. Menghini, *Le cause della precarietà e le norme del diritto del lavoro*, in AA.VV. (a cura di), *Scritti in onore di Edoardo Ghera*, Cacucci, Bari, vol. 1, 2008.
20. Constitutional Law Proposal Mazziotti di Celso and others: 'Amendment to Article 38 of the Constitution to ensure intergenerational equity in social security and welfare' (No. 3478) presented on 4 December 2015.

are carried out by organs and institutions set up or integrated by the State according to principles of equity, reasonableness and non-discrimination among generations.'

The second (*Preziosi*[21]), aimed at '*ensuring the fairness and sustainability of social security treatments*', proposes inserting the following sentence after the second paragraph of Article 38 of the Constitution: '*The social security system is aimed at ensuring the adequacy of the treatments, solidarity and equity among generations and financial sustainability.*'

The proposals under investigation intend to raise political awareness on the issue of non-discrimination among generations. And to this end, the proponents hope for constitutional interventions in order to include in the Constitutional Charter a principle that protects the future generations from policies that charge the costs of the previous onto present and future generations. For this reason, both projects of reform of constitutional law stand, in line with the Sustainable Development paradigm, on the concept of non-discrimination, as well as on that of solidarity and equity among generations, considering them as key values to face the problems of sustainability of the pension system due to the constant aging of the population, constituting a potentially and severely destabilizing factor of the system itself.[22]

A constitutional reform project of this type could stimulate significant structural reforms of the pension system and, more generally, new labour policies, which go beyond the continuous and progressive increase of the retirement age in correspondence with the extension of life expectancy.[23] If, in fact, the mechanism for adjusting the retirement age to the life expectancy established by the Fornero Law can undoubtedly have the merit of increasing the pension system contribution area (leaving aside any evaluation regarding the obligation to work until old age, precluding the possibility of dedicating oneself to other interests in the last years of life), the need for further solidarity-type interventions aimed at guaranteeing adequate pensions for the current young people and the new generations is evident.

On this point, the adoption of a Sustainable Development logic could induce the legislator to provide for figurative contributions for pension purposes in periods of non-employment (in the light of job insecurity) or interventions to support (youth) employment, to broaden the tax base, or, with a view to the full realization of the principle of solidarity, to carry out a levy on 'more generous' pensions to protect actuarial and intergenerational equity:[24] asking pensioners in condition of relative wealth and who received more to participate in the distribution of the sacrifices

---

21. Constitutional Law Proposal Preziosi and others: 'Amendment to Article 38 of the Constitution to ensure the fairness and sustainability of social security benefits' (No. 3858) presented on 15 May 2016, being examined by the Commission from 25 May 2017.
22. M. Cinelli, *La sfida demografica al sistema delle pensioni tra immaginario e realtà*, in *Riv. dir. sic. soc.*, 2003, 2, p. 433; R. Blanpain, *Le differenze di trattamento e la discriminazione connessa all'età: una società per tutte le età*, in *Dir. rel. ind.*, 2005, 4, p. 942.
23. In the two-year period of 2016-2017, the retirement age in Italy was expected to be 66 years and 7 months for men and 65 years and 7 months for women (64 years and 3 months and 63 and 7 months, respectively, the average for OECD countries: Cfr. Report OECD, *Pensions at a Glance 2017: How Does ITALY Compare?* 5 December 2017, OECD). The threshold was raised for 2018 to 66 years and 7 months for men and women, and to 67 for 2019.
24. T. Boeri, T. Nannicini, *Non per cassa, ma per equità*, 30 maggio 2013, lavoceinfo.

required by the adjustment of the intergenerational balance of incomes does not seem to be in conflict with the principles of our Constitution.[25] In this way, it would be possible to limit the burden, for the current generations of young workers, of investing in supplementary pension funds[26] in order to avoid the risk of not receiving an adequate pension upon retirement from working life.

The importance of intergenerational solidarity has also been sanctioned several times by the Constitutional Court: with sentence n. 88 of 2014, the Court recognized the new principle of public debt sustainability as a responsibility towards future generations. According to the Court, the new principles introduced by the constitutional law n. 1 of 2012 on the balanced budget[27] and, in particular, that of the sustainability of public debt, imply a responsibility that, in the implementation of the 'founding' constitutional principles (sentence n. 264 of 2012) of solidarity and equality, is not only pertaining to institutions but also to all citizens reciprocally, including those of future generations.[28]

Similar interventions would also be in line both with the introduction of the balanced budget principle in the Constitutional Charter and with what is promoted by the European Social Pillar in terms of protection and social inclusion: '*a) Retired employees and self-employed workers have the right to a pension commensurate with their contributions and that guarantees an adequate income. Women and men have equal opportunities to earn pension rights. b) Every person of advanced age has the right to resources that guarantee a decent life.*[29]

The adoption of social security policies inspired by the paradigm of Sustainable Development could therefore result, also in the matter of pensions, useful for a revision of the constitutionally protected principles that are too often ignored in the processes of construction of norms and in political decisions.

25. On this point, it should be noted that in recent years the legislator has repeatedly intervened on higher-value pensions through solidarity contributions consisting of an extraordinary levy made on incomes exceeding a certain amount. On the merits, the Constitutional Court, with sentence 173 of 2016, rejected the various questions of constitutionality relating to this last solidarity contribution, excluding its fiscal nature and considering that it is a solidarity contribution within the social security system, exceptionally justified by the contingent and serious crisis of the system itself. The Court also considered that this contribution respects the principle of progressivity and, while undeniably entailing a sacrifice for the affected pensioners, is nonetheless sustainable since it is applied only to higher pensions (from fourteen to over thirty times higher than the minimum pensions).
26. Cfr. G. Sigillò Massara, *L'insostenibile tensione verso il welfare mix, tra fondi di solidarietà bilaterali e previdenza complementare*, in *Riv. dir. sic. soc.*, 2017, 3, pp. 481-498; G. Castellani, *Il rilancio della previdenza complementare: luci e ombre di una rivoluzione incompiuta*, in *Riv. dir. sic. soc.*, 2017, 3, pp. 565-592.
27. The Fiscal Compact has had as its effect the transposition in Art. 81 of the Constitution of the balanced budget by force of the constitutional law of 20 April 2012, n. 1.
28. About the topic, L. Menghini, *I contrasti tra Corte EDU e Corte Costituzionale sulle leggi retroattive che eliminano i diritti di lavoratori e pensionati: qualche idea per un avvio di soluzione*, in *Riv. giur. lav. prev. soc.*, 2012, 2, pp. 362-380.
29. European Commission, Recommendation (EU) 2017/761 of the Commission of 26 April 2017 on the European pillar of social rights, Objective 15.

[C] Gender Inequality and Gender Pay Gap

Despite the equality of opportunity is one of the traditional objectives of labour law, and although the two genders have long been legally placed on a level playing field (at least formally) both by national and European sources, the statistical data show how full and effective equality between men and women in the field of labour is still far from being achieved.[30]

In fact, the gender pay gap, and more broadly, the gender gap (in terms of not only pay but also employment, market access, career opportunities and, consequently, pension coverage) is a complex phenomenon, attributable to a series of interconnected factors, including those of social-cultural origin. In fact, in addition to direct discrimination (i.e., the case in which women are paid less than men even when they carry out the same work in the same position), which are expressly prohibited and sanctioned by the law,[31] the gender gap derives from a multiplicity of coexistent factors, among which the differences between man and woman are noted in terms of education, work

30. With reference to the *gender gap*, although in Europe between 2008 and 2016 the gender gap in employment rates progressively decreased, stabilizing over the past two years at an average of 10.4 percentage points (from 13.7 in 2008), in Italy it settled at 18.4 points in 2016 (compared to 22.9 in 2008). *See* 'The Labour Market Report: Slow Recovery and Disparities in Social Groups', ISTAT 2017. Despite the higher level of education of women in active age (53.8% of women have a diploma or degree compared to 49.2% of men, mainly due to the higher incidence of university graduates), in 2016 the employment rate for women between the ages of 15 and 64 stood at 48.1 percent, with a distance of 18.4 percentage points compared to men (66.5 percent), with a gender gap in employment rates much lower in the Centre-North (about -15 percentage points) than in the South (-23.6 percentage points). Furthermore, 25.9% of women who want to work do not find employment against 18.2% of men, and the gender gap is five times higher than in Europe (7.7 points versus 1.7). *See* Bes Report, 'Fair and Sustainable Wellness in Italy: Work and Reconciliation of Life Times', ISTAT, 15 December 2017, p. 61. If reference is made to the recent OECD data, the situation does not change: the gap appears both in terms of annual income (Italy has a 45% gap, against an OECD average of 38%), and in terms of earnings for full-time workers (Italy 6%, OECD 10%), and in terms of employment (Italy 28%, OECD 21%) (OECD (2017), OECD Employment Outlook 2017, OECD Publishing, Paris, http://dx.doi.org/10.1787/empl_outlook-2017-en, pp. 31-33). If we then consider the gaps that can be found in the most diverse areas ranging from education to health, from work to life expectancy up to the acquisition of power in the political field, the gender gap in terms of opportunities in Italy between men and women not only continues to widen over the years but marks a dramatic decline: in the global ranking compiled by the Word Economic Forum, Italy, compared to last year, loses 32 positions, falling to 82nd out of a total of 144 countries taken in a survey (Top of the rankings: Ireland, Norway, Finland, Sweden. The last: Yemen, Pakistan Syria, Chad, Iran and Mali. *Source:* World Economic Centre, The Global Gender Gap Report 2017, November 2017.
31. It constitutes direct discrimination, pursuant to Art 25 of the Law 125/1991, '*any act, pact or behaviour that produces a prejudicial effect discriminating against male or female workers on the basis of their sex and, in any case, less favourable treatment than that of another male worker or another female worker in similar situation*'. With reference, for example, to the principle of equal pay, this is constitutionally protected in Italy, pursuant to Art 37, according to which the working woman has the same rights and 'for equal work' has the right 'to the same wages that belong to the male worker'. The concept is also reiterated in Art. 28 of D. lgs. 198/2006, entitled 'Prohibition of Pay Discrimination', which provides in the first paragraph for the prohibition of 'any direct or indirect discrimination, concerning any aspect or condition of remuneration, as regards the same job or any other job with an equal value' and, in the second paragraph, 'the obligation to adopt common criteria for men and women in 'professional classification systems for the purpose of determining remuneration', which must be 'processed in order to eliminate

experience, school career choices, number of hours worked, type of work sector, type of activity performed, as well as the choice (or burden) of taking care of parents or of carrying out unpaid housework.[32]

In light of the gender inequity detected, the legislator recently intervened with the Jobs Act,[33] in order to increase the participation of women in the labour market and their professional development, protecting motherhood and enhancing parenting experience. The most significant changes include the provision of greater flexibility in taking compulsory maternity leave (paid leave of 30%, usable up to the child's 6 years of age (8 for low income groups) and unpaid up to 12 years of age; automaticity of benefits for working mothers registered in the Special Fund for independent workers (failure to pay contributions by the buyer will not jeopardize the use of maternity benefits), the equalization of the rights of adoptive and foster parents in parental leave; the introduction of a three-month leave for female employees who are victims of gender-based violence and included in protection programmes, which can also be used on an hourly basis.[34]

Undoubtedly, these are goals that have long been advocated, especially in the process of extending the protections so far recognized only to women employees, therefore in line with the general trend of widening the protection provisions also to those who are outside the sphere of subordination, but nevertheless, we cannot certainly consider these measures as a solution to the problem of gender inequality and the gender pay gap.

---

discrimination' (article as amended by Legislative Decree 25 January 2010, n. 5 of Implementation of Directive 2006/54/EC on the principle of equal opportunities and equal treatment of men and women in matters of employment and occupation).

32. About the issue of gender discrimination: M. Barbera, *Discriminazioni ed eguaglianza nel rapporto di lavoro*, Giuffrè, Milano, 1991; L. Menghini, *Efficacia diretta delle fonti comunitarie esaurienti ed effetti dissuasivi nella discriminazione per sesso*, in *Riv. giur. lav.*, 1994, 45, p. 696; M. Barbera, *L'eguaglianza come scudo e l'eguaglianza come spada*, in *Riv. giur. lav.*, 2002, 1, pp. 805 ss; M. Barbera, *Eguaglianza e differenza nella nuova stagione del diritto antidiscriminatorio*, in *Dir. lav. rel. ind.*, 2003, p. 399; D. Gottardi, *Dalle discriminazioni di genere alle discriminazioni doppie e sovrapposte: le transizioni*, in *Dir. lav. rel. ind.*, 2004, p. 447; M. Barbera (a cura di), *Il nuovo diritto antidiscriminatorio: il quadro comunitario e nazionale*, Giuffrè, Milano, 2007; F. Guarriello, *Il ruolo delle istituzioni e della società civile nel nuovo diritto antidiscriminatorio*, ivi; D. Gottardi (a cura di), *Il diritto antidiscriminatorio tra teoria e prassi applicativa*, Ediesse, Roma, 2009; F. Guarriello, *Discriminazioni (divieto di)*, (con M. C. Cimaglia), in P. Lambertucci, *Dizionari del diritto privato promossi da N. Irti, Diritto del lavoro*, Giuffrè, Milano, 2010, pp. 177-187; A. Lassandari, *Le discriminazioni nel lavoro. Nozione, interessi, tutele*, Cedam, Padova, 2010; G. De Simone, *Tra il dire e il fare. Obiettivi e tecniche delle politiche per il lavoro femminile nella riforma Fornero*, in *Lav. dir.*, 2012, p. 589; S. Scarponi (a cura di), *Diritto e genere. Analisi interdisciplinare e comparata*, Cedam, Padova, 2014; L. Calafà, *D.lgs. 11 aprile 2006, n. 198 codice delle pari opportunità, Commentario Breve alle leggi sul Lavoro*, Cedam, Padova, 2018, pp. 2307-2312.
33. D. lgs. 15 giugno 2015, n. 80, Misure per la conciliazione delle esigenze di cura, di vita e di lavoro (in attuazione dell'articolo 1, commi 8 e 9, della Law 183/2014).
34. For more detailed analysis, refer to: B. Caruso, *La tutela della maternità dopo il Jobs Act*, in F. Besenghi, A. Russo (a cura di), *Flessibilità, sicurezza e occupazione alla prova del Jobs Act*, Giappichelli, Torino, 2016; E. Dagnino, M. Menegotto, L. M. Pelusi, M. Tiraboschi (a cura di), *Guida pratica al lavoro agile dopo la legge n. 81/2017*, Adapt University Press, Modena, 2017; M. L. Vallauri, *Tutela della salute a sostegno della genitorialità*, in L. Fiorillo, A. Perulli (a cura di), *Il Jobs act del lavoro autonomo e del lavoro agile, Il nuovo diritto del lavoro*, Giappichelli, Torino, 2018, pp. 125-138.

The realization of gender equality and the improvement of the living conditions of women (as hoped for by Objective 5 of *MDGs*) or the promotion of lasting, inclusive and sustainable economic growth, of full and productive employment and a decent job for all (MDGs, Objective 8), certainly cannot be fulfilled in the light of these minimal (albeit important) legislative innovations, although this umpteenth regulatory intervention demonstrates the fundamental role played by labour law in achieving equality of opportunity, in the terms proposed by the *Capability Approach* and by Sustainable Development.

The contribution that the labour law discipline can give in this respect is essential, in terms both of prevention of discrimination as well as of promotional measures that attribute specific advantages, such as a better reconciliation of care-giving time and working hours, through particular prohibition techniques or with flexible schedule arrangements. Again, the legislator could envisage corporate *welfare* mechanisms, recognizing tax or social security contributions reliefs for entrepreneurs who promote such benefits or providing public services that relieve women of care tasks at a more reasonable price than those practiced on the market, since some women renounce the occupation because they receive less salary than what they spend on the nursery school of their children or in *baby-sitting* services. Such interventions could compensate for disadvantaged situations, contributing to achieving effective equality between men and women, in terms of substantial equality.

In this perspective, the working woman will be able to benefit from the freedom 'to be able to do' or 'to be what she wants to do or be', as suggested by the theory of capabilities applied to labour law, reconciling the role of worker and mother with greater flexibility, without having to forcefully renounce one or the other status.[35]

§4.02 LABOUR LAW: A SUSTAINABILITY LAW

In light of the value similarities found between the Sustainable Development paradigm and labour law, as well as of the concrete and potential applications of the Sustainable Development paradigm to labour law, the opportunity to elect Sustainable Development as a new theoretical reference model for the subject, in order to ponder about its effects on labour law and for labour law, represents an unprecedented and promising research perspective.

35. Note how the *child-gap*, that is to say the distance between the number of desired children (2) and the number of children actually had (1) is due for the most part to the problematic relationship between women and work. If the woman does not work, caring for children is not a problem, but the family's economic situation remains vulnerable and the expansion of the family itself is likely to cause severe strains on the family budget. If the woman works, the economic situation is more prosperous and stable, but combining work and children becomes a big problem given the scarcity of nursery schools, high costs and reduced hours, to the point that many women are forced to stop working after having their first baby. The ISTAT data confirms for 2016 (latest available data) the tendency to decrease in fertility underway since 2010. The average number of children per woman dropped to 1.34 (1.46 in 2010). The sharp contraction of the first children, from 283,922 in 2008 to 227,412 in 2016 (-20% for the first children and -16% for the children of the next order), affects all areas of the country. *Source:* ISTAT, birth rate and fecundity of the resident population, Report Year 2016 of 28 November 2017.

In the first place, the adoption of this principle as a framework for labour law discipline could be useful in order to overcome the current impasse of the labour law discipline in regulating in a fair and effective way the employment relationship, as well as the labour market, in the light of the profound changes that have taken place in the current phase of economic globalization.

This could happen in two subsequent steps, that is to say in a prior revision of the normative data and in a (possible) subsequent modification of the latter.

More specifically, the promotion of this new axiological paradigm could (first step) induce a revision and reinterpretation of the current legislation in order to preserve its protective function (due process guarantee), rediscovering its foundations, values and original ratio. In particular, what is proposed is a revision of labour law and its Constitutional principles,[36] nowadays largely in crisis, in order to relaunch the social and economic legitimacy of the subject as it is functional to the adoption of a truly sustainable development model.

In the same way, I suggest to commentators, witnesses of this convulsive mutation of the matter, as well as to the legislator, advocate of this process, to stop and ideally rediscover the original identity of the matter and to identify the point (or points) of its crisis. If it is true that the continuous pushes external to flexibility have diverted the course of the evolution of the discipline, it is equally true that the latter has eventually accepted to be bent by them in order to go along with them, ending up sacrificing its actual foundational values. Perhaps because this was really the only way forward. Or maybe because it was considered to be as such.

Sustainable Development could guide the commentator and the legislator in this backwards process, acting as a torch in order for the rediscovery of the discipline's foundations (and for their possible, consequent revision), as well as for identifying any alternative ways that could be undertaken in the light of sustainable growth.

Such an operation of profound revision of the values and functions of labour law in the perspective of sustainability could be useful not only for decision-makers but also in a judicial field, in order to support in an interpretative way a more adequate promotion of social values, and a more appropriate reconciliation compared to economic values, also on the basis of the work of the European and international courts.[37]

---

36. Concerning the issue of labour law within the Constitution, refer to: G. F. Mancini, sub Art. 4, in G. Branca (a cura di), *Commentario della Costituzione*, Zanichelli-Il Foro Italiano, Bologna-Roma, 1975; L. Gaeta (a cura di), *Costantino Mortati e 'Il lavoro nella Costituzione': una ri-lettura*, Giuffrè, Milano, 2005; A. Apostoli, *L'ambivalenza costituzionale del lavoro tra libertà e diritto sociale*, Giuffrè, Milano, 2005; A. Alaimo, *Il diritto sociale al lavoro nei mercati integrati*, Giappichelli, Torino, 2009; E. Ghera, A. Pace (a cura di), *L'attualità dei principi fondamentali della Costituzione in materia di lavoro*, Jovene, Napoli, 2009; P. Lambertucci, *Il diritto al lavoro tra principi costituzionali e discipline di tutela: brevi appunti*, in *Riv. it. dir. lav.*, 2010, 1, pp. 91 ss; G. Zagrebelsky, *Fondata sul lavoro*, Einaudi, Torino, 2013; L. Gaeta (a cura di), *Prima di tutto il lavoro. La costituzione di un diritto all'Assemblea Costituente*, Ediesse, Roma, 2014; A. Occhino, *I diritti sociali nell'interpretazione costituzionale*, in *Riv. dir. sic. soc.*, 2017, 1, pp. 3-28; E. Longo, *I diritti sociali nella Costituzione italiana: un percorso di analisi*, in *Riv. dir. sic. soc.*, 2017, 2, pp. 201-236.
37. For more detailed information on the application of the principle of Sustainable Development in court, please refer to §1.06 'Jurisprudential Remarks'.

Such a hermeneutical activity could be very helpful in guiding the already initiated genetic mutation of labour law,[38] so that the evolutionary process of the matter (the actual 'development' of the latter) does not deny the fundamental backbone of the discipline of the twentieth century, but consider it rather as a starting value base for the development of 'sustainable' norms more suitable to the new context, profoundly changed due to the important social, economic, political and technological transformations that have taken place over the past decades.

Adopting Sustainable Development as a new paradigm for labour law discipline could then (second step) allow the adoption of new rules, in the terms proposed in this research work, that is to say of standards' schemes that are more consistent with the needs of a correct balance and reconciliation between different and, at times, conflicting axiological interests, but being actually pertaining to the context of sustainability, thanks to the necessary reference to the values of equity, solidarity and equality, in line with what is suggested not only by Sustainable Development but also by the *Capability Approach*.

A legislative intervention of this kind should concern both national legislation (for the purpose, for example, of reducing labour market conflicts between *insiders* and *outsiders*, reducing the *gender gap*, improving the sustainability of the pension system and guaranteeing the universality of social safety nets), and, even more urgently, international legislation.

The principle of Sustainable Development, already widely present in the European and international institutional and jurisprudential fabric, could also be useful in the construction of an international labour law that is more modern and interrelated with the economic dynamics compared to the traditional one, for example, by becoming integrated with international trade regulations.[39]

As a matter of fact, labour law, like any policy or reform, can no longer be considered a purely national matter: the legal boundaries of sovereignty are fading

38. V. Speziale, *La mutazione*, in M. P. Iadicicco, V. Nuzzo (a cura di), *Le riforme del diritto del lavoro. Politiche e tecniche normative*, Editoriale Scientifica, Napoli, 2016, in *Dir. lav. mer.* 2016.
39. Regarding the matter of social clauses, and, more generally, about the social dimension in the international trade market regulation, refer to: M.-A. Moreau, *Normes sociales, droit du travail et mondialisation*, Dalloz, Paris, 2006; W. Benedek, K. De Feyter, F. Marrella (eds), *Economic Globalisation and Human Rights*, Cambridge University Press, Cambridge, 2007; A. Perulli, *Diritti sociali fondamentali e regolazione del mercato nell'azione esterna dell'Unione Europea*, in *Riv. giur. lav.*, 2013, 2, pp. 321-345; J. M. Siroën, *Labour Provisions in Preferential Trade Agreements: Current Practice and Outlook*, in *International Labour Review*, 2013; A. Perulli, *Clausola sociale*, in *Enciclopedia del diritto*, Giuffrè, Milano, 2014, vol. VII, pp. 187-211; A. Perulli, *Fundamental Social Rights, Market Regulation and EU External Action*, in *International Journal of Comparative Labour Law and Industrial Relations*, 2014, vol. 30, pp. 27-48; R. Zahn, D. Mangan, *Labour Standards and Sustainable Development: Unpicking the EU's Approach*, in *International Journal of Comparative Labour Law and Industrial Relations*, 2015, vol. 31, n. 3, pp. 233-241; S. Leader, *I diritti sociali nell'economia globale*, in *Riv. giur. lav.*, 2015, 3, p. 753; V. Brino, *Hard and Soft Law Instruments for Regulating Multinational Enterprises: An Uphill Struggle Towards Global Responsibility?*, in AA.VV. (eds), *Employment Relations and Transformation of the Enterprise in the Global Economy*, Giappichelli, Torino, 2016; T. Treu, *Globalizzazione e diritti umani. Le clausole sociali dei trattati commerciali e negli scambi internazionali fra imprese*, in *Stato e Mercato*, 2017, 1; F. Marrella, *Manuale di diritto del commercio internazionale*, Cedam, Padova, 2017.

away and the economy is entirely globalized. Transnational, stateless and mobile companies on the global chessboard[40] choose the most favourable legal order for their economic and corporate strategies and, consequently, the advanced protection systems of the industrialized countries are in crisis because they are unable to sustain the competitive pressure of the less-protective legal systems. A dangerous vortex is therefore created, giving rise to dangerous phenomena of regulatory *dumping*, that is to say downward policies to attract foreign investment and social *dumping*, which sees companies looking for regulatory systems that guarantee savings in labour costs, independently from the consequences this may cause on workers.[41]

It is such rapid and widespread a *race to the bottom* that it could constitute a powerful vector of returning to competition among workers,[42] reducing labour law to a competition law based on reducing the cost of labour,[43] all the more so in the current context of the fourth industrial revolution, where work on online platforms has allowed the real-time competition of crowd-workers residing in every corner of the world.

These processes of flexibilization and deregulation of the discipline, started in order to respond to the competitive pressures of the less-protective systems, could be stopped, or at least controlled, if the labour law discipline integrates the values proposed by the Sustainable Development paradigm, with a view to a more equitable reconciliation between the economic and social interests at stake.

However, this twofold process of reinterpretation and writing of the rules cannot disregard the abandonment of the results-based logic of development, which leads to perceive social and labour standards as *subsidiary social goods* that can readily be dismissed in the event that they hinder the pursuit of economic growth.[44] However, *labour standards* are not just a by-product of other development goals and cannot be considered as a mere tool for achieving economic goals.[45] Rather, social rights such as freedom of association, collective bargaining and trade union action are constitutive of a participatory process that confer legitimacy and sustainability to development,[46] so that labour law should be conceived, even in economic terms, as one of the institutions which holds together, in the name of a core of shared values, a society with advanced

40. Cfr. A. Perulli, *Globalizzazione e Dumping sociale, quali rimedi?*, in *Lav. dir.*, 2011, 1, p. 15.
41. Cfr. V. Brino, *Diritto del lavoro, concorrenza e mercato, Le prospettive dell'Unione Europea*, Cedam, Padova, 2012, p. 19.
42. Cfr. M. Rigau, *Droit du travail ou droit de la concurrence sociale. Essai sur un droit de la dignité de l'Homme du travail (re)mis en cause*, Bruylant, Bruxelles, 2009.
43. The reference here is to 'à *un droit de la concurrence fondée sur la réduction de cout de la main-d'œuvre*', Cfr. G. Lyon-Caen, *L'infiltration du Droit du travail par le Droit de la concurrence*, in *Droit Ouvrier*, 1992, p. 319.
44. In this sense, *see* T. Novitz, *Core Labour Standards Conditionalities: A Means by Which to Achieve Sustainable Development?*, in J. Fandez, C. Tan (eds), *International Economic Law, Globalization and Developing Countries*, Edward Elgar, Cheltenham, 2010, p. 236.
45. L. Gallino, *Il Lavoro non è una merce. Contro la flessibilità*, Laterza, Bari, 2007.
46. T. Novitz, *Core Labour Standards Conditionalities: A Means by Which to Achieve Sustainable Development?*, in J. Fandez, C. Tan (eds), *International Economic Law, Globalization and Developing Countries*, Edward Elgar, Cheltenham, 2010, p. 237.

economic development:[47] in short, a 'cement of society' and not an unnatural constraint on economic growth.

The labour law discipline has been in fact summoned, since its inception, to become the promoter of the so-called *non-trade issues* and to achieve a balanced reconciliation between human values (of occupational stability, of personal fulfilment, of a dignified existence, of a fair remuneration, social security assistance, development of their own *capabilities*) and the need for effectiveness of the production system (of flexibility, productivity, profit and regulatory certainty) which generates the resources that are necessary to satisfy the above-mentioned values.

In this sense, the international and national legislator should provide for a series of new instruments, actions and policies that ensure a trend reversal in the process of erosion of the foundations of the labour law discipline, promoting a greater consideration of the social pillar among regulatory actors, in the awareness of its necessity for general development, because the pursuit of apparently conflicting axiological interests can generate a virtuous circle.

In this way, labour law could safeguard its own space with respect to other branches of law, avoiding becoming an appendix of commercial law[48] and at the same time demonstrating its legal strength with regards to the challenges posed by the changes within the context.

In conclusion, we must reflect on the virtuous linkage between Sustainable Development and labour law. If, as we have seen, the subject matter needs a paradigm shift to be adapted to the context of the third millennium without repudiating its deep roots, at the same time, labour law is legitimized as an integral part of a Sustainable Development project. As authoritative doctrine has significantly stated, the contribution of labour law to Sustainable Development could take the form of a multiplicity of measures: through the protection of workers from old and new social risks; in the promotion of *decent* and quality work; in the dissemination of investments in education and personal skills, essential for equality of opportunity (according to the theory of the *Capability Approach*); in an active use of private and public welfare institutions aimed at increasing personal opportunities and fighting poverty and inequality; in the promotion of a collective voice and in the participation of the worker in the workplace and in the public sphere; in achieving flexibility in the employment relationship associated with security in the labour market and in support of *labour-friendly* use of technological and organizational innovations.[49]

---

47. R. Del Punta, *L'economia e le ragioni del diritto del lavoro*, in *Giorn. dir. lav. rel. ind.*, 2001, 3, p. 7.
48. L. Gaeta, *Il lavoro e il diritto. Un percorso storico*, Cacucci, Bari, 2013, p. 100; L. Gaeta, *Appunti dal corso di diritto del lavoro*, Giappichelli, Torino, 2018, p. 79; in the same terms, Speziale: 'with the exclusion or secondary importance attributed to functions, values and objectives other than economic ones, it empties the axiological content of law and reduces legal science to an "appendix" of economics (and of economic science), of which it constitutes the theoretical formalization applied to the regulatory framework'. Cfr. V. Speziale, *La mutazione genetica del diritto del lavoro*, in M. P. Iadicicco, V. Nuzzo (a cura di), *Le riforme del diritto del lavoro. Politiche e tecniche normative*, Editoriale Scientifica, Napoli, 2016, p. 49.
49. T. Treu, *Labour Law and Sustainable Development*, in *WP C.S.D.L.E. 'Massimo D'Antona'.INT – 130/2016*, p. 27.

The paradigm of Sustainable Development could therefore constitute the most suitable value background in the labour law's paradigm shift operation which, far from being subordinated to the pressures of the standard economy, may allow a new and wider legitimacy of labour law as a 'sustainability law'.

Annexes

ANNEX 1

The Most Significant Evolutionary Stages of Sustainable Development

- **1972 – Stockholm Conference of the United Nations on the Human Environment:** this is the first important conference that addresses the themes of Sustainable Development, the *United Nations Conference on the Human Environment*. The issue of environmental protection is examined in detail together with economic and social issues. The opportunity to undertake actions having as a compelling goal for humanity 'to defend and improve the environment for present and future generations' is thereby affirmed.
- **1983 – Birth of the UN World Commission on Environment and Development**: the United Nations Commission for Sustainable Development (CSD) is established, which must guarantee effective and concrete continuation of the decisions taken in Stockholm.
- **1987 – Brundtland Report of the World Commission on the Environment and Development**: in the Brundtland Report 'Our common future', Sustainable Development is defined as 'the development that satisfies human needs without compromising the ability of future generations to satisfy their own'.
- **1992 – Rio de Janeiro, UN Conference on Environment and Development (Earth Summit)**: representatives of 172 Countries participated in the Conference of Rio de Janeiro or UNCED (United Nations Conference on Environment and Development, 3-14 June 1992). The planet's environmental problems and their links with the problems of social and economic development were discussed. At the conclusion of the Conference, the following provisions were unanimously approved:
  - i) the Rio Declaration (a commitment to environmental protection and Sustainable Development);
  - ii) a Declaration of Principles on the Management, Conservation and Sustainable Development of Forests;

iii) Agenda 21, a broad and articulated program of action that constitutes a sort of manual for the 21st century Sustainable Development of the planet, full of programmatic objectives for economic and social dimensions, conservation and management of resources for the development and strengthening of social forces and implementation tools.

At the Rio Conference, over 150 countries signed two International Conventions:

- the United Nations Convention on Biological Diversity, whose art. 8, lett. e) deals in particular with the promotion of sustainable and ecologically rational development in areas adjacent to protected areas to strengthen the protection of the latter.
- the United Nations Convention on Climate Change; Article. 2 hopes that the parties will work 'to ensure that economic development can continue at a sustainable pace'; Article. 3.4 establishes that the parties have the 'right' and the 'duty' to promote Sustainable Development.

- **1994 – United Nations Convention to combat Desertification and Drought:** this is a legally binding international agreement linking the environment and development to sustainable land management. According to its art. 4.2, lett. b: 'the parties give due attention, within the relevant international and regional bodies, to the situation of affected developing country Parties with regard to international trade, marketing arrangements and debt with a view to establishing an enabling international economic environment conducive to the promotion of sustainable development.'
- **1997 – Kyoto Protocol**: provision of policies and measures for the reduction of greenhouse gas emissions by industrialized countries. Among the measures adopted there is the promotion of scientific research on alternative energies and incentives for forms of sustainable economy. Developed Countries are urged to cooperate with developing countries to achieve sustainable development.
- **1998 – Declaration on the principles and fundamental rights in the work of the ILO**: the Declaration shows the commitment of the ILO to 'mobilize all its capacities for regulatory action, technical cooperation and research in all fields of its competence, with particular regard to employment, vocational training and working conditions, to ensure that, in the context of a global strategy of economic and social development, economic and social policies are mutually reinforcing in order to promote sustainable development on a large scale'.
- **1999 – The concept of Decent Work sees the light**: in 1999 the Director-General of the ILO, Juan Somavia, presented the Decent Work Report to the International Labour Conference in which he stated that 'the primary objective The ILO's mission is to ensure that all men and women have access to productive work, in conditions of freedom, equality, security and human dignity. '
- **2000 – Cartagena Protocol on Biosafety**: 'commercial and environmental agreements should support each other and should be aimed at achieving a Sustainable Development' (Preamble).

- **2000 – Millennium Summit – UN General Assembly on the New Millennium**: the Millennium Development Goals (MDGs) (2000-2015) are elaborated: elimination of extreme poverty and hunger, achievement of universal primary education, promotion of 'gender equality and women's empowerment, measurement of infant mortality, improvement of maternal health, fight against HIV and malaria, environmental sustainability and encouragement for global participation in development.
- **2001 – European Union, Green Paper on Corporate Social Responsibility (CSR)**: CSR is the voluntary adoption by companies of social and environmental objectives in their commercial activities and in their relations with the subjects involved. The Commission emphasizes that CSR programs contribute to the EU's sustainable development.
- **2001 – European Commission, European Strategy for Sustainable Development:** 'All policies must consider Sustainable Development as a fundamental issue. In particular, in the next review exercises of some common policies it will be necessary to evaluate how they will be able to make a more positive contribution to Sustainable Development '.
- **2002 – Johannesburg UN Conference (Rio + 10)**: the realization of the goals set in Rio de Janeiro is encouraged and new political commitments are defined by all countries on the path to Sustainable Development. A monitoring of the works is agreed and the more specific objectives identified in the field of Sustainable Development, identifying three components (or 'pillars') of sustainability: social development, economic development and environmental protection.
- **2002 – Johannesburg Declaration on Sustainable Development:** 'it is necessary to promote and strengthen the three inseparable pillars of Sustainable Development, environmental protection and economic and social development, at local, national, continental and global level' (Principle 5).
- **2005 – Social Agenda (Social Policy Agenda) of the European Union 2005-2009:** relaunch of the Lisbon Strategy. The Agenda identifies two main groups of actions, related to the strategic objectives of employment (prosperity objective) and equal opportunities and inclusion (solidarity objective).
- **2005 – Decade of Education for Sustainable Development (DESS)**: the United Nations General Assembly entrusted UNESCO with the task of coordinating and promoting the activities of the proclaimed Decade for the period 2005-2014.
- **2008 – ILO Declaration on Social Justice for a Fair Globalization**: the Declaration 'offers managers and decision makers a balanced approach that relates to individuals and productive solutions at the national level, while providing a common platform for international governance. A text that contributes to the political coherence in favour of Sustainable Development within national strategies, among international organizations and in the context of development cooperation, incorporating objectives of social, economic and environmental nature'. The concept of decent work devised by the ILO was established in 1999, placing it at the heart of the Organization's

policies for achieving its objectives: employment, promotion and guarantee of social rights, protection and social security, promotion of social dialogue.

- **2010 – Communication from the European Commission EUROPE 2020, A strategy for smart, sustainable and inclusive growth:** Europe 2020 presents three mutually reinforcing priorities: i) smart growth: developing an economy based on knowledge and innovation; ii) sustainable growth: promoting greener, more competitive and more efficient economy; iii) inclusive growth: promoting an economy with a high rate of employment that favours social and territorial cohesion.
- **2012 – Rio de Janeiro UN Conference (RIO + 20)**: renewal of the commitment to Sustainable Development, to consider the Green Economy within Sustainable Development and to clearly formulate an institutional framework for Sustainable Development.
- **2015 – United Nations Agenda 2030, 17 Sustainable Development Goals:** a 15-year action program for people, the planet and prosperity signed in September 2015 by the governments of the 193 UN member States, including 17 Goals for Sustainable Development. These goals are based on the Millennium Development Goals and aim at completing what they failed to accomplish.
- **2017 – ILO recommendation n. 205 on employment and decent work for peace and resilience**: the Recommendation provides Member States with a guide on the measures to be taken to create jobs and decent work for the purposes of prevention, recovery, peace and resilience with respect to situations of crisis arising from conflicts and disasters.
- **2017 – The European Commission proclaims the 'European Social Pillar':** the new European Social Pillar legitimizes new and effective rights for citizens in 3 different categories: i) fair opportunities and access to the labour market; ii) fair working conditions; iii) security and social inclusion.

ANNEX 2

The Ten Principles of the UN Global Compact

Corporate sustainability starts with a company's value system and a principles-based approach to doing business. This means operating in ways that, at a minimum, meet fundamental responsibilities in the areas of human rights, labour, environment and anti-corruption. Responsible businesses enact the same values and principles wherever they have a presence, and know that good practices in one area do not offset harm in another. By incorporating the Ten Principles of the UN Global Compact into strategies, policies and procedures, and establishing a culture of integrity, companies are not only upholding their basic responsibilities to people and planet, but also setting the stage for long-term success.

The Ten Principles of the United Nations Global Compact are derived from: the Universal Declaration of Human Rights, the International Labour Organization's Declaration on Fundamental Principles and Rights at Work, the Rio Declaration on Environment and Development, and the United Nations Convention Against Corruption.

Human Rights

Principle 1: Businesses should support and respect the protection of internationally proclaimed human rights; and
Principle 2: make sure that they are not complicit in human rights abuses.

Labour

Principle 3: Businesses should uphold the freedom of association and the effective recognition of the right to collective bargaining;
Principle 4: the elimination of all forms of forced and compulsory labour;
Principle 5: the effective abolition of child labour; and

Principle 6: the elimination of discrimination in respect of employment and occupation.

Environment

Principle 7: Businesses should support a precautionary approach to environmental challenges;
Principle 8: undertake initiatives to promote greater environmental responsibility; and
Principle 9: encourage the development and diffusion of environmentally friendly technologies.

Anti-Corruption

Principle 10: Businesses should work against corruption in all its forms, including extortion and bribery.

ANNEX 3

The UN Millennium Development Goals (MDGs)

The United Nations Millennium Development Goals are eight goals that all 191 UN member states have agreed to try to achieve by the year 2015. The United Nations Millennium Declaration, signed in September 2000 commits world leaders to combat poverty, hunger, disease, illiteracy, environmental degradation, and discrimination against women. The MDGs are derived from this Declaration, and all have specific targets and indicators.

The Eight Millennium Development Goals are:

1. to eradicate extreme poverty and hunger;
2. to achieve universal primary education;
3. to promote gender equality and empower women;
4. to reduce child mortality;
5. to improve maternal health;
6. to combat HIV/AIDS, malaria, and other diseases;
7. to ensure environmental sustainability; and
8. to develop a global partnership for development.

ANNEX 4

The UN Sustainable Development Goals (SDGs)

The Sustainable Development Goals are the blueprint to achieve a better and more sustainable future for all. They address the global challenges we face, including those related to poverty, inequality, climate change, environmental degradation, peace and justice. The 17 Goals are all interconnected, and in order to leave no one behind, it is important that we achieve them all by 2030.

The Sustainable Development Goals are:

GOAL 1: No Poverty. End poverty in all its forms everywhere

GOAL 2: Zero Hunger. End hunger, achieve food security and improved nutrition and promote sustainable agriculture

GOAL 3: Good Health and Well-being. Ensure healthy lives and promote well-being for all at all ages

GOAL 4: Quality Education. Ensure inclusive and equitable quality education and promote lifelong learning opportunities for all

GOAL 5: Gender Equality. Achieve gender equality and empower all women and girls

GOAL 6: Clean Water and Sanitation. Ensure availability and sustainable management of water and sanitation for all

GOAL 7: Affordable and Clean Energy. Ensure access to affordable, reliable, sustainable and modern energy for all

GOAL 8: Decent Work and Economic Growth. Promote sustained, inclusive and sustainable economic growth, full and productive employment and decent work for all

GOAL 9: Industry, Innovation and Infrastructure. Build resilient infrastructure, promote inclusive and sustainable industrialization and foster innovation

GOAL 10: Reduced Inequality. Reduce inequality within and among countries

GOAL 11: Sustainable Cities and Communities. Make cities and human settlements inclusive, safe, resilient and sustainable
GOAL 12: Responsible Consumption and Production. Ensure sustainable consumption and production patterns
GOAL 13: Climate Action. Take urgent action to combat climate change and its impacts
GOAL 14: Life Below Water. Conserve and sustainably use the oceans, seas and marine resources for sustainable development
GOAL 15: Life on Land. Protect, restore and promote sustainable use of terrestrial ecosystems, sustainably manage forests, combat desertification, and halt and reverse land degradation and halt biodiversity loss
GOAL 16: Peace and Justice Strong Institutions. Promote peaceful and inclusive societies for sustainable development, provide access to justice for all and build effective, accountable and inclusive institutions at all levels
GOAL 17: Partnerships to achieve the Goal. Strengthen the means of implementation and revitalize the global partnership for sustainable development

ANNEX 5

Goal n. 8 of the UN Sustainable Development Goals 'Promote Lasting, Inclusive and Sustainable Economic Growth, Full and Productive Employment and Decent Work for All': Targets, Indicators and Progress in 2019

Goal 8: Targets and indicators

Goal 8. Promote sustained, inclusive and sustainable economic growth, full and productive employment and decent work for all

Target 8.1: Sustain per capita economic growth in accordance with national circumstances and, in particular, at least 7 per cent gross domestic product growth per annum in the least developed countries

- **Indicator 8.1.1:** Annual growth rate of real GDP per capita

Target 8.2: Achieve higher levels of economic productivity through diversification, technological upgrading and innovation, including through a focus on high-value added and labour-intensive sectors

- **Indicator 8.2.1:** Annual growth rate of real GDP per employed person

Target 8.3: Promote development-oriented policies that support productive activities, decent job creation, entrepreneurship, creativity and innovation, and encourage the formalization and growth of micro-, small- and medium-sized enterprises, including through access to financial services

- **Indicator 8.3.1:** Proportion of informal employment in non-agriculture employment, by sex

Target 8.4: Improve progressively, through 2030, global resource efficiency in consumption and production and endeavour to decouple economic growth from environmental degradation, in accordance with the 10-Year Framework of Programmes on Sustainable Consumption and Production, with developed countries taking the lead

- **Indicator 8.4.1:** Material footprint, material footprint per capita, and material footprint per GDP
- **Indicator 8.4.2:** Domestic material consumption, domestic material consumption per capita, and domestic material consumption per GDP

Target 8.5: By 2030, achieve full and productive employment and decent work for all women and men, including for young people and persons with disabilities, and equal pay for work of equal value

- **Indicator 8.5.1:** Average hourly earnings of female and male employees, by occupation, age and persons with disabilities
- **Indicator 8.5.2:** Unemployment rate, by sex, age and persons with disabilities

Target 8.6: By 2020, substantially reduce the proportion of youth not in employment, education or training

- **Indicator 8.6.1:** Proportion of youth (aged 15-24 years) not in education, employment or training

Target 8.7: Take immediate and effective measures to eradicate forced labour, end modern slavery and human trafficking and secure the prohibition and elimination of the worst forms of child labour, including recruitment and use of child soldiers, and by 2025 end child labour in all its forms

- **Indicator 8.7.1:** Proportion and number of children aged 5-17 years engaged in child labour, by sex and age

Target 8.8: Protect labour rights and promote safe and secure working environments for all workers, including migrant workers, in particular women migrants, and those in precarious employment

- **Indicator 8.8.1:** Frequency rates of fatal and non-fatal occupational injuries, by sex and migrant status
- **Indicator 8.8.2:** Level of national compliance of labour rights (freedom of association and collective bargaining) based on International Labour Organization (ILO) textual sources and national legislation, by sex and migrant status

Target 8.9: By 2030, devise and implement policies to promote sustainable tourism that creates jobs and promotes local culture and products

- **Indicator 8.9.1:** Tourism direct GDP as a proportion of total GDP and in growth rate

- **Indicator 8.9.2:** Proportion of jobs in sustainable tourism industries out of total tourism jobs

Target 8.10: Strengthen the capacity of domestic financial institutions to encourage and expand access to banking, insurance and financial services for all

- **Indicator 8.10.1:** (a) Number of commercial bank branches per 100,000 adults and (b) number of automated teller machines (ATMs) per 100,000 adults
- **Indicator 8.10.2:** Proportion of adults (15 years and older) with an account at a bank or other financial institution or with a mobile-money-service provider

Target 8.a: Increase Aid for Trade support for developing countries, in particular least developed countries, including through the Enhanced Integrated Framework for Trade-related Technical Assistance to Least Developed Countries

- **Indicator 8.a.1:** Aid for Trade commitments and disbursements

Target 8.b: By 2020, develop and operationalize a global strategy for youth employment and implement the Global Jobs Pact of the International Labour Organization

- **Indicator 8.b.1:** Existence of a developed and operationalized national strategy for youth employment, as a distinct strategy or as part of a national employment strategy

Progress of Goal 8 in 2019

Inclusive and sustainable economic growth can drive progress and generate the means to implement the Sustainable Development Goals. Globally, labour productivity has increased and unemployment is back to pre-financial crisis levels. However, the global economy is growing at a slower rate. More progress is needed to increase employment opportunities, particularly for young people, reduce informal employment and the gender pay gap and promote safe and secure working environments to create decent work for all.

- In 2017, the global growth rate of real GDP per capita was 1.9 per cent and is expected to remain at about 2 per cent from 2018 to 2020. This is significantly less than the 3 per cent rate attained in 2010 and slightly higher than the 2015 rate of 1.63 per cent. Real GDP growth rate for least developed countries is expected to increase from 4.5 per cent in 2017 to 5.7 per cent in 2020, which is less than the 7 per cent envisioned by the 2030 Agenda.
- Since the global economic downturn of 2009, labour productivity (measured as GDP per employed person) has been increasing in the world, recording

positive annual growth rates consistently since 2010. In 2018, the world's labour productivity increased by 2.1 per cent, its highest annual growth since 2010.

- Informal employment, which has an impact on the adequacy of earnings, occupational safety and health and working conditions, remains pervasive: in three quarters of countries with data on the subject, more than half of all persons employed in non-agriculture sectors are in informal employment.
- Based on data for 62 countries, the median hourly gender pay gap stood at 12 per cent. The median gender pay gap exceeded 20 per cent in managerial and professional occupations, among workers in crafts and related trades and among plant machine operators and assemblers.
- The global unemployment rate has finally recovered from the global economic crisis. In 2018, the global unemployment rate stood at 5.0 per cent – matching pre-crisis levels. Youth were three times more likely to be unemployed than adults.
- In 2018, one fifth of the world's youth were not in education, employment or training, meaning that they were neither gaining professional experience nor acquiring or developing skills through educational or vocational programmes in their prime years. There is a stark gender difference. Young women were more than twice as likely as young men to be unemployed or outside the labour force and not in education or training.
- Many workers around the world are exposed to undue risks in their workplaces. Based on recent data from some 55 countries, a median of 3 deaths occurred per 100,000 employees and a median of 889 non-fatal injuries occurred per 100,000 employees.
- Access to finance is on the rise globally, but the mode of access seems to be changing with growing reliance on technology. From 2010 to 2017, the number of automated teller machines (ATMs) per 100,000 adults grew by close to 50 per cent from 45 to 66 globally, and from 2.3 to 5.8 in the least developed countries. The number of commercial bank branches per 100,000 adults grew by only 2 per cent between 2010 and 2017, with more customers using digital banking solutions.
- In 2017, aid-for-trade commitments increased to $58 billion and more than doubled when compared to the 2002-2005 baseline, when they represented $23.1 billion. In absolute terms, the increase was highest in the agriculture sector ($1.7 billion), the industry sector ($1.0 billion) and in banking and financial services ($1.0 billion)

Source: United Nations E/2019/68 Economic and Social Council, 8 May 2019 Report of the Secretary-General, Special edition: progress towards the Sustainable Development Goals, available at: https://undocs.org/E/2019/68

ANNEX 6

The European Pillar of Social Rights in 20 Principles

Preamble

1. Pursuant to Article 3 of the Treaty on European Union, the aims of the Union are inter alia to promote the well-being of its peoples and to work for the sustainable development of Europe based on balanced economic growth and price stability, a highly competitive social market economy, aiming at full employment and social progress, and a high level of protection and improvement of the quality of the environment. The Union shall combat social exclusion and discrimination, promote social justice and protection, equality between women and men, solidarity between generations and protection of the rights of the child.
2. Pursuant to Article 9 of the Treaty on the Functioning of the European Union, the Union, in defining and implementing its policies and activities, shall take into account requirements linked to the promotion of a high level of employment, the guarantee of adequate social protection, the fight against social exclusion and a high level of education, training and protection of human health.
3. Article 151 of the Treaty on the Functioning of the European Union provides that the Union and the Member States, having in mind fundamental social rights such as those set out in the European Social Charter signed at Turin on 18 October 1961 and in the 1989 Community Charter of the Fundamental Social Rights of Workers, shall have as their objectives the promotion of employment, improved living and working conditions, so as to make possible their harmonisation while the improvement is being maintained, proper social protection, dialogue between management and labour, the development of human resources with a view to lasting high employment and the combating of exclusion.

4. Article 152 of the Treaty on the Functioning of the European Union provides that the Union recognises and promotes the role of the social partners at its level, taking into account the diversity of the national systems. It is to facilitate dialogue between them and respect their autonomy.
5. The Charter of Fundamental Rights of the European Union, first proclaimed at the Nice European Council on 7 December 2000, safeguards and promotes a number of fundamental principles that are essential for the European social model. The provisions of this Charter are addressed to the institutions, bodies, offices and agencies of the Union with due regard for the principle of subsidiarity and to the Member States only when they are implementing Union law.
6. The Treaty on the Functioning of the European Union contains provisions laying down the powers of the Union relating inter alia to the freedom of movement of workers (Articles 45 to 48), the right of establishment (Articles 49 to 55), social policy (Articles 151 to 161), the promotion of dialogue between management and labour (Article 154), including agreements concluded and implemented at Union level (Article 155), equal pay for men and women for equal work (Article 157), the contribution to the development of quality education and vocational training (Articles 165 and 166), Union action complementing national policies and fostering cooperation in the field of health (Article 168), economic, social and territorial cohesion (Articles 174 to 178), the formulation, and the surveillance of the implementation, of the broad guidelines of the economic policies (Article 121), the formulation, and the examination of the implementation of the employment guidelines (Article 148) and more generally, the approximation of legislation (Articles 114 to 117).
7. The European Parliament has called for a solid European Pillar of Social Rights to reinforce social rights and deliver a positive impact on people's lives in the short and medium term and enable support for European construction in the 21st century.
    1. Leaders of 27 Member States have stressed that economic and social insecurity needs to be addressed as a matter of priority and called for the creation of a promising economic future for all, safeguards for our way of life and the provision of better opportunities for youth.
    2. The leaders of 27 Member States and of the European Council, the European Parliament and the European Commission made a commitment to work towards a social Europe in the Rome agenda. That commitment is based on the principles of sustainable growth and the promotion of economic and social progress, as well as cohesion and convergence, while upholding the integrity of the internal market; a Union taking into account the diversity of national systems and the key role of social partners; a Union which promotes equality between women and men as well as rights and equal opportunities for all; a Union which fights unemployment, discrimination, social exclusion

and poverty; a Union where young people receive the best education and training and can study and find jobs across the continent; a Union which preserves our cultural heritage and promotes cultural diversity.

3. The social partners have committed to continue contributing to a Europe that delivers for its workers and enterprises.

8. The completion of the European single market in the last decades has been accompanied by the development of a solid social acquis which has resulted in progress in the freedom of movement, living and working conditions, equality between women and men, health and safety at work, social protection and education and training. The introduction of the euro has provided the Union with a stable common currency shared by 340 million citizens in nineteen Member States, facilitating their daily lives and protecting them against financial instability. The Union has also enlarged significantly, increasing economic opportunities and promoting social progress across the continent.
9. Labour markets and societies are evolving quickly, with new opportunities and new challenges arising from globalisation, the digital revolution, changing work patterns and societal and demographic developments. Challenges, such as significant inequality, long-term and youth unemployment or intergenerational solidarity, are often similar across Member States although in varying degrees.
10. Europe has shown its resolve to overcome the financial and economic crisis, and as a result of determined action, the Union economy is now more stable, with employment levels at an unprecedented high and a steady fall in unemployment. However, the social consequences of the crisis have been far-reaching – from youth and long-term unemployment to the risk of poverty – and addressing those consequences remains an urgent priority.
11. To a large extent, the employment and social challenges facing Europe are a result of relatively modest growth, which is rooted in untapped potential in terms of participation in employment and productivity. Economic and social progress are intertwined, and the establishment of a European Pillar of Social Rights should be part of wider efforts to build a more inclusive and sustainable growth model by improving Europe's competitiveness and making it a better place to invest, create jobs and foster social cohesion.
12. The aim of the European Pillar of Social Rights is to serve as a guide towards efficient employment and social outcomes when responding to current and future challenges which are directly aimed at fulfilling people's essential needs, and towards ensuring better enactment and implementation of social rights.
13. A stronger focus on employment and social performance is particularly important to increase resilience and deepen the Economic and Monetary Union. For this reason, the European Pillar of Social Rights is notably conceived for the euro area but it is addressed to all Member States.

14. The European Pillar of Social Rights expresses principles and rights essential for fair and well-functioning labour markets and welfare systems in 21st century Europe. It reaffirms some of the rights already present in the Union acquis. It adds new principles which address the challenges arising from societal, technological and economic developments. For them to be legally enforceable, the principles and rights first require dedicated measures or legislation to be adopted at the appropriate level.
15. The principles enshrined in the European Pillar of Social Rights concern Union citizens and third-country nationals with legal residence. Where a principle refers to workers, it concerns all persons in employment, regardless of their employment status, modality and duration.
16. The European Pillar of Social Rights shall not prevent Member States or their social partners from establishing more ambitious social standards. In particular, nothing in the European Pillar of Social Rights shall be interpreted as restricting or adversely affecting rights and principles as recognised, in their respective fields of application, by Union law or international law and by international agreements to which the Union or all the Member States are party, including the European Social Charter signed at Turin on 18 October 1961 and the relevant Conventions and Recommendations of the International Labour Organisation.
17. Delivering on the European Pillar of Social Rights is a shared political commitment and responsibility. The European Pillar of Social Rights should be implemented at both Union level and Member State level within their respective competences, taking due account of different socio-economic environments and the diversity of national systems, including the role of social partners, and in accordance with the principles of subsidiarity and proportionality.
18. At Union level, the European Pillar of Social Rights does not entail an extension of the Union's powers and tasks as conferred by the Treaties. It should be implemented within the limits of those powers.
19. The European Pillar of Social Rights respects the diversity of the cultures and traditions of the peoples of Europe, as well as the national identities of the Member States and the organisation of their public authorities at national, regional and local levels. In particular, the establishment of the European Pillar of Social Rights does not affect the right of Member States to define the fundamental principles of their social security systems and manage their public finances, and must not significantly affect the financial equilibrium thereof.
20. Social dialogue plays a central role in reinforcing social rights and enhancing sustainable and inclusive growth. Social partners at all levels have a crucial role to play in pursuing and implementing the European Pillar of Social Rights, in accordance with their autonomy in negotiating and concluding agreements and the right to collective bargaining and collective action.

Chapter I Equal opportunities and access to the labour market

1. Education, training and life-long learning

Everyone has the right to quality and inclusive education, training and life-long learning in order to maintain and acquire skills that enable them to participate fully in society and manage successfully transitions in the labour market.

2. Gender equality

a. Equality of treatment and opportunities between women and men must be ensured and fostered in all areas, including regarding participation in the labour market, terms and conditions of employment and career progression.
b. Women and men have the right to equal pay for work of equal value.

3. Equal opportunities

Regardless of gender, racial or ethnic origin, religion or belief, disability, age or sexual orientation, everyone has the right to equal treatment and opportunities regarding employment, social protection, education, and access to goods and services available to the public. Equal opportunities of under-represented groups shall be fostered.

4. Active support to employment

a. Everyone has the right to timely and tailor-made assistance to improve employment or self-employment prospects. This includes the right to receive support for job search, training and requalification. Everyone has the right to transfer social protection and training entitlements during professional transitions.
b. Young people have the right to continued education, apprenticeship, traineeship or a job offer of good standing within 4 months of becoming unemployed or leaving education.
c. People unemployed have the right to personalised, continuous and consistent support. The long-term unemployed have the right to an in-depth individual assessment at the latest at 18 months of unemployment.

Chapter II Fair working conditions

5. Secure and adaptable employment

a. Regardless of the type and duration of the employment relationship, workers have the right to fair and equal treatment regarding working conditions, access to social protection and training. The transition towards open-ended forms of employment shall be fostered. b. In accordance with legislation and collective agreements, the necessary flexibility for employers to adapt swiftly to changes in the economic context shall be ensured. c. Innovative forms of work that ensure quality working conditions shall be fostered. Entrepreneurship and self-employment shall be encouraged. Occupational mobility shall be facilitated. d. Employment relationships that lead to precarious working conditions shall be prevented, including by prohibiting abuse of atypical contracts. Any probation period should be of reasonable duration.

6. Wages

a. Workers have the right to fair wages that provide for a decent standard of living.
b. Adequate minimum wages shall be ensured, in a way that provide for the satisfaction of the needs of the worker and his / her family in the light of national economic and social conditions, whilst safeguarding access to employment and incentives to seek work. In-work poverty shall be prevented.
c. All wages shall be set in a transparent and predictable way according to national practices and respecting the autonomy of the social partners.

7. Information about employment conditions and protection in case of dismissals

a. Workers have the right to be informed in writing at the start of employment about their rights and obligations resulting from the employment relationship, including on probation period.
b. Prior to any dismissal, workers have the right to be informed of the reasons and be granted a reasonable period of notice. They have the right to access to effective and impartial dispute resolution and, in case of unjustified dismissal, a right to redress, including adequate compensation.

8. Social dialogue and involvement of workers

a. The social partners shall be consulted on the design and implementation of economic, employment and social policies according to national practices. They shall be encouraged to negotiate and conclude collective agreements in matters relevant to them, while respecting their autonomy and the right to collective action. Where appropriate, agreements concluded between the social partners shall be implemented at the level of the Union and its Member States.
b. Workers or their representatives have the right to be informed and consulted in good time on matters relevant to them, in particular on the

transfer, restructuring and merger of undertakings and on collective redundancies. c. Support for increased capacity of social partners to promote social dialogue shall be encouraged.

9. Work-life balance

Parents and people with caring responsibilities have the right to suitable leave, flexible working arrangements and access to care services. Women and men shall have equal access to special leaves of absence in order to fulfil their caring responsibilities and be encouraged to use them in a balanced way.

10. Healthy, safe and well-adapted work environment and data protection

a. Workers have the right to a high level of protection of their health and safety at work.
b. Workers have the right to a working environment adapted to their professional needs and which enables them to prolong their participation in the labour market.
c. Workers have the right to have their personal data protected in the employment context.

Chapter III Social protection and inclusion

11. Childcare and support to children

a. Children have the right to affordable early childhood education and care of good quality.
b. Children have the right to protection from poverty. Children from disadvantaged backgrounds have the right to specific measures to enhance equal opportunities.

12. Social protection

Regardless of the type and duration of their employment relationship, workers, and, under comparable conditions, the self-employed, have the right to adequate social protection.

13. Unemployment benefits

The unemployed have the right to adequate activation support from public employment services to (re)integrate in the labour market and adequate unemployment benefits of reasonable duration, in line with their contributions and national eligibility rules. Such benefits shall not constitute a disincentive for a quick return to employment.

14. Minimum income

Everyone lacking sufficient resources has the right to adequate minimum income benefits ensuring a life in dignity at all stages of life, and effective access to enabling goods and services. For those who can work, minimum income benefits should be combined with incentives to (re)integrate into the labour market.

15. Old age income and pensions

a. Workers and the self-employed in retirement have the right to a pension commensurate to their contributions and ensuring an adequate income. Women and men shall have equal opportunities to acquire pension rights.
b. Everyone in old age has the right to resources that ensure living in dignity

16. Health care

Everyone has the right to timely access to affordable, preventive and curative health care of good quality.

17. Inclusion of people with disabilities

People with disabilities have the right to income support that ensures living in dignity, services that enable them to participate in the labour market and in society, and a work environment adapted to their needs.

18. Long-term care

Everyone has the right to affordable long-term care services of good quality, in particular home-care and community-based services.

19. Housing and assistance for the homeless

a. Access to social housing or housing assistance of good quality shall be provided for those in need.
b. Vulnerable people have the right to appropriate assistance and protection against forced eviction.
c. Adequate shelter and services shall be provided to the homeless in order to promote their social inclusion.

20. Access to essential services

Everyone has the right to access essential services of good quality, including water, sanitation, energy, transport, financial services and digital communications. Support for access to such services shall be available for those in need.

Bibliography

AGNOLI M. S. (a cura di), *Generazioni sospese. Percorsi di ricerca sui giovani Neet*, Franco Angeli, Milano, 2014

ALAIMO A., *I servizi all'impiego e l'art. 4 Cost. dopo le recenti riforme del mercato del lavoro*, in *Dir. lav. rel. ind.*, 2004, 2

ALAIMO A., *Il diritto sociale al lavoro nei mercati integrati*, Giappichelli, Torino, 2009

ALES E., *Diritto del lavoro, diritto della previdenza sociale, diritti di cittadinanza sociale: per un «sistema integrato» di microsistemi*, in *Arg. dir. lav.*, 2001, 3

ALES A., *Diritti sociali e discrezionalità del legislatore nell'ordinamento multilivello: una prospettazione giuslavoristica*, in *Giorn. dir. lav. rel. ind.*, 2015, 147, 3

ALIBRANDI G., *Infortuni sul lavoro e malattie professionali*, Giuffrè, Milano, 1979

ALKIRE S., *Using the Capability Approach: Prospective and Evaluative Analysis*, in F. COMIM, M. QIZILBASH, S. ALKIRE (eds), *The Capability Approach. Concepts, Measures and Applications*, Cambridge University Press, Cambridge, 2008

ALLAMPRESE A., ORLANDINI G., *Licenziamenti e regole di mercato. Il caso greco davanti alla Corte di Giustizia (prime note sulla sentenza AGET Iraklis)*, Roma, 31 gennaio 2017, http://www.cgil.it/licenziamenti-regole-mercato-caso-greco-davanti-alla-corte-giustizia-ue/.

ALSTON P., *Core Labour Standards and the Transformation of the International Labour Rights Regime*, in *European Journal of International Law*, 2004

ANNIBALLI V., *Rapporto di lavoro e solidarietà: verso un modello pluridimensionale*, Franco Angeli, Milano, 2017

APOSTOLI A., *L'ambivalenza costituzionale del lavoro tra libertà e diritto sociale*, Giuffrè, Milano, 2005

ARRIGO G., *I contratti di solidarietà*, in AA.VV. (a cura di), *Il diritto del lavoro negli anni ottanta*, Editoriale Scientifica, Napoli, 1988

ARROW K. H., *Scelte sociali e valori individuali*, ETAS, Milano, 1963

ARTHURS H., *Labour Law After Labour*; in G. DAVIDOV, B. LANGILLE (eds), *The Idea of Labour Law*, Oxford University Press, Oxford, 2011

AUER P., *La flexicurity nel tempo della crisi*, in *Dir. rel. ind.*, 2011, 21

AVIO A., *I diritti inviolabili nel rapporto di lavoro*, Giuffrè, Milano, 2001

BALANDI G. G., *Per una definizione del diritto della sicurezza sociale*, in *Politica del diritto*, 1984

BALANDI G. G., *Lavoro e diritto alla protezione sociale*, in *Lav. dir.*, 1997

BALANDI G. G., *Sulla possibilità di misurare la solidarietà*, in *Rechtsgeschichte*, 2004, 6

BALDASSARRE A., voce *Diritti sociali*, in *Enciclopedia Treccani*, Roma, 1989

BALLESTRERO M. V., *Eguaglianza, parità, differenza*, in *Lavoro '80*, 1988

BALLESTRERO M. V, *Eguaglianza e differenze nel diritto del lavoro. Note introduttive*, in *Lav. dir.*, 2004, 3-4

BALLESTRERO M. V., *La riforma del lavoro: questioni di costituzionalità*, in *Lav. dir.*, 2015, 1

BALLESTRERO M. V., DE SIMONE G. (a cura di), *Massimo Roccella, Manuale di Diritto del Lavoro*, Giappichelli, Torino, 2012

BALZARINI R., *Contratti speciali di lavoro*, in U. BORSI, F. PERGOLESI (diretto da), *Trattato di diritto del lavoro*, 3rd ed., Cedam, Padova, 1958, II

BARBERA M., *Sub Art. 2 Costituzione*, in G. BRANCA (a cura di), *Commentario alla Costituzione*, Zanichelli-Il Foro Italiano, Bologna-Roma, 1975

BARBERA M., *Discriminazioni ed eguaglianza nel rapporto di lavoro*, Giuffrè, Milano, 1991

BARBERA M., *Dopo Amsterdam. I nuovi confini del diritto sociale comunitario*, Promodis Italia, Brescia, 2000

BARBERA M., *L'eguaglianza come scudo e l'eguaglianza come spada*, in *Riv. giur. lav.*, 2002, 1

BARBERA M., *Eguaglianza e differenza nella nuova stagione del diritto antidiscriminatorio*, in *Dir. lav. rel. ind.*, 2003

BARBERA M. (a cura di), *Il nuovo diritto antidiscriminatorio: il quadro comunitario e nazionale*, Giuffrè, Milano, 2007

BARBIERI M., *Il rapporto tra l'art. 8 e l'accordo interconfederale del 28 giugno 2011*, in *Riv. giur. lav*, 2012, 3

BARCELLONA P., *La solidarietà come fatto e come diritto*, in *Lav. dir.*, 1996, 4-5

BARNAND C., *The Financial Crisis and the Euro Plus Act: A Labour Lawyer's Perspective*, in *International Law Journal*, 2012

BARRACO E., *Il collegato lavoro: un nuovo modus operandi per i pratici e, forse, un nuovo diritto del lavoro*, in *Lav. Giur.*, 2010, 4

BARRAL V., *Sustainable Development in International Law: Nature and Operation of an Evolutive Legal Norm*, in *European Journal of International Law*, 2012

BASSANINI F., TIBERI G. (a cura di), *Le nuove istituzioni europee. Commento al Trattato di Lisbona*, il Mulino, Bologna, 2010

BAYLOS GRAU A., *La desconstitucionalización del trabajo en la reforma laboral del 2012*, in *Revista de Derecho Social*, 2013, vol. 61

BECK U., *Il lavoro nell'epoca della fine del lavoro. Tramonto delle sicurezze e impegno civile*, Einaudi, Torino, 2000

BELL S., MORSE S., *Sustainability Indicators, Measuring the Immeasurable?*, 2nd ed., Earthscan, London Washington D.C., 2008

BENASSI G., *Clausole generali e giudice del lavoro: l'art. 30, primo comma, della legge n. 183 del 2010*, in *Arg. dir. lav.*, 2012, 1

BENEDEK W., DE FEYTER K., MARRELLA F. (eds), *Economic Globalisation and Human Rights*, Cambridge University Press, Cambridge, 2007

BERLIN I., *Quattro saggi sulla libertà*, Milano, Feltrinelli, 1989

BERTON F., RICCHIARDI M., SACCHI S., *Flex-insecurity. Perché in Italia la flessibilità diventa precarietà*, il Mulino, Bologna, 2009

BIFULCO R., D'ALOIA A., *Le generazioni future come nuovo paradigma del diritto costituzionale*, in R. BIFULCO, A. D'ALOIA (a cura di), *Un diritto per il futuro. Teorie e modelli della responsabilità intergenerazionale*, Jovene, Napoli, 2008

BLANPAIN R., *Le differenze di trattamento e la discriminazione connessa all'età: una società per tutte le età*, in *Dir. rel. ind.*, 2005, 4

BLANPAIN R., COLUCCI M. (a cura di), *L'Organizzazione Internazionale del Lavoro*, Jovene, Napoli, 2007

BOBBIO N., *Eguaglianza e libertà*, Einaudi, Torino, 1995

BOERI T., GALASSO V., *Contro i giovani: come l'Italia sta tradendo le nuove generazioni*, Mondadori, Milano, 2007

BOLOGNA G., *Manuale della sostenibilità*, Edizioni Ambiente, Milano, 2008

BONFANTI A., *Imprese multinazionali, diritti umani e ambiente. Profili di diritto internazionale pubblico e privato*, Giuffrè, Milano, 2012

BOSSELMANN K., *The Principle of Sustainability: Transforming Law and Governance*, Ashgate, London, 2008

BOYCE J. K., KLEMER A. R., TEMPLET P. H., WILLIS C. E., *Power Distribution, the Environment, and Public Health: A State-Level Analysis*, in *Ecological Economics*, 1999, vol. 1, n. 29

BOZZAO P., *La tutela previdenziale del lavoratore discontinuo. Problemi e prospettive del sistema di protezione sociale*, Giappichelli, Torino, 2005

BOZZAO P., *I nuovi trattamenti di disoccupazione: a piccoli passi verso l'Europa*, in A. PERULLI, L. FIORILLO (a cura di), *Contratto a tutele crescenti e Naspi, Decreti legislativi 4 marzo 2015, n. 22 e n. 23*, Giappichelli, Torino, 2015

BRINO V., *Diritto del lavoro, concorrenza e mercato, Le prospettive dell'Unione Europea*, Cedam, Padova, 2012

BRINO V., *Hard and Soft Law Instruments for Regulating Multinational Enterprises: an Uphill Struggle Towards Global Responsibility?* in AA.VV. (eds), *Employment Relations and Transformation of the Enterprise in the Global Economy*, Giappichelli, Torino, 2016

BROLLO M., *I contratti di solidarietà*, in F. NERI (a cura di), *Le politiche del lavoro negli anni '80*, p. 189-203, Franco Angeli, Milano, 1989

BROLLO M., *Il difficile e tardivo incontro tra giovani e lavoro*, in L. MARIUCCI, *Dopo la flessibilità, cosa? Le nuove politiche del lavoro*, il Mulino, Bologna, 2006

BROLLO M., *Il lavoro a tempo parziale tra flessibilità e sicurezza*, in F. CARINCI, M. MISCIONE (a cura di), *Il collegato lavoro 2008. L. 24 dicembre 2007, n. 247*, vol. 11, pp. 277-306, Ipsoa, Milano, 2008

BROLLO M., *Lavoro a tempo parziale dopo la l. n. 92/2012: meno flex, più security*, in *Il lavoro nella giurisprudenza*, 2012, 10

BROLLO M., *La disciplina delle mansioni dopo il Jobs Act*, in *Arg. dir. lav.*, 2015, 6

Brollo M., *La mobilità professionale dei lavoratori dopo il Jobs Act: spunti dal caso Fiat/FCA*, in *Riv. it. dir. lav.*, 2016

Brollo M., Filì V., *Le donne tra il desiderio di un figlio e la certezza del lavoro*, in M. Brollo, S. Serafin (a cura di), *Donne, politica e istituzioni tra desiderio e certezza*, pp. 67-82, Forum Editrice Universitaria Udinese, Udine, 2008

Brollo M., Marazza M. (a cura di), *Diritto del lavoro e mercato. L'impatto delle riforme del lavoro nell'analisi giuridica dei dati sull'occupazione*, Cedam, Padova, 2015

Bronstein A., *International and Comparative Labour Law: Current Challenges*, Palgrave Macmillan, London, 2009

Cagnin V., *Crisi e diritto del lavoro: la via della sostenibilità*, in *IANUS*, 2012, 7

Cagnin V., *L'Unione europea e il Sistema di preferenze tariffarie generalizzate*, in *Riv. giur. lav.*, 2015, 4

Cagnin V., *Art. 10, L. 81 del 22 maggio 2017 ed il nuovo sportello di servizi al lavoro per i lavoratori autonomi: funzioni, soggetti coinvolti e criticità contestuali*, in A. Perulli, L. Fiorillo (a cura di), *Il Jobs act del lavoro autonomo e del lavoro agile*, Giappichelli, Torino, 2017.

Cagnin V., *Gig-economy ed il problema qualificatorio dei gig-workers; uno sguardo oltreconfine*, in A. Perulli (a cura di), *Lavoro Autonomo ed Economia delle Piattaforme*, Cedam, Padova, 2018

Calafà L., *D.lgs. 11 aprile 2006, n. 198 codice delle pari opportunità, Commentario Breve alle leggi sul Lavoro*, Cedam, Padova, 2018

Canavesi G., Ales E., *Il sistema previdenziale italiano. Principi, struttura ed evoluzione*, Collana Fondazione Marco Biagi, Giappichelli, Torino, 2017

Capron M., *Evaluer les stratégies de développement durable des entreprises: l'utopie mobilisatrice de la performance globale (en collaboration avec Françoise Quairel)*, in *La Revue de l'Organisation Responsable*, 2006, 1

Carabelli U., *I profili di incostituzionalità dell'art. 8 con riferimento all'efficacia erga omnes dei contratti collettivi da esso previsti*, in *Riv. giur. lav.*, 2012

Carinci F., *Al capezzale del sistema contrattuale: il giudice, il sindacato, il legislatore*, in *WP C.S.D.L.E. 'Massimo D'Antona'*, n. 133/2011

Carinci F., *Il diritto del lavoro che verrà (in occasione del congedo di un amico)*, in *Arg. dir. lav*, 2014, 3

Carinci F., *Licenziamento e tutele differenziate*, in O. Mazzotta (a cura di), *Lavoro ed esigenze dell'impresa fra diritto sostanziale e processo dopo il Jobs Act*, Giappichelli, Torino, 2017

Carinci M. T., *Il dialogo fra Pino Santoro Passarelli e la dottrina. Dalla parasubordinazione al lavoro economicamente dipendente: la rivincita di un'idea*, in *Arg. dir. lav.*, 2007, 4-5

Carinci M. T., *Clausole generali, certificazione e limiti al sindacato del giudice. A proposito dell'art. 30, l. n. 183 del 2010*, in O. Mazzotta (a cura di), *Il diritto del lavoro dopo il 'collegato' (Legge 4 novembre 2010, n. 183)*, in *Quaderni di Questione Lavoro*, 2011, 1

Carinci M. T., *Il rapporto di lavoro al tempo della crisi: modelli europei e flexicurity 'all'italiana' a confronto*, in *Giorn. dir. lav. rel. ind.*, 2012, 4

Carter I., *La libertà eguale*, Feltrinelli, Milano, 2010

CARUSO B., *Occupabilità, formazione e 'capability' nei modelli giuridici di regolazione dei mercati del lavoro*, in *Giorn. dir. lav. rel. ind.*, 2007, 1

CARUSO B., *I diritti sociali fondamentali dopo il Trattato di Lisbona (tanto tuonò che piovve)*, in *WP C.S.D.L.E. 'Massimo D'Antona'.INT – 81/2010*

CARUSO B., *Verso il diritto del lavoro della responsabilità*, in *WP C.S.D.L.E. 'Massimo D'Antona'.IT – 283/2015*

CARUSO B., *'The Bright Side of the Moon': politiche del lavoro personalizzate e promozione del welfare occupazionale*, in *Riv. it. dir. lav.* 2016, 2

CARUSO B., *Nuove traiettorie del diritto del lavoro nella crisi europea. Il caso italiano*, in B. CARUSO, G. FONTANA (a cura di), *Lavoro e diritti sociali nella crisi europea. Un confronto fra costituzionalisti e giuslavoristi*, il Mulino, Bologna, 2015

CARUSO B., *Impresa, lavoro, diritto nella stagione del Jobs Act*, in *Giorn. dir. lav. rel. ind.*, 2016

CARUSO B., *La rappresentanza delle organizzazioni di interessi tra disintermediazione e re-intermediazione*, in *Arg. dir. lav.*, 2017, 3

CARUSO B., *La tutela della maternità dopo il Jobs Act*, in F. BESENGHI, A. RUSSO (a cura di), *Flessibilità, sicurezza e occupazione alla prova del Jobs Act*, Giappichelli, Torino, 2016

CASALE G., *Il diritto internazionale del lavoro ed il ruolo della Organizzazione internazionale del lavoro*, in F. CARINCI, A. PIZZOFERRATO (a cura di), *Diritto del lavoro dell'Unione europea*, Commentario diretto da F. CARINCI, *Diritto del lavoro e dell'Unione europea*, UTET, Torino, 2010, vol. IX

CASSESE S., *Il diritto globale*, Einaudi, Torino, 2009

CASTEL R., *L'insicurezza sociale. Che cosa significa essere protetti*, Einaudi, Torino, 2004

CASTELLANI G., *Il rilancio della previdenza complementare: luci e ombre di una rivoluzione incompiuta*, in *Riv. dir. sic. soc.*, 2017, 3

CATAUDELLA A., *Spunti sulla tipologia dei rapporti di lavoro*, in *Dir. lav.*, 1983, 1.

CAZZETTA G., *Giuslavorisi e costruzione della memoria nell'Italia repubblicana*, in G. CAZZETTA, G. G. BALANDI (a cura di), *Diritti e lavoro nell'Italia repubblicana: materiali dall'incontro di studio, Ferrara, 24 ottobre 2008*, Giuffrè, Milano, 2009

CAZZETTA G., BALANDI G. G. (a cura di), *Diritti e lavoro nell'Italia repubblicana: materiali dall'incontro di studio, Ferrara, 24 ottobre 2008*, Giuffrè, Milano, 2009

CAZZOLA G., *Lo Stato sociale tra crisi e riforme: il caso Italia*, il Mulino, Bologna, 1994

CELLA G. P., *Solidarietà e coesione sociale*, in M. NAPOLI (a cura di), *La solidarietà*, Vita e Pensiero, Milano, 2009

CENTOFANTI S., *Le nuove norme, non promulgate, di limitazione della tutela giurisdizionale dei lavoratori*, in *Lav. giur.*, 2010, 4

CENTOFANTI S., *L'articolo 8 d. l. n. 138/2011 conv. in l. n. 148/2011: una norma lesiva dei principi del diritto del lavoro*, in *Lav. giur.*, 2011, 11

CESTER C., *La norma inderogabile: fondamento e problema del diritto del lavoro*, in *Giorn. dir. lav. rel. ind.*, 2008

CESTER C., *I licenziamenti nel Jobs Act*, in*WP C.S.D.L.E. 'Massimo D'Antona'.IT – 273/2015*

CINELLI M., *Diritto della previdenza sociale*, Giappichelli, Torino, 2001

CINELLI M., *La sfida demografica al sistema delle pensioni tra immaginario e realtà*, in *Riv. dir. sic. soc.*, 2003, 2

CINELLI M., *Problemi di diritto della previdenza sociale*, Giappichelli, Torino, 1989.

CINELLI M., FERRARO G. (a cura di), *Il contenzioso del lavoro nella Legge 4 novembre 2010, n. 183 (Collegato Lavoro)*, Giappichelli, Torino, 2011

CINELLI M., FERRARO G., MAZZOTTA O. (a cura di), *Il nuovo mercato del lavoro dalla Riforma Fornero alla legge di stabilità 2013*, Giappichelli, Torino, 2013

CINELLI M., GIUBBONI S., *Il diritto della sicurezza sociale in trasformazione*, Giappichelli, Torino, 2005

CLARKSON M. B. E., *A Risk Based Model of Stakeholder Theory*, in *Proceedings of the 2nd Toronto Conference on Stakeholder Theory, Centre for Corporate Social Performance and Ethics*, University of Toronto, Toronto, 1994

COLANTONIO A., *Social Sustainability: Linking Research to Policy and Practice*, Oxford Brookes University, Oxford, 2009

COMIM F., QIZILBASH M., ALKIRE S. (eds), *The Capability Approach. Concepts, Measures and Applications*, Cambridge University Press, Cambridge, 2008

COMMON M., PERRINGS C., *Towards an Ecological Economics of Sustainability*, in *Ecological Economics*, 1992, vol. 6, n. 1

CONAGHAN J., FISCHL R. M., KLARE K., *Labour Law in an Era of Globalization. Transformative Practices & Possibilities*, Oxford University Press, Oxford, 2002

CORAZZA L., ROMEI R. (a cura di), *Diritto del lavoro in trasformazione*, il Mulino, Bologna, 2014

CORAZZA L., ROMEI R., *Il puzzle delle trasformazioni*, in L. CORAZZA, R. ROMEI (a cura di), *Diritto del lavoro in trasformazione*, il Mulino, Bologna, 2014

CORSO M., *Sfide e prospettive della rivoluzione digitale: lo smart working*, in *Dir. rel. ind.*, 2017, 4

COSTA P., *Cittadinanza sociale e diritto del lavoro nell'Italia repubblicana*, in G. CAZZETTA, G. G. BALANDI (a cura di), *Diritti e lavoro nell'Italia repubblicana: materiali dall'incontro di studio, Ferrara, 24 ottobre 2008*, Giuffrè, Milano, 2009

COSTANZA R. (ed.), *Ecological Economics: The Science and Management of Sustainability*, Columbia University Press, New York, 1991.

COUNTOURIS N., KOUKIADAKI A., *The Glass Half Full: Collective Redundancies, Public Interest, and the (Unfulfilled) Potential of Europe's 'Highly Competitive Social Market Economy'*, in *Giorn. dir. lav. rel. ind.*, 2017, 153, 1

CRAIG J. D. R., LINK M. S., *Globalization and the Future of Labour Law*, Cambridge University Press, Cambridge, 2006

D'ALOJA A., *Eguaglianza sostanziale e diritto diseguale. Contributo allo studio delle azioni positive nella prospettiva costituzionale*, Cedam, Padova, 2002

D'ANTONA M., *Diritto al lavoro e politiche per l'occupazione*, in *Riv. giur. lav.*, 1999, 3

D'ANTONA M., *Diritto del lavoro di fine secolo: una crisi d'identità?*, in *Riv. giur. lav.*, 1998, 1

D'ANTONA M., *La grande sfida delle trasformazioni del lavoro: ricentrare la tutela sulle esigenze del lavoratore come soggetto*, in F. AMATO (a cura di), *I 'destini' del lavoro. Autonomia e subordinazione nella società post-fordista*, Franco Angeli, Milano, 1998

D'ANTONA M., *Il diritto al lavoro nella Costituzione e nell'ordinamento comunitario*, in *Riv. giur. lav.*, 1999

DAGNINO E., MENEGOTTO M., PELUSI L. M., TIRABOSCHI M. (a cura di), *Guida pratica al lavoro agile dopo la legge n. 81/2017, Formule contrattuali - Schemi operativi - Mappatura della contrattazione collettiva*, ADAPT University Press, Modena, 2017

DAGNINO E., MOSCARITOLO I., *Diritto alla disconnessione: un diritto di nuova generazione?*, in Boll. Adapt, 19 settembre 2016

DAHRENDORF R., *Per un nuovo liberalismo*, Laterza, Roma-Bari, 1988

DALY H. E., COBB J. B., *For the Common Good*, Beacon Press, Boston, 1989.

DAVICO L., *Lo sviluppo sostenibile. Le dimensioni sociali*, Carocci, Roma, 2004

DAVIDOV G., *The Reports of My Death are Greatly Exaggerated: 'Employee' as A Viable (Though Over-Used) Legal Concept*, in G. DAVIDOV, B. LANGILLE (eds), *Boundaries and Frontiers of Labour Law: Goals and Means in the Regulation of Work*, Hart Publishing, Oxford, 2006

DAVIDOV G., LANGILLE B. (eds), *Boundaries and Frontiers of Labour Law: Goals and Means in the Regulation of Work*, Hart Publishing, Oxford, 2006

DAVIDOV G., LANGILLE B, *Introduction: Goals and Means in the Regulation of Work*, in G. DAVIDOV, B. LANGILLE (eds), *Boundaries and Frontiers of Labour Law*, Hart Publishing, Oxford, 2006

DAVIDOV G., LANGILLE B. (eds), *The Idea of Labour Law*, Oxford University Press, Oxford, 2011

DAVIES P., *Lavoro subordinato e lavoro autonomo*, in *Dir. rel. ind.*, 2000

DE LUCA TAMAJO R., *La norma inderogabile nel diritto del lavoro*, Jovene, Napoli, 1976

DE LUCA TAMAJO R., *Crisi economica e relazioni industriali: prime osservazioni sull'art. 8 del d.l. 13 agosto 2011*, in *Cuore&Critica.it*, 2011

DE LUCA TAMAJO R., *Prime valutazioni e questioni di legittimità costituzionale dell'art. 8 l. n. 148 del 2011*, in *Arg. dir. lav.*, 2012, 1

DE LUCA TAMAJO R., *Il problema dell'inderogabilità delle regole a tutela del* lavoro: passato e presente, in Giorn. dir. lav. rel. ind., 2013, 4

DE LUCA TAMAJO R., *La (in)derogabilità della normativa lavoristica ai tempi del Jobs Act*, in *Labor*, 2016, 5-6

DE LUCA TAMAJO R., *Concorrenza e diritto del lavoro*, in A. PERULLI (a cura di), *L'idea di diritto del lavoro, oggi. In ricordo di Giorgio Ghezzi*, Cedam, Padova, 2016

DE LUCA TAMAJO R., *Jobs Act e cultura giuslavoristica*, in *Dir. lav. merc.*, 2016, 1

DE LUCA TAMAJO R., FLAMMIA R., PERSIANI M., *La crisi della nozione di subordinazione e della sua idoneità selettiva dei trattamenti garantistici. Prime proposte per un nuovo approccio sistematico in una prospettiva di valorizzazione di un tertium genius: il lavoro coordinato*, in AA.VV. (a cura di), *Subordinazione e autonomia: vecchi e nuovi modelli*, UTET, Torino, 1998

DE LUCA TAMAJO R., VENTURA L. (a cura di), *Il diritto del lavoro nell'emergenza*, Jovene, Napoli, 1979

DE SIMONE G., *Problemi d'identità: il «cittadino lavoratore» e l'evoluzione del diritto del lavoro*, in *Lav. dir.*, 1995

De Simone G., *Tra il dire e il fare. Obiettivi e tecniche delle politiche per il lavoro femminile nella riforma Fornero*, in *Lav. dir.*, 2012

Deakin S., *Economic Approaches to the Evaluation of Labour Law: Comparing Coase, Hayek and Sen*, in A. Perulli (a cura di), *Efficacia e diritto del lavoro*, Padova, Cedam, 2008

Deakin S., *The Contribution of Labour Law to Economic and Human Development*, in G. Davidov, B. Langille (eds), *The Idea of Labour Law*, Oxford University Press, Oxford, 2011

Deakin, S., Supiot A. (eds), *Capacitas: Contract Law, Capabilities and the Legal Foundations of the Market*, Hart Publishing, London, 2009

Deakin S., Wilkinson F., *Il diritto del Lavoro e la teoria economica. Una rivisitazione*, in *Giorn. dir. lav. rel. ind.*, 1999, 84, 4

Deakin S., Wilkinson F., *'Capabilities', ordine spontaneo del mercato e diritti sociali*, in *Dir. merc. lav.*, 2000, 2

Defraigne J.-C. et al. (a cura di), *Les modèles sociaux en Europe. Quel avenir face à la crise?*, Bruylant, Bruxelles, 2012

Del Boca A., Mundo A., *L' inganno generazionale. Il falso mito del conflitto* per il lavoro, Università Bocconi Editore, Milano, 2017

Del Punta R., *L'economia e le ragioni del diritto del lavoro*, in *Giorn. dir. lav. rel. ind.*, 2001, 1

Del Punta R., *Ragioni economiche, tutela dei lavoratori e libertà del soggetto*, in *Riv. it. dir. lav.*, 2002, 1

Del Punta R., *Responsabilità sociale dell'impresa e diritto del lavoro*, in *Lav. dir.*, 2006, 1

Del Punta R., *Economic Challenge to Labour Law*, in A. Lyon-Caen, A. Perulli (eds), *Valutare il diritto del Lavoro, Evaluer le Droit du Travail, Evaluate Labour Law*, Cedam, Padova, 2010

Del Punta R., *La stabilità reale nell'epoca dell'instabilità*, in *Dir. lav. merc.*, 2010

Del Punta R., *Epistemologia breve del diritto del lavoro*, in L. Nogler, L. Corazza (a cura di), *Risistemare il diritto del lavoro. Liber amicorum Marcello Pedrazzoli*, Franco Angeli, Milano, 2012 e in *Lav. dir.*, 2013, 1

Del Punta R., *Leggendo the Idea of Justice di Amartya Sen*, in *Giorn. dir. lav. rel. ind.*, 2013, 138, 2

Del Punta R., *Verso l'individualizzazione dei diritti?*, in L. Corazza, R. Romei (a cura di), *Diritto del lavoro in trasformazione*, il Mulino, Bologna, 2014

Del Punta R., *Labour Law and the Capability*, in *International Journal of Comparative Labour Law and Industrial Relations*, 2016, vol. 32, 4

Del Punta R., *Diritto del Lavoro* (nona edizione), Giuffrè, Milano, 2017

Delfino M., *Diritti sociali e flexicurity*, in *Riv. it. dir. lav.*, 2009, 3

Dell'Olio M., *La subordinazione nell'esperienza italiana*, in *Arg. dir. lav.*, 1998

Diaz Aznarte M. T., *Crisi economica e riforma del diritto del lavoro in Spagna. Le ricette neoliberali producono occupazione?*, in *Riv. giur. lav.*, 2015, 4

Di Paola L. (a cura di), *Il licenziamento. Dalla Legge Fornero al Jobs Act*, Giuffrè, Milano, 2016

Di Turi C., *Globalizzazione dell'economia e diritti fondamentali in materia di lavoro: il ruolo dell'OIL e dell'OMC*, Giuffrè, Milano, 2007

Donata G., Guarriello F. (a cura di), *Massimo Roccella. Manuale di diritto del lavoro,* Sesta edizione, Giappichelli, Torino, 2015

Du Pisani J. A., *Sustainable Development – Historical Roots of the Concept*, in *Environmental Sciences*, 2006, vol. 3, n. 2

Dupuy P. M., *Ou en est le droit international de l'environnement à la fin du siècle?*, in *Rev. Gén. Droit Int. Pub.*, 1997

Ehrenfeld J. R., *Sustainability Needs to Be Attained, Not Managed, Sustainability,* in *Science, Practice & Policy*, 2008, 4

Elkingtonm J., *Cannibals with Forks: The Triple Bottom Line of 21st Century Business*, Capstone, Oxford, 1997

Escande Varniol M.-C., et al. (a cura di), *Quel droit social dans une Europe en crise?*, Larcier, Bruxelles, 2012

Esposito M., Gaeta L., Santucci R., Viscomi A., Zoppoli A., Zoppoli L., *Istituzioni di diritto del lavoro e sindacale. Mercato, contratto e rapporti di lavoro*, Giappichelli, Torino, 2014

Falasca G., *I servizi privati per l'impiego*, Giuffrè, Milano, 2006

Fauvarque-Gobin L., *La conciliazione vita-lavoro nella Loi travail*, in L. Casano, G. Imperatori, C. Tourres (a cura di), *Loi travail: prima analisi e lettura*, in *ADAPT Labour Studies e-Book series*, 2016

Fergola P., *La teoria del recesso e il rapporto di lavoro*, Giuffrè, Milano, 1985

Ferrando García F., *El reforzamiento del poder de direccion tras la reforma laboral de 2012*, in *Revista de Derecho Social*, 2013, vol. 61

Ferrante V., *Responsabilità sociale dell'impresa e lavoro subordinato*, in *Lav. dir.*, 2006, 1

Ferrarese M. R., *Diritto sconfinato: Inventiva giuridica e spazi nel mondo globale*, Laterza, Roma, 2015

Ferraresi M., *Responsabilità sociale dell'impresa e diritto del lavoro*, Cedam, Padova, 2012

Ferraro G., *Politiche dell'impiego e crisi occupazionale nella legge n. 236*, in *Lav. inf.*, 1993, 19

Ferraro G., *Dal lavoro subordinato al lavoro autonomo*, in *Giorn. dir. lav. rel. ind.*, 1998

Ferraro G., *Il contratto collettivo oggi dopo l'art. 8 del decreto n. 138/2011*, in *WP C.S.D.L.E. 'Massimo D'Antona'.IT – 129/201*

Ferraro G., *Il controllo giudiziale sui poteri imprenditoriali*, in M. Cinelli, G. Ferraro (a cura di), *Il contenzioso del lavoro nella Legge 4 novembre 2010, n. 183 (Collegato Lavoro)*, Giappichelli, Torino, 2011

Fievet G., *Réflexions sur le concept de développement durable: prétentions économiques, principes stratégiques et protection des droits fondamentaux*, in *Rev. Belge Droit Int.*, 2001

Filì V., *Le deleghe per il riordino della normativa in materia di servizi per l'impiego e incentivi all'occupazione*, in F. Carinci, M. Miscione (a cura di), *Il Collegato lavoro 2008. L. n. 24 dicembre 2007, n. 247*, Ipsoa, Milano, 2008

FINNEMORE M., TOOPE J. S., *Alternatives to 'Legalization': Richer Views of Law and Politics*, in A. BETH, S. STEINBERG, S. RICHARD (eds), *International Law and International Relations*, Cambridge University Press, Cambridge, 2007

FIORAVANTI M., *Costituzione italiana: articolo 2*, Carocci, Roma, 2017

FIORILLO L., *Il lavoro agile: continua il processo di ridefinizione del Diritto del lavoro*, in L. FIORILLO, A. PERULLI (a cura di), *Il jobs act del lavoro autonomo e del lavoro agile*, Giappichelli, Torino, 2018

FIORILLO L., PERULLI A. (a cura di), *Il jobs act del lavoro autonomo e del lavoro agile*, Giappichelli, Torino, 2018

FONTANA G., *Dall'inderogabilità alla ragionevolezza*, Giappichelli, Torino, 2010

FORTUNE J., HUGHES J., *Modern Academic Myths*, in F. A. STOWELL, R. L. ISON, R. ARMSON, J. HOLLOWAY, S. JACKSON, S. MCROBB (eds), *System for Sustainability: People, Organizations and Environments*, Plenum Press, New York and London, 1997

FREEDLAND M. R., COUNTOURIS N., *Diritti e doveri nel rapporto tra disoccupati e servizi per l'impiego in Europa*, in *Dir. lav. rel. ind.*, 2005, 4

FREEDLAND M., PRASSL J. (eds), *Viking, Laval and Beyond*, Hart Publishing, Oxford and Portland, Oregon, 2014

FREEMAN R. E., *Strategic Management: A Stakeholder Approach*, Pitman, Boston, 1984

FREY C. B., OSBORNE M. A., *The Future of Employment: How Susceptible Are Jobs to Computerization?*, in *Oxford Martin School Working Paper*, Oxford, 17 September 2013

GAETA L., *In tema di frammentazione della subordinazione: a proposito di un paio di sfasature e di un viaggio nel passato*, in M. D'ANTONA (a cura di), *Politiche di flessibilità e mutamenti di diritto del lavoro: Italia e Spagna*, Editoriale Scientifica, Napoli, 1990

GAETA L., *Verso un diritto diseguale senza diseguaglianze*, in L. GAETA, L. ZOPPOLI (a cura di), *Il diritto diseguale: la legge sulle azioni positive*, Giappichelli, Torino, 1992

GAETA L., *Contro l'unificazione tra lavoro autonomo e subordinato*, in F. Amato (a cura di), *I 'destini' del lavoro. Autonomia e subordinazione nella società post-fordista*, Franco Angeli, Milano, 1998

GAETA L. (a cura di), *Costantino Mortati e 'Il lavoro nella Costituzione': una ri-lettura*, Giuffrè, Milano, 2005

GAETA L., *Il lavoro e il diritto. Un percorso storico*, Cacucci, Bari, 2013

GAETA L., *La dialettica stabilità-precarietà*, in L. CORAZZA, R. ROMEI (a cura di), *Diritto del lavoro in trasformazione*, il Mulino, Bologna, 2014

GAETA L. (a cura di), *Prima di tutto il lavoro. La costituzione di un diritto all'Assemblea Costituente*, Ediesse, Roma, 2014

GAETA L. *Appunti dal corso di diritto del lavoro*, Giappichelli, Torino, 2018

GALLINO L., *Il lavoro non è una merce. Contro la flessibilità*, Laterza, Bari, 2007

GARILLI A., *L'art. 8 l. n. 148 del 2011 nel sistema delle relazioni sindacali*, in *Arg. dir. lav.*, 2012, 1

GAROFALO D., *Le novità in tema di servizi per l'impiego e di politica attiva del lavoro*, in F. CARINCI (a cura di), *La politica del lavoro del Governo Renzi, Atti del X*

Seminario di Bertinoro-Bologna del 23-24 ottobre 2014, ADAPT University Press, Modena, 2015

GAROFALO D., *Lavoro, impresa e trasformazioni organizzative, Relazione alle giornate di studio Aidlass 2017, Frammentazione organizzativa e lavoro: rapporti individuali e collettivi*, Cassino, 18-19 Maggio 2017

GAROFALO M. G., *Solidarietà e lavoro*, in M. NAPOLI (a cura di), *La solidarietà*, Vita e Pensiero, Milano, 2009

GAZIER B., *La strategia europea per l'occupazione nella tempesta: il ripristino di una prospettiva a lungo termine*, in *Dir. rel. ind.*, 2011, 1

GEORGESCU-ROEGEN N., *Energia e miti economici*, Torino, Boringhieri, 1982

GHERA E., *Il nuovo diritto del lavoro. Subordinazione e lavoro flessibile*, Giappichelli, Torino, 2006

GHERA E., *Subordinazione, statuto protettivo e qualificazione del rapporto di lavoro*, in *Giorn. dir. lav. rel. ind.*, 2006, 1

GHERA E., GAROFALO D. (a cura di), *Le tutele per i licenziamenti e per la disoccupazione involontaria nel Jobs Act*, Cacucci, Bari, 2015

GHERA E., PACE A. (a cura di), *L'attualità dei principi fondamentali della Costituzione in materia di lavoro*, Jovene, Napoli, 2009

GIANFORMAGGIO L., *Politica della differenza e principio di eguaglianza. Sono veramente incompatibili?*, in *Lav. dir.*, 1992

GIANNOTTI P., *Gli orientamenti comunitari e internazionali in materia di collocamento*, in P. OLIVELLI (a cura di), *Il 'collocamento' tra pubblico e privato*, Giuffrè, Milano, 2003

GIORGIS A., *La costituzionalizzazione dei diritti all'uguaglianza sostanziale*, Jovene, Napoli, 1999

GIUBBONI S., *I diritti sociali nell'Unione europea dopo il Trattato di Lisbona. Paradossi, rischi e opportunità*, in *Relazione al convegno Diritto civile e principi costituzionali europei e italiani*, svoltosi a Perugia il 25 e 26 marzo 2011

GIUBBONI S., *Profili costituzionali del contratto di lavoro a tutele crescenti*, in *WP C.S.D.L.E. 'Massimo D'Antona'.IT – 246/2015*

GIUBBONI S., *Diritto del lavoro europeo. Una introduzione critica*, Cedam Wolters Kluwer, Milano, 2017

GIUFFRÈ F., *La solidarietà nell'ordinamento costituzionale*, Giuffrè, Milano, 2002

GIUGNI G., *Introduzione allo studio della autonomia collettiva*, Giuffrè, Milano, 1960

GIUGNI G., *Mansioni e qualifica del rapporto di lavoro*, Napoli, Jovene, 1963

GIUGNI G., *Prospettive del diritto del lavoro per gli anni '80*, in AA.VV. (a cura di), *Atti del VII Congresso nazionale di diritto del lavoro – AIDLASS, svoltosi a Bari nelle giornate del 23-25 aprile 1982*, Giuffrè, Milano, 1983

GOLDIN A., *Some Defining Components of a Labour Law Influx*, Pompeu Fabra University, Barcelona, 2013

GOODLAND R., LEDEC G., *Neoclassical Economics and Principles of Sustainable Development*, in *Ecological Modelling*, 1987, vol. 38, nos 1-2

GOTTARDI D., *Dalle discriminazioni di genere alle discriminazioni doppie e sovrapposte: le transizioni*, in *Dir. lav. rel. ind.*, 2004

GOTTARDI D. (a cura di), *Il diritto antidiscriminatorio tra teoria e prassi applicativa*, Ediesse, Roma, 2009

GOTTARDI D., *La condivisione delle responsabilità genitoriali in salsa italiana*, in *Lav. dir*, 2012

GOTTARDI D., *Riforme strutturali e prospettiva Europea di Flexicurity: andata e ritorno*, in *Lav. dir.*, 2015, 2

GOTTARDI D., GUARRIELLO F. (a cura di), *Massimo Roccella, Manuale di diritto del Lavoro, Mercato del lavoro e rapporti di lavoro*, Giappichelli, Torino, 6a edizione, 2015

GOW D., *Poverty and Natural Resources: Principles for Environmental Management and Sustainable Development*, in *Environmental Impact Assessment Review*, 1992

GRAGNOLI E., PERULLI A. (a cura di), *La riforma del mercato del lavoro e i nuovi modelli contrattuali. Commentario al decreto legislativo 10 settembre 2003, n. 276*, Cedam, Padova, 2004

GRAMOLATI A., MARI G., TRENTIN B., *Lavoro, libertà, conoscenza*, Firenze University Press, Firenze, 2010

GRANDI M., *Lavoro e valori: note sulla prospettiva assiologica di Luigi Mengoni*, in *Arg. dir. lav.*, 2006

GUARRIELLO F., *Il ruolo delle istituzioni e della società civile nel nuovo diritto antidiscriminatorio*, in M. BARBERA (a cura di), *Il nuovo diritto antidiscriminatorio: il quadro comunitario e nazionale*, Giuffrè, Milano, 2007

GUARRIELLO F., *Discriminazioni (divieto di)*, (con M.C. CIMAGLIA), in P. LAMBERTUCCI, *Dizionari del diritto privato promossi da N. Irti, Diritto del lavoro*, Giuffrè, Milano, 2010

GUARRIELLO F., LEONARDI S. (a cura di), *Globalizzazione e relazioni industriali*, Ediesse, Roma, 2003

HABERMAS J., *Fatti e norme. Contributi a una teoria discorsiva del diritto e della democrazia*, Guerini e Associati, Milano, 1992

HANDY C., *The Changing Shape of Work and Life*, in *Policy Studies*, 1982, 2

HEINEN J. T., *Emerging, Diverging and Converging Paradigms on Sustainable Development*, in *International Journal of Sustainable Development and World Ecology*, 1994, vol. 1

HEMERIJCK A., *Come cambia il modello sociale europeo*, in *Stato e mercato*, 2002

HEPPLE B., *The Future of Labour Law*, in *Comparative Labor Law & Policy Journal*, 1996, vol. 17

HEPPLE B. (ed.), *Social Rights and Labour Rights in a Global Context*, Cambridge University Press, Cambridge, 2002

HEPPLE B., *Diritto del lavoro, diseguaglianza e commercio globale*, in *Giorn. dir. lav. rel. ind.*, 2003

HEPPLE B., *Labour Laws and Global Trade*, Hart Publishing, Oxford, 2005

HEPPLE B., *Diritto del lavoro e crisi economica. Lezioni dalla storia europea*, in *Dir. lav. rel. ind.*, 2009

HUGON A., *Les mutations du droit de l'entreprise et l'objectif de développement durable*, Université de Limoges, 10 novembre 2010

HYDE A., *The Idea of the Idea of Labour Law: A Parable*, in G. DAVIDOV, B. LANGILLE (eds), *The Idea of Labour Law*, Oxford University Press, Oxford, 2011

HYDE A., *What Is Labour Law?, in* G. DAVIDOV, B. LANGILLE (eds), *Boundaries and Frontiers of Labour Law*, Hart Publishing, Oxford, 2006

ICHINO A., *A chi serve il diritto del lavoro, Riflessioni interdisciplinari sulla funzione economica e la giustificazione costituzionale dell'inderogabilità delle norme giuslavoristiche,* in *Riv. it. dir. lav.*, 1994

ICHINO A, ICHINO P., *A chi serve il diritto del lavoro,* in *Riv. it. dir. lav.*, 1994, 1

ICHINO P., *Il collocamento impossibile. Problemi e obiettivi della riforma del mercato del lavoro,* De Donato, Bari, 1982

ICHINO P., *Subordinazione e autonomia nel diritto del lavoro,* Giuffrè, Milano, 1989

ICHINO P. *Il lavoro e il mercato. Per un diritto del lavoro maggiorenne,* Mondadori, Milano, 1996.

ICHINO P., *Il dialogo tra economia e diritto del lavoro,* in *Riv. it. dir. lav.*, 2001, I

ICHINO P., *Il contratto di Lavoro II,* in A. CICU, F. MESSINEO, L. MENGONI (diretto da), *Trattato di diritto civile e commerciale,* Giuffrè, Milano, 2003

ICHINO P., *La stabilità del lavoro e l'uguaglianza,* in *Riv. it. dir. lav.*, 2005, 1

ICHINO P., *Come il metodo sperimentale può contribuire al progresso del diritto del lavoro,* in *Riv. it. dir. lav.*, 2011, 1

ICHINO P., *Inchiesta sul lavoro. Perché non dobbiamo avere paura di una grande riforma,* Mondadori, Milano, 2011

ICHINO P., *La riforma dei licenziamenti e i diritti fondamentali dei lavoratori,* in L. NOGLER, L. CORAZZA (a cura di), *Risistemare il diritto del lavoro. Liber amicorum Marcello Pedrazzoli,* Franco Angeli, Milano, 2012

JABAREEN Y. *A New Conceptual Framework for Sustainable Development,* in *Environmental, Development and Sustainability,* 2008, vol. 10

JEAMMAUD A., *Il diritto del lavoro alla prova del cambiamento,* in *Lav. dir.*, 1997, 3

JEAMMAUD A., *Le droit du travail dans le capitalisme, questions de fonctions et de fonctionnement,* in *WP C.S.D.L.E. 'Massimo D'Antona'.INT – 41/2005*

JONAS H., *Il Principio di Responsabilità,* Einaudi, Torino, 2014

JUNKER K. W., *The Progression of the Sustainability Concept in Environmental Law,* in *Umwelt und Gesundheit Online,* 2012, 5

KAHN L. M., *The Impact of Employment Protection Mandates on Demographic Temporary Employment Patterns: International Microeconomic Evidence,* in *Economic Journal,* 2007, vol. 117 (521)

KAYA I., *Implications of the Danube River Dispute on International Environmental Law,* in *Review of International Law & Politics,* 2008, vol. 4, no. 16

KELSEN H., *ReineRechtslehre,* Wien, 1960; trad. it.: T. TREVES (a cura di), *La dottrina pura del diritto,* Einaudi, Torino, 1966

KIDD C. V., *The Evolution of Sustainability,* in *Journal of Agricultural and Environmental Ethics,* 1992, vol. 5, no. 1

KLASSEN G. A. J., OPSCHOOR J. B., *Economics of Sustainability or the Sustainability of Economics: Different Paradigms,* in *Ecological Economics,* 1991, vol. 4, n. 2

KOTT S., DROUX J. (eds), *Globalizing Social Rights: The International Labour Organization and Beyond,* Palgrave Macmillan, London, 2013

KRUGMAN P., *Il ritorno dell'economia della depressione e la crisi del 2008,* Garzanti, Milano, 2009

KUHN T. S., *La tensione essenziale: cambiamenti e continuità nella scienza*, Einaudi, Torino, 1985

KUHN T. S., *La struttura delle rivoluzioni scientifiche*, Einaudi, Torino, 1995

LA FORGIA S., *Il lavoro dignitoso, il lavoro decente e il lavoro purchessia, in Liber amicorum. Spunti di diritto del lavoro in dialogo con Bruno Veneziani*, Cacucci, Bari, 2012

LAI M., *Evoluzione tecnologica e tutela del lavoro: a proposito di smart working e di crowd working*, in *Dir. rel. ind.*, 2017, 4

LAI M., RICCIARDI L., *La nuova disciplina del lavoro agile*, in *Dir. prat. lav.*, 2016

LAMBERTI M., *L'accordo individuale e i diritti del lavoratore agile*, in L. FIORILLO, A. PERULLI (a cura di), *Il jobs act del lavoro autonomo e del lavoro agile*, Giappichelli, Torino, 2018

LAMBERTUCCI P., *Efficacia dispositiva del contratto collettivo e autonomia individuale*, Cedam, Padova, 1990

LAMBERTUCCI P., *Politiche dell'impiego e promozione dell'occupazione*, in G. SANTORO PASSARELLI (a cura di), *Flessibilità e diritto del lavoro*, Giappichelli, Torino, 1996

LAMBERTUCCI P., *La disciplina della promozione dell'occupazione dopo il d. lgs. n. 276/2003*, in *Arg. dir. lav.*, 2004, 3

LAMBERTUCCI P, *Il diritto al lavoro tra principi costituzionali e discipline di tutela: brevi appunti*, in *Riv. it. dir. lav.*, 2010, 1

LAMBERTUCCI P., *Globalizzazione e diritto del lavoro: brevi spunti di riflessione*, in *Dir. merc. lav.*, 2010, 1

LAMBERTUCCI P., *Il diritto al lavoro tra principi costituzionali e discipline di tutela: brevi appunti*, in *Riv. it. dir. lav.*, 2010, 1

LAMBERTUCCI P., *La contrattazione collettiva di prossimità e gli assetti contrattuali del Testo unico del 2014: modelli di relazioni industriali a confronto*, in *Dir. mer. lav.*, 2014, 1-2

LAMBERTUCCI P., *I poteri del datore di lavoro nello Statuto dei lavoratori dopo l'attuazione del c.d. jobs act del 2015: primi spunti di riflessione*, in *Arg. dir. lav.*, 2016, 3

LAMBERTUCCI P., *Il lavoratore disabile tra disciplina dell'avviamento al lavoro e tutela contro i licenziamenti: brevi note a margine dei provvedimenti attuativi del c.d.* Jobs Act *alla 'prova' della disciplina antidiscriminatoria*, in *Arg. dir. lav.*, 2016, 6

LANGILLE B., *Labour Law's Back Pages*, in G. DAVIDOV, B. LANGILLE (eds), *Boundaries and Frontiers of Labour Law: Goals and Means in the Regulation of Work*, Hart Publishing, Oxford, 2006

LANGILLE B., *Labour Law's Theory of Justice*, in G. DAVIDOV, B. LANGILLE (eds), *The Idea of Labour Law*, Oxford University Press, Oxford, 2011

LANGILLE B., *'Hard Law Makes Bad Cases': The International Labour Organization (Nervously) Confronts New Governance Institutions*, in *International Journal of Comparative Labour Law and Industrial Relations*, 2016, vol. 32, 4

LASSANDARI A., *Le discriminazioni nel lavoro. Nozione, interessi, tutele*, Cedam, Padova, 2010

LASSANDARI A., *Dopo l'accordo del 28 giugno 2011 (e l'art. 8 della l. n. 148): incertezze, contraddizioni, fragilità*, in *Lav. dir.*, 2012, 1

LASSANDARI A., *Problemi di rappresentanza e tutela collettiva dei lavoratori che utilizzano le tecnologie digitali*, in *Riv. giur. lav.*, 2017, 2

LEADER S., *I diritti sociali nell'economia globale*, in *Riv. giur. lav.*, 2015, 3

LEVINAS E., *Autrement qu'être ou au-delà de l'essence*, 1974, trad. it. di S. PETROSINO, M. T. AIELLO, *Altrimenti che essere o al di là dell'essenza* (introd. di S. PETROSINO), Jaca Book, Milano, 1983

LINDBECK A., SNOWER D. J., *The Insider-Outsider Theory of Employment and Unemployment*, MIT Press, Cambridge Mass., London, 1988

LO FARO A., *Compatibilità economiche, diritti del lavoro e istanze di tutela dei diritti fondamentali. Qualche spunto di riflessione dal caso italiano*, in *Giorn. dir. lav. rel. ind*, 2014, 2

LOI P., *Un'introduzione al tema del lavoro nella gig economy*, in *Riv. giur. lav.*, 2017, 2

LOKIEC P., *Il faut sauver le droit du travail*, Odile Jacob, Paris, 2015

LONGO E., *I diritti sociali nella Costituzione italiana: un percorso di analisi*, in *Riv. dir. sic. soc.*, 2017, 2

LOUIS M., *L'Organisation Internationale du Travail et le* travail décent. *Un agenda social pour le multilateralisme*, l'Harmattan, Paris, 2011

LOWE V., *Sustainable Development and Unsustainable Arguments*, in A. BOYLE, D. FREESTONE (eds), *International Law and Sustainable Development: Past Achievements and Future Challenges*, Oxford University Press, Oxford, 1999

LOWE V., *The Politics of Law Making: Are the Method and Character of Norm Creation Changing?*, in M. BYERS (ed.), *The Role of Law in International Politics: Essays in International Relations and International Law*, Oxford University Press, Oxford, 2001

LOY G., *Riflessioni su specialità, tipo e sottotipo nel lavoro subordinato*, in M. PEDRAZZOLI (a cura di), *Lavoro subordinato e dintorni*, il Mulino, Bologna, 1989

LOY G. (a cura di), *Diritto del lavoro e crisi economica. Misure contro l'emergenza ed evoluzione legislativa in Italia, Spagna e Francia*, Ediesse, Roma, 2011

LOY G., *Flessicurezza e precarietà*, in *Riv. giur. lav*, 2013, 1

LUNARDON F., *L'evoluzione del concetto di subordinazione nell'elaborazione dottrinale*, in *Quad. dir. lav. rel. ind.*, 1998

LYON-CAEN A., SACHS T., *L'ADN d'une réforme*, in *Revue de droit du travail*, 2013

LYON-CAEN A., SACHS T., *La legge sulla «sécurisation de l'emploi»: DNA di una riforma*, in *Lav. dir.*, 2013

LYON-CAEN G., *La crise du droit du travail*, in F. GAMILLSCHEG et al., *In Memoriam Sir Otto Kahn Freund*, Munich, C.H. Beck'sche Verlagsbuchhandlung, Munich, 1980

LYON-CAEN G. *L'infiltration du Droit du travail par le Droit de la concurrence*, in *Droit Ouvrier*, 1992

LYON-CAEN G., *Le droit du travail: une tecnique reversible*, Dalloz, Paris, 1995

MAGNANI M., *Diritto dei contratti di lavoro*, Giuffrè, Milano, 2009

MAGNANI M., *Crisi d'impresa tra diritto del lavoro e mercato*, in *Arg. dir. lav.*, 2017, 6.

MAGNI S. F., *Etica delle capacità. La filosofia pratica di Sen e Nussbaum*, il Mulino, Bologna, 2006

MANCINI G. F., *sub art. 4*, in G. BRANCA (a cura di), *Commentario della Costituzione*, Zanichelli-Il Foro Italiano, Bologna-Roma, 1975

Mantini P., *Per una nozione costituzionalmente rilevante di ambiente*, in *Riv. giur. amb.*, 2006, 2

Marazza M., *Il regime sanzionatorio dei licenziamenti nel Jobs Act*, in *Arg. dir. lav.*, 2015, 2

Marazza M., *Dei poteri (del datore di lavoro), dei controlli (a distanza) e del trattamento dei dati (del lavoratore)*, in *Arg. dir. lav.*, 2016, 3

Maresca A., *Concorrenza tra ordinamenti e diritto del lavoro*, in A. Plaia (a cura di), *La competizione tra ordinamenti giuridici, Mutuo riconoscimento e scelta della norma più favorevole nello spazio giuridico europeo*, Giuffrè, Milano, 2007

Mariucci L., *Il diritto del lavoro della seconda Repubblica*, in *Lav. dir.*, 1997, 2

Mariucci L., *Autonomia individuale e collettiva: l'attualità di un vecchio dilemma*, in *Lav. dir.*, 2008, 2

Mariucci L., *Le politiche del lavoro di fronte alla crisi*, in *Riv. it. dir. lav.*, 2009, 3

Marrella F., *Manuale di diritto del commercio internazionale*, Cedam, Padova, 2017

Massi E., *Il ricambio generazionale. Il contratto di solidarietà espansiva*, in *Dir. prat. lav.*, 2017, 7.

Massimiani C., *La qualità del lavoro nell'esperienza dell'OIL e nelle politiche sociali europee*, Lulu Press, Raleigh, 2010

Mazzotta O., *La giustizia del lavoro nella visione del 'collegato': la disciplina dei licenziamenti*, in M. Cinelli, G. Ferraro (a cura di), *Il contenzioso del lavoro nella Legge 4 novembre 2010, n. 183 (Collegato Lavoro)*, Giappichelli, Torino, 2011

Mazzotta O. (a cura di), *Lavoro ed esigenze dell'impresa fra diritto sostanziale e processo dopo il Jobs Act*, Giappichelli, Torino, 2017

McEntire D. A., *The History, Meaning and Policy Recommendations of Sustainable Development: A Review Essay*, 2005, vol. 4, n. 2

Meliadò G., *Concorrenza e politiche sociali*, in A. Baylos Grau, B. Caruso, M. D'Antona, S. Sciarra (a cura di), *Dizionario di diritto del lavoro comunitario*, Monduzzi, Milano, 1996

Menghini L., *Autonomia e subordinazione: sollecitazioni dottrinali e risposte della giurisprudenza*, in *Riv. giur. lav.*, 1991, 42

Menghini L., *Efficacia diretta delle fonti comunitarie esaurienti ed effetti dissuasivi nella discriminazione per sesso*, in *Riv. giur. lav.*, 1994, 45

Menghini L., *Le cause della precarietà e le norme del diritto del lavoro*, in AA.VV. (a cura di), *Scritti in onore di Edoardo Ghera*, Cacucci, Bari, vol. 1, 2008

Menghini L., *I contrasti tra Corte EDU e Corte Costituzionale sulle leggi retroattive che eliminano i diritti di lavoratori e pensionati: qualche idea per un avvio di soluzione*, in *Riv. giur. lav. prev. soc.*, 2012, 2

Mengoni L., *Diritto e valori*, il Mulino, Bologna, 1985

Mengoni L., *Fondata sul lavoro: la Repubblica tra diritti inviolabili e doveri inderogabili di solidarietà*, in M. Napoli (a cura di), *Costituzione, lavoro e pluralismo sociale*, Vita e Pensiero, Milano, 1998

Mitcham C., *The Concept of Sustainable Development: Its Origins and Ambivalence*, in *Technology in Society*, 1995, vol. 17, n. 3

Moffatt I., *The Evolution of Sustainable Development Concept: A Perspective from Australia*, in *Australian Geographical Studies*, 1992, vol. 30

MONTUSCHI L, TULLINI P. (a cura di), *Lavoro e responsabilità sociale dell'impresa*, Zanichelli, Bologna, 2006

MORALES ORTEGA J. M., *Movilidad geográfica y modificaciones sustanciales tras la reforma de 2012: ¿una mal entendida flexiseguridad?*, in *Temas Laborales*, 2013, vol. 119

MOREAU M.-A., *Normes sociales, droit du travail et mondialisation*, Dalloz, Paris, 2006

MORTATI C., *Art. 1, Commento sub art. 1 Costituzione*, in G. BRANCA (a cura di), *Commentario Costituzione, Principi fondamentali, sub artt. 1-12*, Zanichelli-Il Foro italiano, Bologna-Roma, 1975

MUNN R. E., *Towards Sustainable Development*, in *Atmospheric Environment*, 1992, vol. 26, n. 15

NAPOLI M. (a cura di), *La responsabilità sociale delle imprese*, Vita e Pensiero, Milano, 2005

NAPOLI M., *Globalizzazione e rapporti di lavoro*, Vita e Pensiero, Milano, 2006

NAPOLI M. (a cura di), *La solidarietà*, Vita e Pensiero, Milano, 2009

NAPOLI M., *Prefazione. La solidarietà da riscoprire*, in NAPOLI M. (a cura di), *La solidarietà*, Vita e Pensiero, Milano, 2009

NAPOLI M., *Lavoro Diritto Valori*, Giappichelli, Torino, 2010

NAPOLI M., OCCHINO A., CORTI M., *I servizi per l'impiego. Art. 2098 c.c.*, Giuffrè, Milano, 2010

NATALINI F., *La riforma dell'Aspi nell'ambito del Jobs Act; nasce la Naspi. Come cambia il sussidio di disoccupazione. Le ulteriori novità: la Dis-Coll e l'Asdi*, in A. PERULLI, L. FIORILLO (a cura di), *Contratto a tutele crescenti e Naspi, Decreti legislativi 4 marzo 2015, n. 22 e n. 23*, Giappichelli, Torino, 2015

NOGLER L., *Ancora su 'tipo' e rapporto di lavoro subordinato nell'impresa*, in *Arg. dir. lav.*, 2002

NOGLER L., *Opinioni sul Collegato Lavoro*, in *Giorn. dir. lav. rel. ind.*, 2011

NOGLER L., *I licenziamenti per giustificato motivo soggettivo o per gusta causa nel d. lgs. n. 23 del 2015*, in *Arg. dir. lav.*, 2015, 1

NOGLER L., CORAZZA L. (a cura di), *Risistemare il diritto del lavoro. Liber amicorum Marcello Pedrazzoli*, Franco Angeli, Milano, 2012

NOVARA G., *Il recesso volontario dal rapporto di lavoro*, Giuffrè, Milano, 1961

NOVELLA M., *Note sulle tecniche limitative dell'autonomia individuale nella disciplina del lavoro a progetto*, in *Lav. dir.*, 2004, 1

NOVELLA M., *L'inderogabilità nel diritto del lavoro. Norme imperative e autonomia individuale*, Giuffrè, Milano, 2009

NOVITZ T., *Core Labour Standards Conditionalities: A Means by Which to Achieve Sustainable Development?*, in J. FANDEZ, C. TAN (eds), *International Economic Law, Globalization and Developing countries*, Edward Elgar, Cheltenham, 2010

NUSSBAUM M., *Diventare persone*, il Mulino, Bologna, 2001

NUSSBAUM M., *Giustizia sociale e dignità umana. Da individui a persone*, il Mulino, Bologna, 2002

NUSSBAUM M. C., *Capacità personale e democrazia sociale*, Diabasis, Reggio Emilia, 2003

NUSSBAUM M., *Creare capacità*, il Mulino, Bologna, 2011

Occhino, A. *I diritti sociali nell'interpretazione costituzionale*, in *Riv. dir. sic. soc.*, 2017, 1

Okun A., *Uguaglianza ed Efficienza. Il Grande Trade Off*, Liguori, Napoli, 1994

Olivieri A., *Le tutele dei lavoratori dal rapporto al mercato del lavoro: alla postmodernità giuridica verso la modernità economica?*, Giappichelli, Torino, 2017

Orlandini G., *Libertà di stabilimento versus diritto al lavoro: ancora un bilanciamento 'sbilanciato' tra libertà economiche e diritti dei lavoratori*, in *Giorn. dir. lav. rel. ind.*, 2017, 153, 1

Papadopoulos T., Roumpakis A., *The Meta-regulation of European Industrial Relations: Power Shifts, Institutional Dynamics and the Emergence of Regulatory Competition*, in *International Labour Review*, 2013, vol. 152

Passaniti P., *Storia del diritto del lavoro*, Giuffrè, Milano, 2006

Pearce D., *Sustainable Development: An Economic Perspective, Gatekeeper Series*, n. 89-01, London Environmental Economic Centre, London, 1989

Pearce D., Markandya A., Barbier E., *Blueprint for a Green Economy*, Earthscan, London, 1989

Pedrazzoli M. (a cura di), *Lavoro subordinato e dintorni. Comparazioni e prospettive*, il Mulino, Bologna, 1989

Pedrazzoli M., *La parabola della subordinazione: dal contratto allo status. Riflessioni su Barassi e il suo dopo*, in *Arg. dir. lav.*, 2002

Pellacani G., *Autonomia individuale e rapporto di lavoro*, Giappichelli, Torino, 2002

Pellacani G., *Il cosiddetto «Collegato Lavoro» e la disciplina dei licenziamenti: un quadro in chiaroscuro*, in *Riv. it. dir. lav.*, 2010, 1

Pelusi L. M., *La disciplina di salute e sicurezza applicabile al lavoro agile*, in *Dir. rel. ind.*, 2017, 4

Pepe V., *Riforma dell'art. 41 della Costituzione per uno sviluppo sostenibile: la sostenibilità come etica pubblica*, in *L'Italia Forestale e Montana / Italian Journal of Forest and Mountain Environments*, 2012, vol. 67, n. 1

Pera G., *I contratti di solidarietà*, in *Giorn. dir. lav. rel. ind.*, 1984

Persiani M., *Il sistema giuridico della previdenza sociale*, Cedam, Padova, 1960

Persiani M., *La tutela dell'interesse del lavoratore alla conservazione del posto*, in G. Mazzoni, L. Riva Sanseverino (a cura di), *Nuovo trattato di diritto del lavoro*, Cedam, Padova, 1971

Persiani M., *Rischio e bisogno nella crisi della previdenza sociale*, in *Atti delle Giornate di studio Aidlass*, Rimini 28-29 aprile 1984, Giuffrè, Milano, 1985

Persiani M., *Diritto della previdenza sociale*, Cedam, Padova, 1998

Persiani M., *Diritto del lavoro*, Cedam, Padova, 2004

Persiani M., *Individuazione delle nuove tipologie tra subordinazione e autonomia*, in *Arg. dir. lav.*, 2005, 1

Persiani M., *Diritto sindacale*, Cedam, Padova, 2015.

Persiani M., Lunardon F., *Fondamenti di diritto sindacale*, Giappichelli, Torino, 2017.

Perulli A., *Il diritto del lavoro tra crisi della subordinazione e rinascita del lavoro autonomo*, in *Lav. dir.*, 1997

Perulli A., *Lavoro autonomo e dipendenza economica, oggi*, in *Riv. giur. lav.*, 2003, 1

PERULLI A., *Lavori atipici e parasubordinazione tra diritto europeo e situazione italiana*, in *Riv. giur. lav.*, 2006, 4

PERULLI A., *Globalizzazione e Dumping sociale, quali rimedi?*, in *Lav. dir.*, 2011, 1

PERULLI A., *Efficient breach, valori del mercato e tutela della stabilità. Il controllo del giudice sui licenziamenti economici in Italia, Francia e Spagna*, in *Riv. giur. lav.*, 2012, 1

PERULLI A., *Il diritto del lavoro tra libertà e sicurezza*, in *Riv. it. dir. lav.*, 2012, 1

PERULLI A. (a cura di), *La responsabilità sociale dell'impresa: idee e prassi*, il Mulino, Bologna, 2013

PERULLI A., *Diritti sociali fondamentali e regolazione del mercato nell'azione esterna dell'Unione Europea* in *Riv. giur. lav.*, 2013, 2

PERULLI A., *La contrattazione collettiva 'di prossimità': teoria, comparazione e prassi*, in *Riv. it. dir. lav.*, 2013, 4

PERULLI A., *La crisi come categoria del discorso e le aporie della nuova disciplina sui licenziamenti economici*, in *Il diritto del lavoro al tempo della crisi, Atti AIDLASS del XVII Congresso Nazionale di Diritto del Lavoro, Pisa, 7-9 giugno 2012*, Giuffrè, Milano, 2013

PERULLI A., *Clausola sociale*, in *Enciclopedia del diritto*, Giuffrè, Milano, 2014

PERULLI A., *Fundamental Social Rights, Market Regulation and EU External Action*, in *International Journal of Comparative Labour Law and Industrial Relations*, 2014, vol. 30

PERULLI A., *Il contratto a tutele crescenti e la Naspi: un mutamento di 'paradigma' per il diritto del Lavoro?*, in A. PERULLI, L. FIORILLO (a cura di), *Contratto a tutele crescenti e Naspi, Decreti legislativi 4 marzo 2015, n. 22 e n. 23*, Giappichelli, Torino, 2015

PERULLI A., *Il controllo giudiziale dei poteri dell'imprenditore tra evoluzione legislativa e diritto vivente* in *Riv. it. dir. lav.*, 2015, 1

PERULLI A., *Observations sur les réformes de la législation du travail en Europe*, in *Revue de Droit du Travail*, 2015, 3

PERULLI A. (a cura di), *L'idea di diritto del lavoro, oggi. In ricordo di Giorgio Ghezzi*, Cedam, Padova, 2016

PERULLI A., *L'idea di diritto del lavoro, oggi*, in A. PERULLI (a cura di), *L'idea di diritto del lavoro, oggi. In ricordo di Giorgio Ghezzi*, Cedam, Padova, 2016

PERULLI A., *Il jobs act del lavoro autonomo e agile: come cambiano i concetti di subordinazione e autonomia nel diritto del lavoro*, in *WP C.S.D.L.E. 'Massimo D'Antona'.IT – 341/2017*

PERULLI A., *La contrattazione collettiva aziendale e il welfare aziendale: caratteristiche e limiti di un modello troppo enfatizzato*, in G. ZILIO GRANDI (a cura di), *Stato sociale, lavoro e welfare aziendale ai tempi del Jobs Act, Nota di Ricerca n. 1/2017*, Università Ca' Foscari, Venezia, 2017

PERULLI A., *Lavoro e tecnica ai tempi di Uber*, in *Riv. giur. lav.*, 2017, 1

PERULLI A., *Una questione di 'valore': il Jobs Act alla prova di costituzionalità*, in *Dir. rel. ind.*, 2017, 4

PERULLI A., FIORILLO L. (a cura di), *Tipologie contrattuali e disciplina delle mansioni: Decreto legislativo 15 giugno 2015, n. 81*, Giappichelli, Torino, 2016

PERULLI A., SPEZIALE V., *L'articolo 8 della legge 14 settembre 2011, n. 148 e la 'rivoluzione di Agosto' del Diritto del lavoro*, in *WP C.S.D.L.E. 'Massimo D'Antona'.IT – 132/2011*

PERULLI A., TREU T. (eds), *Enterprise and Social Rights*, Kluwer, 2017

PERULLI A., TREU T. (eds), *Sustainable Development, Global Trade and Social Rights*, Alphen aan den Rijn, Kluwer, 2018

PESKINE E., *Les accords de maintien dans l'emploi. Ruptures et continuités*, in *Revue de droit du travail*, 2013

PESSI R., *Funzione e disciplina dei contratti di solidarietà*, in *Giorn. dir. lav. rel. ind.*, 1985

PESSI R., *Economia e Diritto del lavoro*, in *Arg. dir. lav.*, 2006

PESSI R., *Indisponibilità del tipo e disponibilità regolativa dell'autonomia collettiva. Sull'art. 8 della manovra bis*, in *Riv. it. dir. lav.*, 2011, 1

PESSI R., *Prime riflessioni sui decreti attuativi del Jobs Act*, in R. PESSI, C. PISANI, G. PROIA, A. VALLEBONA (a cura di), *Jobs Act e licenziamento*, Giappichelli, Torino, 2015

PESSI R., *Tornando su adeguatezza e solidarietà nel welfare*, in *Riv. dir. sic. soc*, 2016, 4

PESSI R., FABOZZI R., *Gli obblighi del datore di lavoro in materia di salute e sicurezza*, in FIORILLO L., PERULLI A. (a cura di), *Il jobs act del lavoro autonomo e del lavoro agile*, Giappichelli, Torino, 2018

PIERSON P., *Dismantling the Welfare State? Reagan, Thatcher, and the Politics of Retrenchment*, Cambridge University Press, Cambridge, 1994

PITTEL K., *Sustainability and Endogenous Growth: New Horizons in Environmental Economics*, Edward Elgar, Cheltenham, 2002

POCHET P., DEGRYSE C., *Social Policies of the European Union*, in *Global Social Policy*, 2010, vol. 10, n. 2

PONZELLINI A. M., *I contratti di solidarietà. Costi e benefici sul piano economico, occupazionale, organizzativo*, bozza del Rapporto Conclusivo, CESOS, Torino, 17 novembre 2015

PROIA G., *Rapporti di lavoro e tipo*, Milano, 1997

PROIA G., *Flessibilità e tutele 'nel' contratto di lavoro subordinato*, in *Giorn. dir. lav. rel. ind.*, 2002

PROIA G., *Metodo tipologico, contratto di lavoro subordinato e categorie definitorie*, in *Arg. dir. lav.*, 2002

PROIA G., *L'accordo individuale e le modalità di esecuzione e di cessazione della prestazione di lavoro agile*, in L. FIORILLO, A. PERULLI (a cura di), *Il jobs act del lavoro autonomo e del lavoro agile*, Giappichelli, Torino, 2018

RADIGHIERI E., *I diritti fondamentali dei lavoratori nel commercio internazionale*, in L.S. ROSSI (a cura di), *Commercio internazionale sostenibile? WTO e Unione europea*, il Mulino, Bologna, 2003

RAUSEI P., *Tutto Jobs Act: Lavoro Autonomo e Smart Work*, Wolters Kluwer Italia, Milano, 2016

RAWLS J., *A Theory of Justice*, Harvard University Press, Cambridge, 1971

RAWLS J., *Political Liberalism*, Columbia University Press, New York, 1993

RAY J-E., *Naissance et avis de décès du droit à la déconnexion: le droit à la vie privée au XXIe siècle*, in *Droit Social*, 2002

Ray J-E., *Grande accélération et droit à la déconnexion*, in *Droit Social*, 2016

Redclift M. R., *Sustainable Development: Exploring the Contradictions*, Methuen, London, 1987

Reich R. B., *Supercapitalismo: come cambia l'economia mondiale e i rischi per la democrazia*, Fazi, Roma, 2008

Renga S., *Mercato del lavoro e diritto*, Franco Angeli, Milano, 1996

Repetto R., *The Global Possible-Resources, Development and the New Century*, Yale University Press, New Haven, 1985, 10

Repetto R., *World Enough and Time*, Yale University Press, New Haven, 1986

Reynaud E. (a cura di), *Le développement durable au cœur de l'entreprise*, Dunod, Paris, 2006

Ricci M., *I servizi per l'impiego dopo le modifiche legislative tra luci e ombre*, in *Arg. dir. lav.*, 2017, 2

Rifkin J., *The End of Work: The Decline of the Global Labor Force and the Dawn of the Post-Market Era*, Putnam Publishing Group, New York, 1995

Rifkin J., *La fine del lavoro, Il declino della forza lavoro globale e l'avvento dell'era post-mercato*, Mondadori, Milano, 2014

Rigau M., *Droit du travail ou droit de la concurrence sociale. Essai sur un droit de la dignité de l'Homme du travail (re)mis en cause*, Bruylant, Bruxelles, 2009

Robé J. P., Mazuyer E., *Faut-il faire une évaluation sociale des entreprises?*, in *Revue* de droit du travail, 2010

Roccella M., *Lavoro subordinato e lavoro autonomo, oggi*, in *WP C.S.D.L.E. 'Massimo D'Antona'.IT – 65/2008*

Rodotà S., *Solidarietà. Un'utopia necessaria*, Laterza, Roma, 2014

Rodriguez-Piñero y Bravo Ferrer M., *La grave crisi del diritto del lavoro*, in *Lav. dir.*, 2012, 1

Rodríguez-Piñero y Bravo Ferrer M., *Globalizzazione, flessicurezza e crisi economica*, in *Riv. giur. lav.*, 2013, 1

Rodríguez-Piñero y Bravo Ferrer M., Valdés Dal-Ré F., Casas Baamonde M. E., *La huida del derecho del trabajo hacia el 'emprendimiento', las reformas de la Reforma Laboral de 2012 y otras reformas: la L 11/2013 y el RDL 11/2013*, in *Relaciones Laborales*, 2013, n. 10

Romagnoli U., *Eguaglianza e differenza nel diritto del lavoro*, in *Giorn. dir. lav. rel. ind.*, 1994

Romagnoli U., *Un diritto da ripensare*, in *Lav. dir.*, 1995

Romagnoli U., *Il diritto del lavoro nel prisma del principio d'eguaglianza*, in *Riv. trim. dir. proc. civ.*, 1997

Romagnoli U., *Giuristi del lavoro. Percorsi italiani di politica del diritto*, Donzelli editore, Roma, 2009

Romero Burillo A. M., *La regulación de la movilidad geográfica tras las reformas laborales 2010-2012*, in *Revista de Derecho Social*, 2013, vol. 64

Rosina A., *NEET. Giovani che non studiano e non lavorano*, Vita e Pensiero, Milano, 2015

Rusciano M., *Il lavoro come diritto: servizi per l'impiego e decentramento amministrativo*, in *Riv. giur. lav.*, 1999

RUSSO M., *La prosecuzione del rapporto di lavoro oltre l'eta` pensionabile tra tutele individuali ed esigenze di ricambio generazionale*, in *Ec. & lav.*, 2015, 3

RUSSO M., *Lavoratori anziani e giovani: tra tutele individuali e tentativi di solidarietà intergenerazionale*, in A. PERULLI (a cura di), *L'idea di diritto del lavoro, oggi. In ricordo di Giorgio Ghezzi*, Cedam, Padova, 2016

SACHS J., *L'era dello sviluppo sostenibile*, Università Bocconi Editore, Milano, 2015

SALENTO A., *Industria 4.0 ed economia delle piattaforme: spazi di azione e spazi di decisione*, in *Riv. giur. lav.*, 2017, 2

SALOMONE R., *La responsabilità sociale dell'impresa: riflessioni a margine di una strategia europea sullo sviluppo sostenibile*, in *Dir. relaz. ind.*, 2004, 2

SALOMONE R., *Preferenze tariffarie generalizzate e core labour standards*, in *Lav. dir.*, 2011

SANDS P., *International Law in the Field of Sustainable Development*, in *British Yearbook of International Law*, 1994

SANDULLI P., *Tutela previdenziale e assistenziale dei lavoratori atipici nell'ordinamento giuridico italiano*, in *Lav. dir.*, 2003, 3

SANTONI F., RICCI M., SANTUCCI R. (a cura di), *Il diritto del lavoro all'epoca del* jobs act, Editoriale Scientifica, Napoli, 2016

SANTORO PASSARELLI F., *Rischio e bisogno nella previdenza sociale*, in *Rivista italiana di previdenza sociale*, 1948, 1

SANTORO PASSARELLI G., *I contratti di solidarietà: due esperienze a confronto*, in *Riv. it. dir. lav.*, 1994, 1

SANTORO PASSARELLI G., *Flessibilità e subordinazione: pluralità di fattispecie o di tutele?*, in AA. VV. (a cura di), *Subordinazione e autonomia: vecchi e nuovi modelli*, in *Quad. dir. lav. rel. ind.*, UTET, Torino, 1998

SANTORO PASSARELLI G., *Efficacia soggettiva del contratto collettivo: accordi separati, dissenso individuale e clausola di rinvio*, in *Riv. it. dir. lav.*, 2010, 1

SANTORO PASSARELLI G., *Accordo interconfederale 28 giugno 2011 e art. 8 d. l. 138/2011 conv. con modif. l. 148/2011*, in *Arg. dir. lav.*, 2011

SANTORO PASSARELLI G., *Diritto dei lavori. Diritto sindacale e rapporti di lavoro*, Giappichelli, Torino, 2013

SANTORO PASSARELLI G., *Autonomia privata individuale e collettiva e norma inderogabile*, in *Riv. it. dir. lav.*, 2015, 1

SANTORO PASSARELLI G., *Appunti sulla funzione delle categorie civilistiche nel diritto del lavoro dopo il Jobs Act*, in *WP C.S.D.L.E. 'Massimo D'Antona'.IT – 290/2016*

SANTORO PASSARELLI G., *Lavoro etero-organizzato, coordinato, agile e telelavoro: un puzzle non facile da comporre nell'impresa in via di trasformazione*, in *Dir. rel. ind.*, 2017, 3

SCARPELLI F., *Autonomia collettiva e autonomia individuale nella regolazione del rapporto dei lavoratori parasubordinati*, in *Lav. dir.*, 1999, 4

SCARPELLI F., *Rappresentatività e contrattazione tra l'accordo unitario di giugno e le discutibili ingerenze del legislatore*, in *WPCSDLE 'Massimo D'Antona'.IT – 127/2001*

SCARPONI S. (a cura di), *Globalizzazione e diritto del lavoro: il ruolo degli ordinamenti sovranazionali*, Giuffrè, Milano, 2001

SCARPONI S., *Globalizzazione e responsabilità sociale delle imprese transnazionali*, in *Lav. dir.*, 2006, 1

SCARPONI S. (a cura di), *Diritto e genere. Analisi interdisciplinare e comparata*, Cedam, Padova, 2014

SCHRIJVER N., *The Evolution of Sustainable Development in International Law: Inception, Meaning and Status*, Brill Nijoff, Leiden, 2008.

SCHUMPETER J. A., *Teoria dello sviluppo economico*, ETAS, Milano, 2002 (Traduzione della sesta edizione tedesca (1964), sulla scorta anche dell'edizione inglese del 1934, della *Theorie der wirtschaftlichen Entwicklung*, 1911, con Introduzione di P. SYLOS LABINI)

SCIARRA S., *L'Europa e il lavoro. Solidarietà e conflitto in tempo di crisi*, Laterza, Roma-Bari, 2013

SCIARRA S., *Ci sara` una solidarieta` europea?*, in *Riv. dir. sic. soc.*, 2016, 1

SCONAMIGLIO R., *Lavoro subordinato: I) Diritto del lavoro*, in *Enc. giur. Treccani*, 1988, XVIII

SEGGER M. C. C., *Sustainable Development Law: Principles, Practices, and Prospects*, Oxford University Press, Oxford, 2004

SEGHEZZI F., *La nuova grande trasformazione. Lavoro e persona nella quarta rivoluzione industriale*, ADAPT University Press, Modena, 2017

SEN A. K., *Inequality Reexamined*, Oxford University Press, New York, 1992

SEN A. K., *Capability and Well-Being*, in M. NUSSBAUM, A. K. SEN (eds), *The Quality of Life*, Clarendon Press, Oxford, 1993

SEN A. K., *Development as Freedom*, Oxford University Press, Oxford, 1999

SEN A. K., *Lo sviluppo è libertà*, Mondadori, Milano, 2000 (ed. orig. 1999)

SEN A. K., *Etica ed economia*, Laterza, Roma-Bari, 2002 (ed. orig. 1987)

SEN A. K., *Razionalità e libertà*, il Mulino, Bologna, 2005

SEN A. K., *The Idea of Justice*, Penguin Group, London, 2009 (trad. it. *L'idea di giustizia*, Mondadori, Milano, 2010

SHAPIRO C., STIGLITZ J. E., *Equilibrium Unemployment as a Worker Discipline Device*, in *The American Economic Review*, 1984, vol. 74, 3

SIGILLÒ MASSARA G., *L'insostenibile tensione verso il welfare mix, tra fondi di solidarietà bilaterali e previdenza complementare*, in *Riv. dir. sic. soc.*, 2017, 3

SIMITIS S., *Il diritto del lavoro ha ancora un futuro?* in *Giorn. dir. lav. rel. ind.*, 1997, 4

SINZHEIMER H., *Arbeitsrechts und Rechtssoziologie*, Europ. Verl.-Anst, Frankfurt, 1976

SIROËN J. M., *Labour Provisions in Preferential Trade Agreements: Current Practice and Outlook*, in *International Labour Review*, 2013

SOLOW R. M., *Sustainability: An Economist's Perspective*, in R. DORFMAN, N. DORFMAN (eds), *Economics of the Environment*, 3rd ed., W. W. Norton, New York, 1991

SOMAINI E, *Uguaglianza*, Donzelli editore, Roma, 2002

SOMMA A., *Dal lavoratore al consumatore. Cittadinanza e paradigma giuslavoristico nell'economia sociale di mercato*, in G. CAZZETTA, G. G. BALANDI (a cura di), *Diritti e lavoro nell'Italia repubblicana: materiali dall'incontro di studio, Ferrara, 24 ottobre 2008*, Giuffrè, Milano, 2009

Speziale V., *L'articolazione della fattispecie,* in F. Carinci (a cura di), *Il lavoro subordinato,* Tomo II, in M. Bessone (diretto da), *Trattato di diritto privato,* vol. XXIV, Giappichelli, Torino, 2007

Speziale V., *Il contratto a tempo indeterminato a tutele crescenti tra law and economics e vincoli costituzionali,* in *WP C.S.D.L.E. 'Massimo D'Antona'. IT – 259/2015*

Speziale V., *La mutazione genetica del diritto del lavoro,* in *Dir. lav. mer.,* 2016, 2

Speziale V., *La trasformazione del diritto del lavoro,* in *Lav. dir.,* 2016, 4

Stone K. V. W., Arthurs H. (eds), *Rethinking Workplace Regulation: Beyond the Standard Contract of Employment,* Russell Sage Foundation, New York, 2013

Stone K. V. W., Arthurs H., *The Transformation of Employment Regimes: A Worldwide Challenge,* in K. V. W. Stone, H. Arthurs (eds), *Rethinking Workplace Regulation,* Russell Sage Foundation, New York, 2013

Stone K. V. W., *Rethinking Labour Law: Employment Protection,* in G. Davidov, B. Langille (eds), *Boundaries and Frontiers of Labour Law,* Hart Publishing, Oxford, 2006

Stone K. V. W., *The Decline of the Standard Contract of Employment in the United States: A Socio-Regulatory Perspective,* in K. V. W. Stone, H. Arthurs (eds), *Rethinking Workplace Regulation: Beyond the Standard Contract of Employment,* Russell Sage Foundation, New York, 2013

Streeck W., *Il modello sociale europeo: dalla redistribuzione alla solidarietà competitiva»,* in *Stato e mercato,* 2000, 1

Stymne S., Jackson T, *Intra-generational Equity and Sustainable Welfare: A Time Series Analysis for the UK and Sweden,* in *Ecological Economics,* 2000, vol. 2, n. 33

Supiot A., *Au-delà de l'emploi,* Flammarion, Paris, 1999

Supiot A., *Lavoro subordinato e lavoro autonomo,* in *Dir. rel. ind.* 2000

Supiot A., *Il futuro del lavoro: trasformazioni dell'occupazione e prospettive della regolazione del lavoro in Europa,* Carocci, Roma, 2003

Supiot A., Barbieri B. (a cura di), *Il futuro del lavoro, Trasformazioni dell'occupazione e prospettive della regolazione del lavoro in Europa,* Carocci, Roma, 2003

Talamo V., *Diversamente agile? Lo Smart Work nelle pubbliche amministrazioni,* in L. Fiorillo, A. Perulli (a cura di), *Il jobs act del lavoro autonomo e del lavoro agile,* Giappichelli, Torino, 2018

Tinti A. R., *A proposito di lavoro «agile» e work-life balance. La conciliazione ingannevole,* in *La rivista Il Mulino,* 27 maggio 2016

Tiraboschi M. (a cura di), *La riforma del collocamento e i nuovi servizi per l'impiego,* Giuffrè, Milano, 2003

Tiraboschi M., *Clausole generali, onere della prova, ruolo del giudice,* in G. Proia, M. Tiraboschi (a cura di), *La riforma dei rapporti e delle controversie del lavoro,* Giuffrè, Milano, 2011

Tiraboschi M. (a cura di), *Le nuove regole del lavoro dopo il Jobs Act,* Giuffrè, Milano, 2016

Tiraboschi M., *Il lavoro agile tra legge e contrattazione collettiva: la tortuosa via italiana verso la modernizzazione del diritto del lavoro,* in *Dir. rel. ind.,* 2017, 4

Tosi A., *Rapporti speciali di lavoro,* in *Enc. giur. Treccani,* 1991

Tosi P., *Autonomia, subordinazione e coordinazione,* in *Labor,* 2017, 2

TREMOLADA M., *Norme della l. n. 183/2010 in materia di certificazione e di limiti al potere di accertamento del giudice*, in M. MISCIONE, D. GAROFALO (a cura di), *Il Collegato lavoro 2010*, Ipsoa, Milano, 2011

TREU, T., *La disciplina legale dei contratti di solidarietà*, in *Dir. lav.*, 1985, 1

TREU T., *Riequilibrio delle tutele e flexicurity*, in M. MAGNANI, M. TIRABOSCHI (a cura di), *La nuova riforma del lavoro, Commentario alla legge 28 giugno 2012, n. 92*, Giuffrè, Milano, 2012

TREU T., *Flessibilità e tutele nella riforma del lavoro*, in *Giorn. dir. lav. rel. ind.*, 2013

TREU T., *Prove di staffetta generazionale*, in *Il Sole 24 ore*, 2 ottobre 2015

TREU T., *Labour Law and Sustainable Development*, in *WP C.S.D.L.E. 'Massimo D'Antona'.INT – 130/2016*

TREU T., *Globalizzazione e diritti umani. Le clausole sociali dei trattati commerciali e negli scambi internazionali fra imprese*, in *Stato e mercato*, 2017, 1

TREU T., *Flessibilità e oltre*, in *WP CSDLE 'Massimo D'Antona'.INT – 135/2017*

TREU T., *Rimedi, tutele e fattispecie: riflessioni a partire dai lavori della Gig economy*, in *Lav. dir.*, 2017, 3-4

TREU T., *Una seconda fase della Flexicurity per l'occupabilità*, in *Dir. rel. ind.*, 2017, 3

TULLINI P., *Indisponibilità dei diritti dei lavoratori: dalla tecnica al principio e ritorno*, in *Giorn. dir. lav. rel. ind.*, 2008

TULLINI P., *Digitalizzazione dell'economia e frammentazione dell'occupazione. Il lavoro instabile discontinuo informale: tendenze in atto*, in *Riv. giur. lav.*, 2016, 4

TULLINI P. (a cura di), *Web e lavoro: Profili evolutivi e di tutela*, Giappichelli, Torino, 2017

TUNKIN G. I., *Remarks on the Juridical Nature of Customary Norms of International Law*, in *California Law Review*, 1961, vol. 49, n. 3

TURSI A., *Responsabilità sociale dell'impresa, «etica d'impresa» e diritto del lavoro*, in *Lav. dir.*, 2006, 1

VALDES DAL RE F., *Il dibattito sulla flessicurezza all'interno dell'Unione Europea*, in G. LOY (a cura di), *Diritto del lavoro e crisi economica*, Ediesse, Roma, 2011

VALLAURI M. L., *Tutela della salute a sostegno della genitorialità*, in L. FIORILLO, A. PERULLI (a cura di), *Il Jobs act del lavoro autonomo e del lavoro agile, Il nuovo diritto del lavoro*, Giappichelli, Torino, 2018

VALLEBONA A., *Il Collegato Lavoro: un bilancio tecnico*, in *Mass. giur. lav.*, 2010

VALLEBONA A., *Giustizia sociale: Eraclito surclassa Sen*, in *Arg. dir. lav.*, 2011

VALLEBONA A., *Istituzioni di diritto del lavoro, il diritto sindacale*, Ottava edizione, Cedam, Padova, 2012

VARDARO G., *Tecnica, Tecnologia e ideologia della tecnica nel diritto del lavoro* in *Pol. dir.*, 1986

VENTURI A., *Costituzione, ambiente e sviluppo sostenibile. Elementi di comparazione giuridica per una revisione costituzionale*, in G. CORDINI, A. VENTURI (a cura di), *Lo sviluppo sostenibile nelle aree protette del Mediterraneo*, Aracne, Roma, 2011

VERDIER J. M., *Pensieri in libertà su «diritti fondamentali» e lotta all'emarginazione*, in *Dir. merc. lav.*, 1999

VERSCHUUREN J., *Sustainable Development and the Nature of Environmental Legal Principles*, in *Potchefstroom Electronic Law Journal*, 2006, vol. 9, n. 1

VIDIRI G., *Il licenziamento disciplinare nel primo decreto attuativo del* Jobs *Act tra luci e (non poche) ombre*, in *Arg. dir. lav.*, 2015, 2

VIDIRI G., *La disciplina delle mansioni nel jobs act: una (altra) riforma mal riuscita*, in *Arg. dir. lav.*, 2016, 3

VILLANI U., *La politica sociale nel Trattato di Lisbona*, in *Riv. giur. lav.*, 2012, 1

VILLANUEVA C., *Community Development and the Futures of Sustainable Communities in the Philippines*, in Y. KAORU (ed.), *Sustainable Global Community in the Information Age: Vision from Future Studies, Praeger Studies on the 21st Century*, Praeger, Santa Barbara, 1997

VOZA R., *Il lavoro reso mediante piattaforme digitali tra qualificazione e regolazione*, in *Riv. giur. lav.*, 2017, 2

WEISS M., *Re-inventing Labour Law?*, in G. DAVIDOV, B. LANGILLE (eds), *The Idea of Labour Law*, Oxford University Press, Oxford, 2011

WEISS M., *International Labour Standards: A Complex Public-Private Policy Mix*, in *International Journal of Comparative Labour Law and Industrial Relations*, 2013, vol. 29

ZAGREBELSKY G., *Un lessico civile*, in N. BOBBIO (a cura di), *Eguaglianza e libertà*, Einaudi, Torino, 1995

ZAGREBELSKY G., *Fondata sul lavoro. La solitudine dell'articolo 1*, Einaudi, Torino, 2013

ZAHN R., MANGAN D., *Labour Standards and Sustainable Development: Unpicking the EU's Approach*, in *International Journal of Comparative Labour Law and Industrial Relations*, 2015, vol. 31, n. 3

ZILIO GRANDI G., GRAMANO E. (a cura di), *La disciplina delle mansioni prima e dopo il Jobs Act. Quadro legale e profili problematici*, Giuffrè, Milano, 2016

ZOLI C., *Le recenti riforme del diritto del lavoro tra continuità e discontinuità*, in L. MARIUCCI (a cura di), *Dopo la flessibilità, cosa? Le nuove politiche del lavoro*, il Mulino, Bologna, 2006

ZOLI C., *Contrattazione in deroga*, in F. CARINCI (a cura di), *Da Pomigliano a Mirafiori: la cronaca si fa storia*, Ipsoa, Milano, 2011

ZOLI C., *La legge n. 183/2010: le novità in materia di licenziamento*, in *Arg. dir. lav.*, 2011, 4-5

ZOLI C., *Dall'accordo interconfederale 28 giugno 2011 all'art. 8 del d. l. n. 138/2011*, in F. CARINCI (a cura di), *Contrattazione in deroga*, Ipsoa, Milano, 2012

ZOLI C., *I licenziamenti per giustificato motivo oggettivo dalla legge n. 604 del 1966 al d. lgs. n. 23 del 2015*, in G. FERRARO (a cura di), *Licenziamenti nel contratto a tutele crescenti*, Cedam, Padova, 2015

ZOLI C., *La disciplina delle mansioni*, in A. PERULLI, L. FIORILLO (a cura di), *Tipologie contrattuali e disciplina delle mansioni: Decreto legislativo 15 giugno 2015, n. 81*, Giappichelli, Torino, 2016

ZOPPOLI A., *Il declino dell'inderogabilità?*, in *Dir. lav. merc.*, 2013

ZOPPOLI L., *Flessibilità del diritto del lavoro e accumulazione di capitale*, in L. MARIUCCI (a cura di), *Dopo la flessibilità cosa? Le nuove politiche del lavoro*, il Mulino, Bologna, 2006

ZOPPOLI L., *Flex/insecurity. La riforma Fornero (l. 28 giugno 2012, n. 92) prima, durante e dopo*, Editoriale Scientifica, Napoli, 2012

ZOPPOLI L., *Contratto a tutele crescenti e altre forme contrattuali*, in *Dir. merc. lav.*, 2015, 2

ZOPPOLI L., *Il 'riordino' dei modelli di rapporto di lavoro tra articolazione tipologica e flessibilizzazione funzionale*, in *Dir. rel. ind.*, 2015, 1

ZOPPOLI L., *Il diritto del Lavoro dalle ideologie alla numerologia? L'insostenibile pesantezza delle politiche, del diritto e dei tecnici del diritto*, in M. BROLLO, M. MARAZZA (a cura di), *Quad. arg. dir. lav.*, 2015, 13

ZOPPOLI L., *Le fonti (dopo il jobs act): autonomia ed eteronomia a confronto* in O. MAZZOTTA (a cura di), *Lavoro ed esigenze dell'impresa fra diritto sostanziale e processo dopo il Jobs Act*, Giappichelli, Torino, 2017

STUDIES IN EMPLOYMENT AND SOCIAL POLICY

1. W. Beck, L. van der Maesen & A. Walker (eds), *The Social Quality of Europe*, 1997 (ISBN 90-411-0456-9).
2. R. Blanpain, M. Colucci, C. Engels, F. Hendrickx, L. Salas & E. De Smyter, *Institutional Changes and European Social Policies after the Treaty of Amsterdam*, 1998 (ISBN 90-411-1018-6).
3. V. Lo: *Law and Industrial Relations: China and Japan after World War II*, 1998 (ISBN 90-411-1075-5).
4. A. Den Exter & H. Hermans (eds), *The Right to Health Care in Several European Countries*, 1998 (ISBN 90-411-1087-9).
5. M. Biagi (ed.), *Job Creation and Labour Law from Protection towards Pro- Action*, 2000 (ISBN 90-411-1432-7).
6. W. Beck, L. van der Maesen, F. Thomése & A. Walker (eds), *Social Quality: A Vision for Europe*, 2000 (ISBN 90-411-1523-4).
7. F. Pennings, *Introduction to European Social Law*, 3rd ed., 2001 (ISBN 90-411-1628-1).
8. J. Murray, *Transnational Labour Regulation: The ILO and EC Compared*, 2001 (ISBN 90-411-1583-8).
9. R. Blanpain & C. Engels (eds), *The ILO and Social Challenges of the 21st Century*, 2001 (ISBN 90-411-1572-2).
10. M. Biagi (ed.), *Towards a European Model of Industrial Relations? Building on the First Report of the European Commission*, 2001 (ISBN 90-411-1653-2).
11. J. Clasen (ed.), *What Future for Social Security? Debates and Reforms in National and Cross-National Perspective*, 2001 (ISBN 90-411-1671-0).
12. A. Numhauser-Henning (ed.), *Legal Perspectives on Equal Treatment and Non-Discrimination*, 2001 (ISBN 90-411-1665-6).
13. R. Blanpain (ed.), *Labour Law, Human Rights and Social Justice* 2001 (ISBN 90-411-1697-4).
14. M.-C. Kuo, H.F. Zacher & H.-S. Chan (eds), *Reform and Perspectives on Social Insurance: Lessons from the East and West*, 2002 (ISBN 90-411-1819-5).
15. P. Foubert, *The Legal Protection of the Pregnant Worker in the European Community*, 2002 (ISBN 90-411-1842-X).
16. M. Biagi (ed.), *Quality of Work and Employee Involvement in Europe*, 2002 (ISBN 90-411-1885-3).
17. F. Pennings, *Dutch Social Security Law in an International Context*, 2002 (ISBN 90-411-1887-X).

18. T. Carney & G. Ramia, *From Rights to Management: Contract, New Public Management and Employment Services*, 2002 (ISBN 90-411-1889-6).
19. R. Blanpain & M. Colucci, *European Labour and Social Security Law, Glossary*, 2002 (ISBN 90-411-1905-1).
20. I.U. Zeytinoglu (ed.), *Flexible Work Arrangements: Conceptualizations and International Experiences*, 2002 (ISBN 90-411-1947-7).
21. J. Berghman, A. Nagelkerke, M. Boos, R. Doeschot & G. Vonk (eds), *Social Security in Transition*, 2002 (ISBN 90-411-1969-8).
22. R. Blanpain, *The Legal Status of Sportsmen and Sportswomen under International, European and Belgian National and Regional Law*, 2003 (ISBN 90-411-1980-9).
23. R. Blanpain & M. Weiss (eds), *Changing Industrial Relations & Modernisation of Labour Law, Liber Amicorum in Honour of Professor Marco Biagi*, 2003 (ISBN 90-411-2008-4).
24. J. Malmberg (ed.), *Effective Enforcement of EC Labour Law*, 2003 (ISBN 90-411-2160-9).
25. M. De Vos (ed.), *A Decade Beyond Maastricht: The European Social Dialogue Revisited*, 2003 (ISBN 90-411-2163-3).
26. M. Sewerynski (ed.), *Collective Agreements and Individual Contracts of Employment*, 2003 (ISBN 90-411-2190-0).
27. R. Blanpain & M. Van Gestel, *Use and Monitoring of E-Mail, Intranet and Internet Facilities at Work: Law and Practice*, 2004 (ISBN 90-411-22-66-4).
28. A. C. Neal (ed.), *The Changing Face of European Labour Law and Social Policy*, 2004 (ISBN 90-411-2312-1).
29. E. Sol & M. Westerveld (eds), *Contractualism in Employment Services: A New Form of Welfare State Governance*, 2005 (ISBN 90-411-2405-5).
30. F. Pennings (ed.), *Between Soft and Hard Law – The Impact of International Social Security Standards on National Social Security Law*, 2006 (ISBN 978-90-411-2491-3).
31. L. Dickens & A. C. Neal (eds), *The Changing Institutional Face of British Employment Relations*, 2006 (ISBN 978-90-411-2541-5).
32. G. Sebardt, *Redundancy and the Swedish Model in an International Context*, 2006 (ISBN 978-90-411-2503-3).
33. A.M. Swiatkowski, *Charter of Social Rights of the Council of Europe*, 2007 (ISBN 978-90-411-2608-5).
34. M. Sargeant (ed.), *The Law on Age Discrimination in the EU*, 2008 (ISBN 978-90-411-2522-4).
35. G. Di Domenico & S. Spattini (eds), *New European Approaches to Long- Term Unemployment: What Role for Public Employment Services and What Market for Private Stakeholders?*, 2008 (ISBN 978-90-411-2614-6.)
36. C. Welz, *The European Social Dialogue under Articles 138 and 139 of the EC Treaty: Actors, Processes, Outcomes*, 2008 (ISBN 978-90-411-2744-0).
37. M. Rönnmar (ed.), *EU Industrial Relations v. National Industrial Relations: Comparative and Interdisciplinary Perspectives*, 2008 (ISBN 978-90-411- 2770-9).

38. F. Pennings, Y. Konijn & A. Veldman (eds), *Social Responsibility in Labour Relations: European and Comparative Perspectives*, 2008 (ISBN 978-90- 411-2783-9).
39. F. Pennings & C. Bosse (eds), *The Protection of Working Relationships: A Comparative Study*, 2011 (ISBN 978-90-411-3289-5).
40. S. Devetzi & S. Stendahl (eds), *Too Sick to Work?: Social Security Reference in Europe for Persons with Reduced Earnings Capacity*, 2011 (ISBN 978-90- 411-3426-4).
41. Ulrich Becker, Frans Pennings & Tineke Dijkhoff (eds), *International Standard Setting and Innovations in Social Security*, 2013 (ISBN 978-90-411-3233-8).
42. E. Ales (ed.), *Health and Safety at Work: European and Comparative Perspective*, 2013 (ISBN 978-90-411-4661-8).
43. F. Pennings, T. Erhag & S. Stendahl (eds), *Non-public Actors in Social Security Administration: A Comparative Study*, 2013 (ISBN 978-90-411-4917-6).
44. A. Neal (ed.), *Cross-Currents in Modern Chinese Labour Law*, 2014 (ISBN 978-90-411-4763-9).
45. B. Waas (ed.), *The Right to Strike: A Comparative View*, 2014 (ISBN 978-90-411-5007-3).
46. A. Ojeda-Avilés, *Transnational Labour Law*, 2015 (ISBN 978-90-411-5858-1).
47. A. Numhauser-Henning & M. Rönnmar, *Age Discrimination and Labour-Law: Comparative and Conceptual Perspectives in the EU and Beyond*, 2015 (ISBN 978-90-411-4979-4).
48. A. Perulli & T. Treu (eds), *Enterprise and Social Rights*, 2017 (ISBN 978-90-411-8234-0).
49. Dr F.C.A. van Haasteren, *Decent Flexibility: The Impact of ILO Convention 181 and the Regulation on Temporary Agency Work*, 2017 (ISBN 978-90-411-9236-3).
50. T. Dijkhoff & L.G. Mpedi (eds), *Recommendation on Social Protection Floors: Basic Principles for Innovative Solutions*, 2018 (ISBN 978-90-411-8623-2).
51. A. Perulli & T. Treu (eds), *Sustainable Development, Global Trade and Social Rights*, 2018 (ISBN 978-90-411-9235-6).
52. M. Mironi & M. Schlachter (eds), *Regulating Strikes in Essential Services: A Comparative 'Law in Action' Perspective*, 2019 (ISBN 978-90-411-8997-4).
53. A. Perulli & T. Treu (eds), *The Role of the State and Industrial Relations*, 2019 (ISBN 978-94-035-0661-6).
54. T. Gyulavári & E. Menegatti (eds), *The Sources of Labour Law*, 2020 (ISBN 978-94-035-0284-7).
55. V. Cagnin, *Labour Law and Sustainable Development*, 2020 (ISBN 978-94-035-2074-2).

www.ingramcontent.com/pod-product-compliance
Ingram Content Group UK Ltd.
Pitfield, Milton Keynes, MK11 3LW, UK
UKHW020818290926
15470UKWH00003B/1237

9 789403 520742